POR

MAKING IT BIG

Binod Chaudhary is the president of the Chaudhary Group (CG Corp Global), a multinational conglomerate with a portfolio of 122 companies spread over five continents and with seventy-six renowned brands in the global market. He is an internationally respected name in FMCG as the man behind Wai Wai noodles, the most iconic brand from CG. His other business interests include electronics, hospitality, infrastructure, education, telecom and realty, which are among the fifteen business verticals he runs within CG. The Chaudhary Group's assets include a controlling stake in Nepal's largest private-sector commercial bank (Nabil Bank) and a string of hotels, and JVs with the Taj (Tata Group), Alila, Fern and the Farm at San Benito, to name a few prominent brands. Chaudhary is also regarded as a leading philanthropist in Nepal. He is an avid trekker and a fitness enthusiast.

With my blessings!

Ravi Shankar

22.2.17

London

MAKING IT BIG

The Inspiring Story of Nepal's First Billionaire in His Own Words

BINOD CHAUDHARY

To:
Dear Rahia,
Compliments!

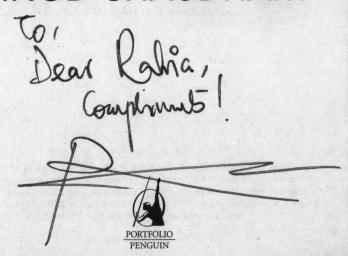

PORTFOLIO
PENGUIN

PORTFOLIO

USA | Canada | UK | Ireland | Australia
New Zealand | India | South Africa | China

Portfolio is part of the Penguin Random House group of companies
whose addresses can be found at global.penguinrandomhouse.com

Published by Penguin Random House India Pvt. Ltd
7th Floor, Infinity Tower C, DLF Cyber City,
Gurgaon 122 002, Haryana, India

Penguin
Random House
India

First published in Nepali as *Binod Chaudhary: Atmakatha* by Nepalaya,
Kathmandu 2013
First published in English in Portfolio by Penguin Books India 2016

ISBN 9780143426035

Typeset in Minion Pro by Manipal Digital Systems, Manipal
Printed at Thomson Press India Ltd, New Delhi

For my father

*'You have to sacrifice something to gain something else,'
my father told me.
That is one piece of fatherly advice I could never accept.
I want everything from life, not one thing at the cost of another.*

My late father, Shri Lunkaran Das Chaudhary

Contents

PART III: REBIRTH

PART IV: MY BUSINESS MANTRAS

A Rebeginning . . .

The clock tower in Kathmandu would soon strike noon. But here, thousands of miles away, in the Chilean capital of Santiago, time hung so heavy that each ticking of the clock felt like an eternity.

Monday, 1 March 2010
4 a.m.–5 a.m.
We were milling around the reception lounge in Kennedy Hotel like a flock of startled birds, trapped with no sign of escape. I could clearly see the hair on my arms standing on end. My mouth felt parched, even though we were in an air-conditioned facility. My legs trembled uncontrollably. My heart was heavy as a rock in my chest. When would this crisis end?

All we wanted was to be able to make one call to Kathmandu—at any cost. But the telephone system was down. Sometimes a call would get through, only to disconnect after a brief ring. Sometimes we could hear a muffled voice at the other end, and our eyes, dulled by many hours of fear and sleeplessness, would suddenly brighten.

But, to our dismay, our desperate screams of 'Hello! Hello!' would fetch only a noise that sounded vaguely like rushing water.

If everything had gone according to plan, we would have been on our way to Rio de Janeiro. Our flight was due to depart at 10 a.m. As we prepared to leave for the airport, the hotel receptionist announced that all roads leading to the airport were closed and that all flights out of the city had been cancelled. Some of the roads were severely damaged and a number of flyovers had crumbled. Many vehicles lay overturned on the roads. At the airport, wide cracks had appeared on the tarmac, and the control tower had completely collapsed.

'They're trying to clear the roads to make way for the ambulances and fire trucks,' the receptionist announced. 'Please have patience.' But patience it was that was running thin, and her exhortation calling for stoicism on our part only made us even more anxious. But there seemed no respite to this crisis, and we had little choice but to ride it out.

The night before, as we were browsing through our itinerary, I had told Lily (a name I lovingly use for my wife Sarika) that Chile had been a great experience. We were excited and wanted to explore Brazil now, especially Rio de Janeiro and Sao Paulo. After our South America trip, we would head directly to Dubai.

Lily, as always, listened to me patiently as she packed. Packing the night before makes life much easier in the morning and allows one to have a sound night's sleep—a simple rule I observe when I travel.

Little did we know that that night would turn out to be our worst nightmare.

3 a.m.–4 a.m.

I was jolted out of my sleep. The bed was shaking. Something fell from the table, smashing on to the floor. The bed continued to shake. I was in a state of shock.

Another loud thumping sound. Something else fell from the table. I jumped out of bed and looked at the clock on the wall. It was 3 a.m. I looked around the room and felt as though we were being sucked into a vortex. Lily woke up with fright. 'An earthquake has struck, Babu, an earthquake!'

She closed her eyes and desperately started to chant, '*Sai Ram, Sai Ram.*' She was praying for help from Sathya Sai Baba, an Indian guru considered to be an avatar of the gods and a divine teacher. The belief is that he performed miracles through the materialization of *vibhuti,* or scented holy ash, which had healing powers. According to his followers, Sai Baba had divine powers, even of bringing the dead back to life. I had the opportunity to meet him before he passed away at the age of eighty-four in April 2011.

As for me, I could neither close my eyes nor see clearly.

The bed started to slide. We felt as though we were dolls in a doll's house shaken violently by an angry child. Things were ricocheting all over the room. The curtains would be dragged to one side by an unseen force, and then to the other side. Nothing remained on the table. Everything was scattered on the floor. If we could get off the bed later, I thought, we would have to tread carefully.

I discovered that when an earthquake shakes a room, it produces a deafening sound, like a huge tree uprooted by a powerful storm, with rattles, bangs, screeches, raps and rasps. Next thing, I thought, the walls would crumble and the whole room would collapse. Our hearts were in our mouths.

'Babu, let's run for cover!' Lily said in a quavering voice.

But where could we run to? We were on the twelfth floor. If a big room like ours could spin like a revolving restaurant, what would be the state of the elevator? It must have crashed to the ground. We thought about taking the stairs, but what if they collapsed as we were going down? Should we just hang on where we were? What if the roof caved in? I did not believe at that moment that I could possibly survive. I was sure that the entire building was about to collapse or that our floor would be torn away and flung into the night to land God alone knew where.

An earthquake follows a pattern. It heralds its arrival with a series of tremors, and after the main quake subsides, there is a number of intermittent aftershocks. After two minutes and forty seconds of continuous tremors, the quake began to subside.

Lily sprang to her feet. 'Babu, I think it's over. Let's go downstairs.'

I hurriedly slipped on my trackpants, a T-shirt, and my shoes. As we were leaving the room, I glanced through the open bathroom door. After having my medicines the night before, I had left a bottle of mineral water beside the sink. I had forgotten to put on the lid. The entire room had been turned upside down, but the water bottle was standing there untouched. I was amazed.

We ran towards the elevator, but it was not working. It had been shut down as a precautionary measure perhaps, I thought; or had it actually crashed to the ground? Could there be people trapped inside?

We rushed towards the stairs. Every step produced a crunching sound as the stairs were littered with shards of broken glass. Many doors were jammed shut, and some hotel staffers were trying to break them down to rescue the guests trapped inside.

A large number of guests had already gathered in the lounge at the reception. Just as they were starting to talk nervously among themselves, a sudden tremor sent the room into a wild convulsion. Everybody was thrown about, like stalks of corn buffeted about by a gale. We were aware about earthquake aftershocks, but this one had happened with such ferocity that it appeared as though the quake was returning in full force. We wanted to go outside, into an open space towards the lawns, but a security guard stopped us. 'Going outside a tall building like this could be fatal,' he said. 'A cable might snap and hit you, or the windows could shatter and fall on your head.'

In a situation like this, the basement is usually considered the safest option for refuge. The hotel's basement had been unlocked, but the power supply had been switched off, probably to prevent short circuits, and it had no lighting or air conditioning. The guests gathered there were drenched in sweat, and had to use their mobile phones for light. It was so unbearable there that we headed back to the lounge.

CNN was already running the breaking news: a massive earthquake measuring 8.8 on the Richter scale, the strongest in the world since 1965, had hit Chile. Its epicentre was Santiago. Lily and I held each other's hands tightly.

Who could have imagined that a journey that began with so much excitement and enthusiasm would lead to such a terrifying night?

Sunday, 14 February 2010
I was on a ten-storeyed ship belonging to Celebrity Infinity Cruises that had just begun its journey to Antarctica from the

Argentinian capital Buenos Aires, with 2000 passengers and 1000 crew on board. The cruise liner offered all the facilities of a five-star hotel: round-the-clock casinos, an ultramodern theatre, a luxury spa, and restaurants that served cuisines from all over the world. It was like a floating city. I was vacationing with Lily, Naresh Khattar—a friend from New Delhi—and his wife Rita (Guddi).

I have always had an appetite for adventure. In 2009, I crossed the 5416-metre-high Thorong La pass on the Annapurna circuit. I have trekked to Kailash Manasarovar. I like to take up challenges and savour that feeling of victory when I complete them. This is my weakness as well as my strength. Some might call me overambitious, or a thrill-seeker, but to me, taking on challenges and succeeding at them is one's strength of will. And if you have strong willpower, there is nothing you cannot achieve. The voyage to Antarctica was a continuation of my quest for adventure.

The Celebrity cruise liner left the shore and soon seemed lost in the deep waters of the Atlantic Ocean under a crystal blue sky. We could not see land until we reached the Falkland Islands.

We experienced rough seas during the first two days of the voyage; something that felt like a perpetual, mild earthquake. We had not experienced anything like that before, and were so afraid we could not sleep. As if this was not enough, our ship was rocked violently by storms too, adding to our sleeplessness. We felt nauseated. At one point, I got so paranoid that I called the reception in the middle of the night, asking, 'What on earth is going on?'

'Sir, this is a normal thing for a cruise liner,' came the reply. I felt embarrassed. 'That idiot,' I thought. 'Patronizing me. Meet me at Thorong La pass if you have the nerve.'

People pride themselves on appearing calm and in control. But Lily's false courage made me laugh. She was trying to soothe me, saying, 'Babu, it can't be helped. We're on the high seas.' I quipped, 'You're so calm, you think it's like boating on Lake Fewa, do you?'

'No,' she snapped, 'I don't think so at all and that's why I'm not as scared as you are.' Khattar's wife loved the way Lily and I teased each other. She burst into laughter.

As the ship sailed farther into the sea, we began to feel better and started enjoying ourselves, making the most of what life on a cruise liner had to offer. Sometimes we went to the deck for the bracing, sometimes numbing, chill of the polar winds. At other times, we played roulette at the casino and ate delicious meals at the restaurants. Sometimes Lily and I simply stayed in our cabin, talking and laughing.

After four days of uninterrupted sailing, the ship arrived at the Falkland Islands, a place with historical ties to the Nepali Gurkhas, whose courage and discipline are legendary. In 1982, Margaret Thatcher had crushed Argentina, largely with the help of the fierce Gurkha soldiers fighting alongside British regiments. One story has it that the Argentinians fled when they heard Britain was dispatching a regiment of Gurkhas to the front.

Four years later, after Britain and Argentina had faced off once again—this time in a World Cup soccer quarter-final match—Argentinian football legend Diego Maradona reportedly said, 'This is a football ground and not a battlefield where the Gurkhas come to the rescue of the Brits.'

Even today, residents of the Falkland Islands are generous in their praise of the Gurkhas' bravery. From the chauffeur to the restaurateurs, everybody who discovered we were from Nepal treated us with immense respect. We felt a little overwhelmed. Thousands of miles away from home, our hearts swelled with pride at being Nepali. Britain still retains this oil-rich archipelago and should be grateful to the Gurkhas for that.

Our next destination was Elephant Island, considered the gateway to Antarctica. Here, all the colours of the world converge into two: the blue of the water and the white of the icebergs—some as big as mountains—floating on it. The sight evokes great tranquillity, much as the sight of the snow-capped peaks of the Himalayas meeting the blue sky does.

I had felt the same way at the Thorong La pass in Nepal as I looked around, standing close to the sky and surrounded by the mighty peaks of the Himalayas. I felt I had escaped the force of gravity and could float away any moment. An experience like that, so far removed from the mundane, has a huge impact on the mind. Most people's lives are so bogged down in trivialities that they find little chance to rise above them. To be surrounded by the majestic heights of the Himalayas or the depths of the ocean leads one to contemplation and a feeling of inner peace. We are in a place where no one can disturb us.

Nobody disturbed us during our voyage, except for a few tourists who could not stop themselves from screaming in delight at the sight of the gigantic icebergs. Some of them ran from one end of the deck to the other, mindless of the frigid polar winds buffeting them. Others stood at the extreme edge of the starboard side, extending their arms as if they were in the movie *Titanic*.

The cruise liner manoeuvred its way safely through the icebergs. We crossed the tail of Antarctica and arrived at Cape Horn Island in Chile two days later.

We were greeted by the penguins. The penguins love human company; these danced like children on meeting us, making us laugh in delight. We took many pictures with them. A film we saw on the ship showed how penguins can travel up to fifty kilometres a day searching for food for their fledglings. While the male goes out in search of food, the female takes care of the chicks. As soon as the male comes back, the female leaves to fetch more food. They know how pressing their task is, because if they cannot find enough food for their chicks, the young ones will die of hunger. There is something to be learnt from them: a lesson in perseverance, a lesson that one should never give up, no matter how daunting a challenge might appear.

From Cape Horn we headed towards the southern-most point of the world. Had we been ants crawling on a globe, we would have been scrambling upside down, feeling as though we were about to fall off.

I have no idea how many people have set foot on Antarctica. Norwegian explorer Roald Amundsen was the first man to reach the South Pole, when he set foot there on 14 December 1911. We landed there on 20 February 2010—eighty-eight years, two months and six days after Amundsen did.

The next day, we arrived at the port of Ushuaia in Argentina. The cruise liner was to dock at some ports in Argentina and Uruguay during the remaining six days of the voyage. I decided to cut the voyage short and visit some other Latin American countries before returning to Kathmandu. Khattar did not like the idea.

'You want to dump us in the middle of the trip?' he protested. I managed to cheer him up while Lily embraced Guddi goodbye. Leaving the Khattars behind, we set out to travel overland from Ushuaia to Mendoza, and from there to Buenos Aires and finally to Santiago in Chile.

Thus it was that we found ourselves in Santiago, where we experienced the worst nightmare of our lives.

28 February 2010
5 a.m.–7 a.m.
One of the hotel staff called out to me, 'Mr Chaudhary, your line is connected.'

A smile spread over Lily's face. She raced to the reception desk and grabbed the receiver. I followed her, hoping the line would stay connected this time.

'Hello, Nirvana,' she said in a single breath.

'Hello, madam, this is Sanjay.' One of our aides had picked up the phone. 'We're at a function at the Chandbagh School. Nirvana Babu is delivering his speech.'

'Get him on the line at once,' Lily said. 'It's an emergency.'

How unnerved Nirvana must have been, to unexpectedly have to take an emergency call from his parents in the middle of his address! But we were left with no other choice. The connection was unreliable and could be lost at any moment.

Lily gave him a detailed account of our ordeal. Nirvana was so upset that he was speechless. We assured him that everything would be all right. How anxious the others at home must have been when he told them about our situation! But talking to him brought us an enormous sense of relief.

As we were returning to the lounge after the phone call, we could hear an elderly lady shouting 'Hello! Hello!' into the phone. The connection had been lost again! Poor thing.

The hotel elevator started working again, two hours after the quake. Neither had it fallen to the ground nor was anybody trapped inside. We used the elevator to return to our room and started to take out our suitcases one by one. As I was pulling out the last suitcase, I again looked into the bathroom. The half-full bottle of mineral water was still intact.

'That's a good omen,' Lily said. 'Don't worry, Babu. The worst is over.'

I wanted to believe her.

The elevator was overcrowded as we descended to the lobby again. The guests in the lobby were rushing back to their rooms, while those in the rooms were emerging with their baggage. Even in the frigid February weather, most of them were in T-shirts, shorts or pyjamas. Nobody had bothered to put on warm clothes. Fear may send a chill up your spine and leave your hair standing on end, but at the same time beads of sweat roll down your face!

We had to wait for a while to get space in the lift. Lily dug out a shawl from a suitcase and wrapped it around her shoulders. 'Babu, should I take out a jacket for you?'

I was still wearing only a T-shirt and trackpants, but I did not feel the need for a jacket. Lily too was feeling warm and was wiping the perspiration from her forehead with the edge of her shawl.

Once we brought our baggage downstairs, I asked the receptionist to call up the airport. It turned out that no one had any idea when flights might resume. I inquired about the state of the roads. After making a few calls, the receptionist said, 'A car might be able to get to the border.'

It is a six-hour drive from Santiago to the small Argentinian border town of Mendoza. We had stayed there for two days on our way to Santiago from Ushuaia. Now, it seemed fate was taking us back there.

'I can't say for sure that the roads are clear,' the receptionist said. This put us in quite a dilemma. Eventually, I decided it was worth taking a chance. I asked Lily for her thoughts. 'Let's give it a go,' she said.

The hotel arranged a car for us.

7 a.m.–noon

The situation outside was chaotic, more frightening than inside the hotel. There were large cracks zigzagging across the roads. A road journey seemed precarious. Upturned vehicles were everywhere, and the bulldozers were out, trying to clear the streets. Flyovers had collapsed along several stretches. We did not see any house intact. Windows had shattered, and roofs and walls had collapsed. The same roads had been bustling with life when we were exploring the town only the day before. Now, our ears were assailed by the screeching sirens of ambulances and fire trucks.

Lily was pointing things out as we passed. 'There's the place we had dinner last night. My God! It's lost its roof. Look! There's the mall where we shopped yesterday. Remember how we had to pause after every few steps to reach the other side of the street without getting run over? Every window has been shattered.' She had not even removed the price tag from the new sunglasses she had bought there. I looked from side to side as Lily pointed things out. I had seen a town built overnight in China. Here I was seeing one devastated overnight.

The Chilean driver spoke very little English. If we asked him something, he would reply in broken English and then lapse into his local dialect. We tried to make sense of what he said, and had a surprisingly good conversation! We could read a lot from his expressive eyes. After all, humans share common emotions.

Approximately twenty-eight kilometres away from the hotel, he suddenly jammed on the brakes. We stuck our necks out of the taxi and looked out. The road was blocked by a flyover that had completely collapsed. Bulldozers had arrived to clear the road, but it was obvious they would not be finished before evening.

'What do we do now?' I asked.

The driver did not answer.

'Is there another route?'

He shook his head, 'No.'

We waited there for a while, but clearly could not go any further. We had no choice but to return to the hotel, dejected.

Some of the guests were glued to the television streaming live news from CNN. A few others were sitting on their suitcases, biting their nails nervously. I did not want to stay there a moment longer after my experience the night before, which had left me shaken to the core. Lily was in a similar state. She did not want to stay there either.

As we could not leave Santiago immediately, we decided to move to Hotel Marriott, a bigger and better place than the Kennedy. It was also in better shape. Even if you cannot escape a crisis, you do feel more secure under a strong roof.

Lily wanted to book a room on the ground floor, or at least no higher than the second floor, so we would have a better chance of running outside if another quake struck. Unfortunately, there were no rooms available on the lower floors, and we found ourselves on the twelfth floor again. Tourists like us who had also moved in from other hotels were crowding the lobby in search of a safer place.

'Well,' I said, 'we'll spend yet another night in the lobby while our luggage occupies the room!'

Lily started to chant 'Sai Ram'.

We tried to contact Kathmandu from the Marriott, but to no avail. We managed, however, to get a call through to a friend of Nirvana's who lived in Rio de Janeiro. She had been briefed about our situation already, and was quite worried about us. We asked her to let people in Kathmandu know that we were okay.

Once again, a fresh sense of relief swept over us.

Tuesday, 2 March 2010

We had experienced more than fifty aftershocks in the preceding twenty-four hours, three of which measured 6.6 on the Richter scale. Though the television signal was weak, CNN kept us updated. When we tried to watch television in our room, the TV would suddenly start to shake and then go dead. When we turned on the tap in the bathroom, the water flowed out of it like a snake. There was some respite downstairs in the lobby, but even there it was only temporary. The tables and sofas would begin to rock and the chandelier sway precariously, its crystals clanging. A glass flower vase slid to the edge of the table. After two sleepless nights in a row, most of the tourists looked exhausted, with eyes as red as tomatoes. Lily's eyes too were slightly swollen. I was in better shape, but having not shaved for a couple of days, probably looked worse than she did.

'Mr Chaudhary,' a receptionist jolted me out of a power nap in the lobby. 'There's a caller on the line from Brazil.'

It must be Nirvana's friend, I thought. Had she come up with a plan to get us out of here? I ran to the reception desk, wiping my eyes.

'Hello, Uncle.' It was Nirvana's friend.

She told me how worried Nirvana was back in Kathmandu. He had even thought about chartering a flight to rescue us but, of course, the airport was still closed. He had also contacted the Indian ambassador in Kathmandu, Rakesh Sood. Sood had briefed Pradeep Kapur, his counterpart in Chile, about our situation.

I asked the receptionist for a piece of paper and jotted down Kapur's number.

Dejection turned to hope as I immediately dialled his number.

'Hello, Mr Kapur . . . This is Binod Chaudhary speaking.'

He responded with familiarity as soon as he heard my name. He said he had been posted at the Indian embassy in Kathmandu from 1996 to 2001, and had actually met me several times. I could not recall him, but when we met, I felt there indeed was something familiar about him.

He personally came to pick us up, and we went to his residence. I silently thanked Sood.

We felt at home with Mr and Mrs Kapur; we felt indescribably relieved, as though we had been brought back from the brink of death. Kapur urged us to stay for a few more days but I turned down his offer.

'I wouldn't stay here even if they let me open a big factory,' I said.

That struck a chord with him, and he laughed.

'Do you have any suggestions about how we can get out of here instead?' I inquired.

'The border with Argentina is just a six-hour drive from here,' he said.

'Mendoza?'

He was taken aback.

'We already tried that but had to turn back,' I said.

'We have information that the road will be cleared by tonight,' he said. 'Mendoza has a small airport. Narrow-bodied planes can land there.'

Our faces lit up.

He advised us that a bus would be safer than a car for the trip along the precarious road. 'If you start tonight, you'll be there in the morning,' he said.

He helped us get tickets at the bus station. Many had heard that the road had reopened. By nightfall, the bus station was crowded.

Wednesday, 3 March 2010

A chilly wind was blowing as we stepped out of the bus in Mendoza.

Lily had wrapped herself in a shawl. I had put on a jacket as it was cold inside the bus during the night. But the jacket alone could not keep me warm any longer. I also put on a sweater and a scarf, and zipped my jacket up to my chin. I felt better.

We walked straight to a telephone booth at the bus station and called home. The line was now clear, and we were connected right away. Lily was so overwhelmed to hear Nirvana's voice that she could not speak. I took the receiver.

'Hello, Nirvana!'

He tried to clear his throat as soon as he heard my voice. He was crying.

'My boy, why haven't your plane arrived?' I asked, trying to cheer him up.

His laughter sounded like a whimper.

From Mendoza, we caught a flight to Buenos Aires and from there, another to Sao Paulo. After that, we went to Dubai and straight onwards to Kathmandu. We arrived after two nights and one day of continuous travel.

Nirvana had come to meet us at Kathmandu airport. My eyes brightened as soon as I saw him. I felt as though I was seeing the light of day for the first time in years. He hugged both of us tightly for a long time, but could not say a word. We were speechless too.

Lily did not step out of the house for two days after we returned to Kathmandu. She stayed inside, continuously chanting 'Sai Ram', and I did not want to stop her. All said and done, we depended on His mercy.

There is a lot worth mentioning from my memories of fifty-seven years. I have deliberately chosen to start this book with the events in Chile because that experience had a profound impact on me. The fear of imminent death and the realization that I might, in fact, have died in that earthquake, left me badly shaken. You lose your nerve in the face of death. Life is hope, a beginning, a dream to be realized, whereas death is the end, a void and extreme desolation. A dreamer lives on hope, always looking forward to the future, not focusing on 'the end' or giving way to despair. But eventually, every dreamer has to wake up too.

The Chilean earthquake pushed me into a period of my life when I could see nothing except the void, despair and 'the end'. I was a man who had set out to conquer the world, but suddenly I had been brought to the realization that my achievements, in which I took so much pride, could have been snatched away from me in a single moment.

Time is fleeting. I want to share something of myself with others. I might have earned billions of dollars, but my most treasured possessions are my experiences and my memories. This is the story of my life.

PART I: BIRTH

1

The Beginning

Many Nepalis call us *Maade*. This could be a colloquial, short form for Marwari, or it could have originally been a disrespectful term intended to belittle us, perhaps out of jealousy.

The Marwaris are among the oldest trading communities in the world. The community, which spread out from the Indian state of Rajasthan in the nineteenth century, has a strong presence in the industrial and commercial sectors in India and Nepal. The Marwaris have achieved this as a result of their willingness to take risks on the basis of their skill as traders.

Marwaris have never received the respect they deserve—whether in Nepali or in Indian society. The Indian author Gurcharan Das has observed this in his book *India Unbound*. Wherever Marwaris have established themselves, they have not been the local entrepreneurs. In India, the Parsis, Khojas and Bhatias dominated the industrial sector in Mumbai, while Gujaratis and Jains dominated in Ahmedabad. The presence of Marwaris in the business sector can be traced only to the years after World War I, but today they are among the most successful of India's entrepreneurs. According to Gurcharan Das, Marwaris own roughly half of the total industrial capital in India. By the year 1997, eight of the top twenty industrial houses in India belonged to Marwaris.

The Marwaris' situation in Nepal is not very different. They control the bulk of the total private industrial capital in Nepal, though there is no formal data to confirm this. The local Newars are another big trading community. If we look at the history of world trade, we realize that local trading communities still dominate local business everywhere. Newars and Marwaris are the dominant trading communities in Nepal.

The word Marwar comes from Jodhpur in the Indian state of Rajasthan. Historically, Jodhpur was known as Marwar. Later, the traders who spread to other parts of Rajasthan, especially Shekhawati, Udaipur, Bikaner, Ramgarh and Fatehpur, were collectively known as Marwaris. Among the Marwaris, those who come from Old Bikaner and the Shekhawati area of Jaipur have been particularly successful.

I would like to quote here from *India Unbound*:

For centuries Marwaris had been bankers and helped finance the land trade between the East and the West, as the great trade route passed through northern Rajasthan. During the Mughal days, they were financiers to many princes, including the emperor's family . . . a Marwari Oswal was a banker to the nawabs of Bengal . . . As the British created a national market during the nineteenth century, there was a huge migration of Marwari traders into the smallest and remotest villages of India. The migrants began as petty shopkeepers (often with capital advanced from a wholesaler from their own community) and slowly graduated to moneylending, then moved up to finance farmers for their commercial crops . . . The railways accelerated the process.

Some Marwaris became hugely successful and created large and famous firms . . . around 1900.

Why the Marwaris turned out to be so spectacularly successful had a lot to do with their wonderful support system, explains Tom Timberg in *The Marwaris*. When a Marwari traveled on business, his wife and children were cared for in a joint family at home. Wherever he went in search of trade, he found shelter and good Rajasthani food in a *basa*, a sort of collective hostel run on a cooperative basis or as a philanthropy by local Marwari merchants . . . When the Marwari needed money, he borrowed from another Marwari trader on the understanding that the loan was payable on demand, "even at midnight", and that he would reciprocate with a similar loan. At the end of the year, they tallied and settled the interest.

I belong to a community with a proud history.

My grandfather was born in Shekhawati in Rajasthan in 1870. We take his birth as the time of origin of the Chaudhary Group. He moved to Nepal when he was less than twenty years old. Nepal was under the control of the Rana regime in those days. Though Nepal was a kingdom, the Shah kings were mere figureheads under the Rana oligarchy. The Rana regime, which assumed power in 1846 following a royal court massacre, was toppled by the first democratic movement in 1951.

Towards the turn of the twentieth century, the Rana prime minister Bir Shumsher had written to four Marwari families in Rajasthan formally inviting them to start trading in Nepal. My father thought the four Marwari families were those of Mangal Sahu (Suraj Mal's family), Maya Ram Bhola Ram (the Tibrewal family), Hanuman Sahu (Banawari Lal Mittal's family) and Mahavir Prasad Brijwala (the Kedia family). My grandfather came to assist Mangal Sahu.

Until the Malla period, Nepal used to be on the trade route between India and Tibet. Nepal's internal trade was comparatively robust. After Chinese traders drove the Newar traders out of Tibet and established their dominance there, trade between India and Tibet through Nepal began to dry up. Some of those Newar traders fled to Sikkim, where they have a strong presence even now.

Nepal's trade sector began to shrink because of external political factors. The local Newar business community somehow sustained the internal trade in the country. The Ranas, who were then just beginning to gain exposure to the outside world, were concerned about Nepal's poor trade environment. It was around the same time that the Marwaris started to spread out from Rajasthan. The Ranas then decided to invite some of them to Nepal to expand trade there. That is how my grandfather and other Marwaris found themselves in Nepal.

Makhan Sahu was what the local residents used to call Mangal Sahu. He sold fabric and clothes in the Makhan area in Kathmandu. My father (Lunkaran Das Chaudhary) told us that grandfather's first job in Nepal was at Makhan Sahu's fabric shop. Though my father had never seen the shop, he had heard about it from my grandfather and my grandmother Saraswoti Devi Chaudhary. Grandfather was about fifty years of age when my father was born. I think he could not afford to have a child earlier, as he had to struggle until late in life to make a living, having left his home and his loved ones behind.

In those days, the Indian cities of Muzaffarpur, Ahmedabad and Bombay (now Mumbai) used to host textile *mundi*s (trading hubs) for Nepal as well as India. Grandfather would go to those mundis, walking all the way up to Birgunj, a Nepali town that borders the Indian town of Raxaul in Bihar. He had to walk for days along the old Indo-Tibetan trade route of Chisapani Gadhi to reach the border. At Raxaul, he would board a train. Having worked with Makhan Sahu for a long time, grandfather had become acquainted with the mundi traders. Soon he decided to start his own business.

We did not have a proper shop then. What we had was a mobile shop of sorts. Grandfather used to hire porters to carry loads of clothes and fabrics around, and sold them wherever he found customers. He was somewhat like a street vendor of today. Father started to help grandfather in the business before he was even ten years old. At family reunions, father used to tell us how our grandfather would visit the palace of the Rana prime minister with porters loaded with clothes: 'If the load was light, he used to carry it himself. I used to go along with him wherever he went.'

Those were the days of Prime Minister Juddha Shumsher. Grandfather used to spread out the clothes in the palace courtyard to display the latest designs of sarees and other clothing. Most of the clothes were ordered by the queens, but even if they had not placed orders, grandfather would head to the palace whenever a fresh consignment arrived from India. The queens used to select their clothes by gesturing from their *khopis*, or private chambers. The purdah system was in place then, and the women were not allowed to mingle with men from outside the family. Being a child, my father, however, was allowed to go straight to the queens' private rooms to deliver the clothes they had selected. We never had to return empty-handed from the palace. The queens would always buy something, perhaps just to show off.

Grandfather established his first proper shop in 1934, just before a powerful earthquake struck Nepal in the same year. Back then, a trader's share of the market was not determined by merely his abilities or the quality of his merchandise. Personal allegiances and animosities, based on racial, linguistic and communal differences, also played a part. 'That guy is a Nepali and this other guy a foreigner!' 'He is a local and the other guy an immigrant!' At a time when a person's 'nationality' was judged on the basis of his language, dress and the food he ate, the Marwaris were as thorns in their side for some local business families. The local traders' grievance was that the government should have trusted in the capability of the indigenous traders instead of inviting the Marwaris to come in. They claimed this would eventually let the foreigners take control of Nepal's trade, and undermine nationalism. In fact, the real reason they resented us was that they did not want to share the market they had monopolized for so long. However, they were not in a position to openly oppose us. To openly attack the families that had been invited to Nepal by the all-powerful Rana prime minister himself would have been perceived as a revolt against the Rana regime, and considered treason.

However, these jealous local business families started to poison the ears of the Rana rulers. As they had good connections with the elite in the Rana oligarchy, they succeeded in convincing some of them that we and some other Marwari families who had come from India should be squeezed out. We had to wait months for petty administrative processes to be completed, whereas the local businessmen enjoyed instant service. They succeeded in turning many of the Ranas against us, though fortunately, not the prime minister himself. Had the day come when we lost his support, we would have either been deported to India, or driven out to the malaria-infested lowland belt of the Terai.

The local traders might have succeeded in their goal had a devastating earthquake not struck the country in 1934.

Half the city of Kathmandu was destroyed in the quake. All the old, mud-walled houses collapsed. The eleven-storeyed Dharahara tower, the pride of the capital, shrank to nine storeys high. Ghantaghar, the clock tower, was damaged. Many people lost their lives and many more were rendered homeless. At the time of the crisis, the Marwaris came to the rescue of the people. They set up camps at Tundikhel, the open space in the heart of Kathmandu, where they treated the injured and gave shelter and food to the homeless. The Marwari women cooked, while the men brought those who had been pulled out of the rubble to Tundikhel for treatment. The entire Marwari community gave whatever it could afford.

Reports of the open camps run by the Marwaris reached the palace, and Juddha Shumsher himself came to inspect them. What he saw there was far removed from the things his brothers and other officials had been telling him about the Marwaris. These Marwaris were providing selfless service to the victims of the earthquake. Right there, Shumsher declared: 'Where did the idea of deporting those who are providing for my people in their hour of need come from? And how dare those who are doing absolutely nothing believe themselves superior? It will be them I will take action against.'

Those who had tried to squeeze us out got swept away themselves, while we received rewards from Juddha Shumsher, who had assumed responsibility for rebuilding the city. A few shops were constructed on Juddha Sadak (Road), and Juddha Shumsher leased one of them to my grandfather for Rs 200 a year. Later, the rent was raised to Rs 500.

Our shop was located just opposite the present-day Bishal Bazaar supermarket. In those days, companies did not have formally registered names. Grandfather was the first person in the country to start a formal and organized clothing company, which he called Bhuramal Lunkaran Das Chaudhary.

The earthquake that shook Kathmandu to its foundations led to the foundation of the Chaudhary Group.

The clothing retail shop was very modest. Our family lived downtown at Indra Chowk in the capital. Every day, grandfather would visit a Ganesha temple at nearby Maru, make a round of the Basantapur area and return to Indra Chowk. There he would visit the temple of Akash Bhairab, an incarnation of Lord Shiva, before opening the shop. He never changed this routine even during the most frigid winters.

'Looking at the face of a customer before looking at the face of God would bring bad luck,' he would say.

He built a small altar in a compartment on the top row of one of the shelves in the shop. There he placed a small statue of Lord Ganesha, who symbolizes luck, and of Laxmi, the Goddess of affluence. He would offer prayers and make offerings of sweetmeats, which he brought from the Ganesha temple. He would also make offerings into a small cash box at the shop. A swastika, symbol of good luck for the Hindus, was painted on the box in vermilion, with the auspicious words *Shubha Lava* written just beneath it. We still have that cash box today.

As the strong aroma of incense permeated the shop, grandfather would settle down to business for the day, sitting on a cushion with a clean white cover. Very few people were out on Juddha Sadak that early in the morning. Only a handful of the folk from Indra Chowk and the surrounding areas would stroll along that road. Grandfather recognized each of them and knew them all by name.

'*Taremam!*' He would greet them waving his right hand.

They would reply, 'Taremam, Sahujee!'

His neighbours and friends called him Sahujee, it being a term of respect to acknowledge his enterprising spirit. If a close friend passed by, he made it a point to invite him into the shop and share with him the sweets offered to the deities.

He was competent in the Newari language. My father too spoke Newari fluently, as do I.

Opening the shop so early in the morning was an exercise in public relations. Morning was when people had some leisure time. Even if a few customers came into the shop, it gave grandfather a chance to interact with the locals, get acquainted with them and build relationships. He always reminded us, 'A good businessman doesn't wait for people to come to him. He reaches out to them.'

Once people were at work and there were fewer customers, he would open his ledgers. He would double and triple check the entries and make the necessary adjustments every day before he returned home late in the evening. He would go over the figures again the next day, slowly moving his lips as he calculated, dipping his pen in the ink. A person who does not take numbers seriously will never be successful in business. This is something father learnt from his father and I from mine. I am now teaching this to my sons.

As the city was sparsely populated and quiet in those days, the chimes of the Ghantaghar clearly resonated at Juddha Sadak.

Father used to arrive at the shop at around 10 a.m., with one hand inside his pocket and the other wiping his eyes.

'You're late again today,' grandfather would chide him. 'Had you gone to bed early, you would have woken up early in the morning.'

Father would just smile. After cupping his hands around an oil lamp at the altar to seek blessings from the deities, he would eat the remaining sweets and then squat beside grandfather to peek at his ledgers.

My father already had a good knowledge of the business as he had followed grandfather around selling clothes before the shop was established. As grandfather entered old age, my father began to contribute more at the shop. Father's duties were to enter the daily transactions in the ledger, clean the shop and show the clothes to the customers. He was getting good training.

After grandfather passed away, father got the key to the cash box. Grandfather had given my father wings and shown him the open sky. My father was full of dreams and determination, but lacking in resources.

When I was born on 14 April 1955, father was trying his hand at enterprises beyond the shop at Juddha Sadak .

There was a high demand for Nepali jute in the international market. Many traders in the town of Biratnagar were making good money exporting it. The jute produced in that town bordering India was considered to be the best, in both quality and quantity.

Biratnagar had become a trading hub for the exporters because of its proximity to the port of Calcutta, now Kolkata. Father opened an office of Bhuramal Lunkaran Das Chaudhary there. That was the first branch of our company outside Kathmandu.

The decision to open the branch was in keeping with the times. The majority of Nepali traders, who had previously limited themselves to internal trade, were now getting into import and export trade. Trade with India was growing. The Nepali towns that were close to the Indian border, such as Biratnagar, Birgunj, Bhairahawa and Nepalgunj, were growing fast.

Father started to export jute to India and to places as far away as Europe from our Biratnagar office, and import clothing from Japan and Korea. The import trade was growing very fast, but the jute export side of the business was sluggish from the beginning. The business families of Biratnagar had almost monopolized the market, and others would have to depend on their grace to flourish. They would allow other entrepreneurs to export jute only when they had enough orders to keep their own jute mills fully functioning.

When I was two years old, father diversified his business interests into construction.

The construction of the Kathmandu–Trishuli road began in 1957. Father took a subcontract. He had taken a huge risk by trying his hand at an enterprise that his forefathers had never undertaken. A businessman who was selling cloth by the metre was now trying to gauge scores of kilometres of road. Father was a neophyte when it came to the construction business. He did not have a team to rely on and had no acquaintance with any of the experts whom he could have consulted. He had simply heard that the Trishuli road was being constructed with Indian assistance and that a subcontractor was required; on that basis alone, he was ready to give it a go.

Father mostly stayed at the construction site until the road was built. Mother used to tell us that he would drop by at home for a few days and sometimes, only a few hours, and then disappear for weeks or months. Sometimes it was hard to recognize him as his face would be smeared with dirt. Sophisticated technology was not available in those days. A contractor had to employ labourers who used their bare hands to construct roads, and father was not a hands-off boss.

'You learn by doing a job, not by watching it being done,' he used to say. 'Supervision is not about being the "big boss". If you lend a hand, you get better results because you're not only showing your workers that you value what they do, but also that nobody can get away with not working when you're part of the team.'

Though I have not travelled much on that seventy-kilometre stretch of road, its construction was an important part of the family journey that has brought us to this point. A person who has big dreams should take on tasks that push his limits. Capability is something you can acquire. This is another lesson I learnt from my father. From that point on, we have kept raising the bar for ourselves.

The experience father gained from the road project, as well as the money he had made from it, encouraged him to take on another. The Soaltee Oberoi, a five-star hotel, was coming up in Kathmandu. Father got the contract to construct it.

He formed a core team for the project. An engineer from Calcutta, V.K. Dhar, was one of the experts in the team. Dhar and father had become friends during father's business trips to Calcutta. Ghan Shyam Das Dhurka, a businessman from Calcutta, was another member. Father became acquainted with him during the days of his jute export business. Dhurka used to operate a jute mill owned by the famous Birla House of India. Birla House had a policy of letting its executive employees run their own businesses, provided they duly informed the board of directors and there were no conflicts of interest. If they failed to comply with this condition, they were fired immediately. Dhurka looked after the financial management of the project.

While Dhar was the engineer and Dhurka looked after the financial matters, the person with overall responsibility for project management was Satya Pal Sachdev. My mother treated him like her brother. In partnership with these members of the core team, father established a construction company called United Builders. His expertise grew with every project. Father had learnt to crawl with the Kathmandu–Trishuli road. When it came to the Soaltee project, he was still only a toddler. And building that five-star hotel was by no means child's play.

I was five or six years old at the time. I used to go along with father to the construction site, the way father followed grandfather about to the palaces of the Ranas. I still vaguely remember dozens of people working at the site, constructing the huge building.

The royal palace had a financial interest in the construction of the Soaltee hotel. Father used to tell us that King Mahendra and Prince Himalaya would visit the site from time to time. However, Prabhakar Shumsher Rana, the great-grandson of Juddha Shumsher, was the one who handled the project on behalf of the royal family. It took almost six years for the hotel to be completed. Everybody was pleased with the end result. However, for father, his hard work did not pay off. The hotel management kept putting off payments to the contractor, citing cash flow problems. There was nothing my father could do, as it was a hotel owned by the royal family. My father has told me that even the hotel accountant, who was a good man, used to candidly tell him that he was embarrassed to face the contractor.

Father had done his job honourably and was now being denied the payment due to him. But how could he, a businessman and a simple commoner, possibly raise his voice in any matter linked to the royal palace?

Father made numerous futile rounds of the hotel, hoping to collect his payment. Eventually, having undertaken a major project for which it was never paid, his construction company was forced to close down.

The toddler had tumbled as soon as he took his first step.

Juddha Sadak was no longer what it used to be in grandfather's time. It had become New Road, the heart of Kathmandu city. One day, father was chatting with his old friend Ramjee Narayan Agrawal during an evening get-together at New Road.

'Lunkaranjee, my son has just graduated from university. He speaks good English and gets along well with westerners. Please find a job for him,' he requested father.

'Let's see,' father said. 'Ask him to come and see me.'

A few days later the son, Binay Agrawal, came to see father. He was well educated, as his father had said, and also quite clever. He was fluent in English and well connected with the elite such as the Ranas, the Thakuris and the Shahs. Through those circles, he was acquainted with many westerners living in Nepal.

At that time, father was planning to open a flooring and furnishing store. Nobody had done a business like that in Nepal before. If people wanted to buy jute flooring or a linen carpet, they had to order it from India. No entrepreneur was importing those products, though there was high demand for them. International organizations were opening their offices in Nepal. Hotels were being built, in view of the prospects for tourism in Nepal. Even the average person was showing more interest in home decor. Father was looking for a reliable assistant who would have a good rapport with the international organizations, the hoteliers as well as ordinary shoppers. He saw that potential in Binay.

'I am opening a flooring and furnishing store,' father told him. 'Would you be interested in looking after it?' Binay agreed.

That was in 1963, when I was eight years old.

The clothing shop that grandfather had opened, thanks to Juddha Shumsher, was now turned into a flooring and furnishing store. Binay became our working partner. The store soon found its market. Tiger Tops hotel, among other such facilities, was about to open. USAID had recently established an office in Kathmandu. We supplied a lot of the furniture and fittings for the new hotels and international organizations.

Soon the demand grew so much that one old shop was not adequate to handle it, and father opened another outlet at nearby Fasikeba, and then yet another in Birgunj. Hotel Panorama stood just across the road from our present-day office at Khichapokhari in New Road. One more outlet was opened on the ground and first floors of the same building. With almost no competition, we had a virtual monopoly.

We shifted to the building at Khichapokhari where our office is located today. It was Binay who mostly looked after the store in that building. I used to call him Binaydai, '*dai*' meaning older brother in Nepali. I used to visit him as soon as I woke up in the morning and as soon as I came home from school in the afternoon. He would buy me peppermints, candies and biscuits. However, he would not make me his centre of attention when he was busy with work. I would then get offended and start to fiddle with things in the shop, at which he would scold me and send me away.

Binay really worked hard in the early years. He helped expand the business a lot, as my father had hoped he would. I do not know what went wrong with Binay later on, but he slipped into some very bad habits. He would get drunk in the morning and come to the office all tipsy. How could the partner of a virtuous man like my father be drunk first thing in the morning? Father tried to persuade him to give up his addiction but he would not listen. When we discovered that Binay had started his own flooring and furnishing business in Birgunj in competition with us, father decided it was best to sever ties with him. My father was an honourable man who gave his business partners a long rope and a lot of independence. But he would not tolerate betrayal of trust. Clearly, Binay could no longer be trusted as a business partner.

'I can't work with you any longer,' father told him one morning. 'Let's go our separate ways.'

Binay was dumbstruck. He then tried to plead innocence, claiming he had not invested a penny of his own money in the Birgunj store and that it belonged to his in-laws. He even promised to give up drinking. But my father would not change his mind. Once he became disillusioned with someone, it was hard to win back his trust.

'I've made my decision,' he told Binay. 'Don't worry, though. I'm not firing you. I'm the one who's quitting.'

Binay stood with his head hanging in shame.

The business that was flourishing so well while my father was at the helm, was ruined by Binay. A person who made bad decisions in terms of his own personal well-being could hardly be trusted to run a business, especially if his heart was not in it. But father could not fire the son of a friend's—not so much because he was kind, but because he feared criticism from his peers.

He settled his stake in the stores for Rs 6 lakh.

The year was 1968.

The demand for imported goods was surging in Nepal. Indian tourists had started flooding in to buy goods from other countries. Two decades after independence from British rule, India had not yet freed its market. Following the socialist economic principles of Jawaharlal Nehru, India was against foreign goods, in line with its 'quit India' policy aimed against the British Empire.

The state may have been opposed to foreign goods, but the Indian people were crazy about them.

Rs 6 lakh was a huge sum of money in those days. My father invested the money in yet another new venture—a department store. To woo Indian tourists as well as affluent Nepalis, the department store had to have an attractive design. Father was conscious of the importance of interiors through his experience in the flooring and furnishing business. He hired a foreign interior designer, Kwalthru, who was based in Kathmandu. He charged almost Rs 25,000 to design the store.

Father started the first department store, Arun Emporium, in Nepal, by leasing the ground and first floors of Meera House, a building owned by the late Juddha Bahadur Shrestha, whom we called Subba Sahib using a local term of respect.

The store was ahead of its time. It had separate departments for women, men and children, as well as separate sections for electrical and household appliances. It introduced world-famous brands such as Weinsil, Dormeuil, Hilltop Blankets and Christian Dior to Nepal. Indian tourists would come looking for our store.

I was thirteen years old at the time.

By then, the times had changed, but the wheel had turned full circle. My father was now visiting the Maru Ganesha temple and the Akash Bhairab temple via Basantapur before he opened the store, very much the way grandfather did.

He had moved the statues of Lord Ganesha and Goddess Laxmi from the old shop to the department store. He would offer prayers and make the offerings of sweets brought from the Ganesha temple. The same old cash box was kept at the store, and father would make offerings into the box as well, just the way grandfather did in the past.

Grandpa used to sit on a white cushion on the ground by the cash box. Father now sat in a revolving chair at the cash counter. He had hired around half a dozen people to assist him. He would wave his hand and greet passers-by, saying, *'Bhagwan sharanam!'*, meaning 'Take refuge in God!'

He knew everybody in the neighbourhood by name. They would reply, 'Bhagwan sharanam, Sahujee!'

By the time I reached the shop, rubbing my eyes, he would have finished his prayers as well as his PR exercises. 'You're late again,' he would scold me, extending the offerings to me, just the way grandfather would to my father at his shop. I would grin, taking the offerings and a morsel of laddoo if there was any on the plate.

Father tried his hand at many different business ventures after grandfather's death. Of them, Arun Emporium was the most successful. He also established a separate import company called Arun Impex. By the beginning of the 1970s, Arun Impex had become a leading import and export company.

Arun Emporium and Arun Impex complemented each other. One was a retailer while the other was an importer. We started to import a wide range of products for which there was strong demand, from foodstuffs and clothes to hardware and construction materials. We also obtained the authorized dealerships for some reputed European brands such as Moulinex S.A. of France and Max Factor of the United Kingdom. We also imported Beck's Beer from Germany.

I started helping my father once the department store came into operation. I was fifteen years old and preparing for the School Leaving Certificate exams.

Sarees made in Japan, Singapore and France were quite popular in Kathmandu those days. These imported sarees became a status symbol for women from the affluent and nouveau riche classes. It was a boon for our business. I handled separate departments—Saree Sansar and Ghar Sansar—within Arun Emporium, to meet this demand. I would stay back at the store late into the night, arranging the sarees on the racks; and I would notify our loyal customers about new arrivals. I would personally visit special customers to tell them about the arrival of new stock, and these sarees were so popular that the customers would come to the store the very next day.

Grandfather used to take bundles of sarees to the palaces under the regime of Juddha Shumsher. I sold sarees at our Khichapokhari store. But our approach was similar. He would go to the customers, carrying the sarees with him. I too went to the customers, carrying the message that new sarees had arrived. My grandfather's was a small, traditional business. Ours was much bigger and better organized. But our selling strategies were essentially the same. The customers would come and, just as my father had done in the past, I would unfold the sarees and lay them out for scrutiny. The customers would check each one carefully until they had made their final choice. After they left, I would have to fold up the heaps of sarees and put them back on the shelves.

Day in and day out, the sarees were folded out and then folded away.

It was best to import the sarees by air but it was difficult to bring in large orders because of the limited air cargo capacity. Those were the days of the 'gift parcel'—the government having formulated a law that waived customs duty on goods brought in by Nepalis from overseas. Many traders were exploiting this provision. Though there was supposedly a cap on the quantity and size of the 'gift parcels', the customs officers always appeared oblivious to that rule, or perhaps they simply did not care about it. Some of the customs officers would 'object' to what was going on, so the traders would bribe them. Some of the traders were having a field day, receiving thousands of 'gift parcels' every day, while we, on the other hand, could not get enough cargo volume to import goods for trade. We faced a stark choice: to resort to sycophancy, and if that did not work, to offer bribes.

I would visit the houses of the employees of what was then called Royal Nepal Airlines (RNAC). It had a monopoly as it was the only carrier of the country. The staff used to act as bosses. I would leave no stone unturned to please them so that they would facilitate our cargo. The day our goods landed in Kathmandu, we would be jubilant.

In the meantime, my father was establishing three factories in Birgunj in partnership with the Kedias and the Jatias. The first, Modern Hosiery Private Limited, opened in 1965. It manufactured socks under the brand name Rhino—a humble attempt to redefine the identity of Nepal, which was traditionally associated with the Mount Everest and Lord Buddha.

Nepal Spinning, Weaving and Knitting Private Limited, the second, was also commissioned in the same year. The factory laid the foundation for the production of synthetic cloth in the country by using imported spools of fibre. Imported fabric dominated the market in Nepal at the time. Though our cloth did not displace imported fabric, it allowed us to take pride in our domestic production.

The third factory, Ratna Stainless Steel Private Limited, came into operation in 1967. The steel utensils produced by that semi-automatic plant were the best in the market.

India had waived customs duty for these products from Nepal, and factories started to mushroom. Many trading houses expanded their business; however, many misused the duty-free facility by exporting raw materials rather than finished products to India. They would smuggle in coils of steel under the pretext of exporting stainless steel products. Others openly took spools of yarn and sold them in the Indian market.

Despite the customs waiver, India had placed a quota on exports from Nepal. Some businesses exploited the quota system by making special arrangements with ministers and other high-ranking government officials to ensure their products were included in the quota. Small entrepreneurs like us were supposed to beg them or the industrial families for a small share of the quota, but father would not do that. Hence, we were somewhat at odds with some of the big business houses.

Father, however, would not give up.

Life as a child

When I was born, everything seemed to be in a state of flux, from our family business to the political climate in the country.

The 1951 revolution had toppled the Rana oligarchy and had laid the foundation for political transformation. People had lofty aspirations. But the delayed general election did not allow the transformation to materialize. There was a yawning gulf between aspiration and reality.

Our family business was in a similar state.

The shop established by my grandfather at Juddha Sadak had laid the foundation for transformation of the family business, but the transformation could not take place as the family lacked capital, and my father was getting frustrated.

I was born under these circumstances at a maternity hospital in the premises of Surendra Bhawan, which has since been renovated and is now the International Club. As destiny would have it, it is the building next door to mine. Every day I go up to the sixth floor for lunch, I look at the building where I was born.

I was raised modestly in our Khichapokhari house. In those days, a row of connected houses lined Khichapokhari. It was a close-knit community, unlike the situation these days when people live isolated from each other in free-standing houses. The connected houses reflected the interconnected lives of the residents. As children, we would jump from one roof to the next. From the veranda of one house, we could reach over to the window of the adjoining house. The courtyards were as big as football fields; still, that sprawling space never seemed large enough for the restless, high-spirited children that we were.

My first school was Judhhodaya Public High School at Chhetrapati, in the vicinity of New Road. I then moved to Nepal Adarsha Vidhya Mandir at nearby Ganabahal. I was not an enthusiastic student. In fact, I would often skip school and loiter around, playing marbles and a local game involving pebbles. When I did attend school, I could not wait to get home, throw my bag down and go out to play right away. I was good at both marbles and the pebble game. The skin on my hands and legs would flake off and the skin on my face dry up from the dirt. During winter, the skin on my face would also develop dark patches. Mother would scold me, 'This boy doesn't care for his health so long as he gets to play.'

She was right.

Once, when I was on my way home from school, I spotted two deflated bicycle tyres. As I was with a group of friends, I acted as though I was indifferent to them, but as soon as we parted company at Khichapokhari, I ran back to Ganabahal. The tyres were still there. I picked them up. They were only punctured. I wanted to get them repaired as soon as I reached home, but my father had returned home early, so I hid the tyres under the staircase.

I could not sleep that night. I was waiting for daybreak so that I could get the tyres repaired. I was also afraid that my father might spot them, so I quietly slipped out of bed several times in the darkness to make sure they were still there.

Next morning, I sneaked out of home with the tyres and went straight to the Ason market in the neighbourhood. The repair man there asked for a rupee per tyre. As I did not have enough money, I asked him to repair one and dumped the other. That did not bother me as I had got it for free.

As he fixed the flat tyre and started to pump air into it, I felt inflated with joy. The tyre was to me what a new bike is to a teenager.

I would always carry a wooden ruler with me. I dug it out of my schoolbag. Now I had a steering prop for the wheel too. What more could a driver ask for? I set off, rolling the tyre along the road with the help of the ruler. I was in school uniform and carrying my schoolbag. Someone I knew could have spotted me and told my parents what I was up to, but the inflated tyre had so enticed me I could not stop playing with it.

I kept running, on and on.

Those days, the sidewalks were largely empty and very few vehicles plied the road.

I paused after running for about an hour. I was panting, and thoroughly drenched in sweat. As I looked around to find out where I had reached, I saw a big airplane parked on my right.

I had reached the airport, which was about five kilometres from home.

I had never seen an aircraft from such a close distance before. I ran to the other side of the road, clutching the tyre. Placing the tyre on the roadside, I sat on it, gaping at the aircraft. Shortly after that, the plane started to taxi and then left the ground to fly like a bird. I immediately sprang to my feet and picked up the tyre. My hands were sweaty and slippery. I wiped them on the sleeves of my shirt and, adjusting my schoolbag, tightening my shoelaces, and grabbing the ruler, I started rolling the tyre again. I was now trying to chase the plane.

I kept running, chasing after the plane for as long as I could see it.

Sometimes I feel I am still chasing it. I spent half a year flying.

When I reached home that evening, even my uniform looked exhausted.

This marathon activity went on for days. I would mostly go towards the airport as it had two advantages: a view of airplanes and less risk of being caught in action, as very few people would have recognized my father in that area. Sometimes, just for a change, I ventured out to other localities such as Thamel, Maharajgunj and Kalimati, but I was always looking over my shoulder in those places, fearing someone might see me and tell my parents.

One day, my fears came true. Father walked straight into my room, took me by the arms, lifted me up and asked sternly, 'Where is that tyre?'

I panicked. How did he know about it? Had he spotted me himself or had someone else told him? I never knew how. When I saw that he was furious, I did not even try to make excuses. Father did not get angry very easily. He would usually keep quiet or simply laugh things off even if we did something wrong. But when he got really angry his earlobes would quiver, and my own hands and legs would start to shake when I saw that. There was no point making excuses; none would be accepted.

'Under the staircase,' I said, so softly that I could hardly hear myself.

He went out of the room without a word. I did not dare to look under the stairs that day, but when I looked the next day, the tyre was gone.

I loved another game—collecting empty cigarette packets.

My friends and I would go around the neighbourhood for hours collecting empty cigarette packets discarded by smokers. We would even search the heaps of waste dumped by the roadside. As soon as I touched them, these empty packets would become cash in my hands, the way rubbish turns into art for some people. My friends and I had given the cigarette packets monetary value, depending on their condition and the brand. A packet that was worn out and faded was valued at only 50 paise. The Charminar brand was the most valuable. Those who collected the highest number of packets became the bankers. Those with none were bankrupt.

We would trade the cigarette packets for marbles. Actually, we would use the cigarette packets as a currency for trading marbles. Everybody was addicted to marbles but that did not mean everybody could bring money from home to buy them. We came up with this idea so that we could still play, even after we lost all the marbles we possessed. If one of us ran out of marbles, he or she could approach a friend and borrow marbles using the cigarette packets as collateral.

I came to realize much later that people had relied on the barter system before the monetary system was introduced, and that was what we too had invented to meet our need for marbles.

Why did we choose cigarette packets? Why did we not use normal paper for the purpose? We could not have, because regular paper was too readily available. To find a few cigarette packets involved at least an hour or two of search, plus we had to look for packets that were in a good shape so that we could maximize our returns. If they were slightly soiled, we had to clean them. It was an income-generating activity. We were into a form of commerce even in our childhood.

I would keep my marbles in an empty spice box under my bed. I would also arrange the cigarette packets in a row under the bed. I would inspect my assets every day after coming home from school, counting all my marbles and all my packets.

Father once caught me playing marbles at Khichapokhari. He did not say anything and his earlobes did not quiver either, but I could tell he was not happy about it, so I went home immediately.

But father never knew about the treasures hidden under my bed.

Once, while my mother was changing my bed linen, she spotted the cigarette packets. 'Why have you collected so many dirty packets?' she asked.

'Those are cash,' I replied.

She laughed heartily.

She was probably happy that a Marwari son was showing an interest in money at such a tender age.

We had a domestic help called Lal Bahadur. His son used to live with us. We all lovingly called him Kanchha, or the youngest one. I called him Kanchha too, even though he was older than I. We became firm friends.

He would regale us with his colourful accounts of life. He was a movie maniac. After watching a movie, he would emulate the style of the protagonist. I was already more into games than studies, and after Kanchha joined the household, I got into movies too. Now I would skip school to go to the cinema. If a new movie had not released, Kanchha and I would hang around town together, trying the food at various cafes.

I got so used to Kanchha being around and so at a loss if he had to leave me to go to work that I even decided to provide for him.

'You look for a room for yourself,' I told him. 'I'll pay for it.'

I was hardly ten then.

He found a room at Tebahal, a stone's throw away from our neighbourhood. I bought bedding and everything else he might need. If I needed money, I would sneak into my father's store, steal things and sell them at another shop. As I was still a boy, I would take Kanchha along with me to sell the stolen goods. I also helped him become a vendor. He ran the business for a while, but then gave it up. He had become a parasite, but I was too fond of him to realize it at that point.

Once, I lifted a whole box of lighter stones from the shop. A box of imported lighter stones would cost around Rs 100, which was a huge sum in those days. We approached a shop at Bhotahity at the other end of New Road trying to sell them, but the shopkeeper figured out where we had stolen the box from. That type of lighter stone was only sold at a handful of outlets. The shopkeeper also happened to be a friend of my father.

'Aren't you Lunkaran Das's son? You stole it from your father's shop, didn't you?' He scolded me. 'Should I tell your father?'

I pleaded with him not to, and promised I would never steal again.

He was a man of principle. He did not tell my father about the incident, being of the view that it was my first mistake. The incident was an eye-opener for me. I realized I was in bad company.

Father never realized what sort of bad company I had fallen into with Kanchha. However, he knew that I was not taking an interest in my studies and that I spent a lot of time fooling around with my friends. This worried him a lot.

Damodar Lamichhane, a son of one of my father's friends, had just returned from Germany after completing an engineering degree. He had started working at what was then called the Technical Training Institute at Thapathali in Kathmandu. A man of discipline and integrity, he is currently a senior advisor at our Chandbagh School.

One day, father invited him to our home.

'My sons are poor students,' he said. 'Would you tutor them?'

Damodar agreed.

He started to tutor me and my younger brother, Basant. Our youngest brother, Arun, was still only a toddler. 'Damodar Sir', as we called him, was shocked at the level of our education. We hardly knew anything. He told my father, 'This is not going to work. You have to put them in a better school.'

'Do as you wish,' father said, and handed over the total responsibility for our education to Damodar.

Damodar found a new school for us—DMPS, at Sanothimi. The school, founded with American assistance, had just opened. The National Vocational Training Centre (NVTC) was located to the right of the road leading to Bhaktapur, a historic town close to Kathmandu. The school was just across the road. He got me and Basant enrolled there when I was a sixth grader.

Our school was far away from home. It did not even have its own bus. We had to walk all the way up to Ratna Park to catch a public bus to school. We had to board it by 9 a.m. to make sure we would not miss the first class, which started at 10 a.m. It was almost an hour's ride. The time we left for school more or less coincided with the time the farmers from Bhaktapur returned home after selling their produce in Kathmandu. Not only that, the civil servants based in Kathmandu but working in Bhaktapur also boarded the bus at the same time. It was rush hour. As soon as the bus arrived, the commuters would rush in and grab all the seats. Kids like us did not stand a chance to get a seat.

I came up with an idea. As soon as the bus came to a halt, we would climb on the tyres and get in through the windows. While the grown-ups would be scrambling to board the bus, we could easily find seats. The idea worked! Never again did we have to travel standing.

In addition to academic subjects, four vocational subjects were taught at the school, and every student had to choose one from among them. Under Industrial Science, the students were taught carpentry. Home Science was about the culinary art, sewing and gardening. Most of the girls opted for it. Agriculture was concerned with farming. The fourth subject was Secretarial Science, which included touch-typing and practical classes on entrepreneurship. I chose that subject.

Jalpa Pradhan was our vocational subject teacher. She told our class, 'I will form a group of students. All you have to do is collect some money and open a small shop at school.'

We were quite bewildered.

'You will learn a few things and make some money too,' she said. 'Who wants to lead the team?'

Silence descended on the classroom, as though it were an examination hall. I promptly raised my hand.

We could not ask for money from our parents to open the shop. As we were day-students, we did not get money for our lunch either. We were at a loss about what to do. I came up with an idea. We would all contribute the money our parents gave us to buy snacks. That way, each could contribute at least one rupee a day.

My classmates accepted the idea, and a Save Money campaign was launched. I would collect the money from my classmates and save it in a piggy bank at home. I had written 'school project' with a red marker on the yellow-coloured, clay piggybank. We also collected money to buy a ledger to maintain the accounts of our investment. Each entry was posted in front of everyone.

We broke the piggy bank open after a month and collected more than Rs 150.

The teacher had told us to stock our shop with items that were in high demand. We bought peppermint candies, colourful erasers, different types of pencil sharpeners and a few other things.

At lunch break, we would gulp down our food, rush to the classroom and drag a few benches and desks to the playground. We would take our stock out and display it on the desks. Initially, other students wondered what we were doing. Some of them asked, 'What are you up to?' We replied, 'Project work.' Then they would look at each other and dig deep into their pockets. We had displayed items that we knew would tempt them. We would sell as much as we could before the bell rang to signal the end of the break.

After the final bell, we would have to show the accounts of our transactions of the day to 'Jalpa Miss'. We would show her the entries posted in the ledger book that we had bought for the purpose.

This was my first baby step into the world of business. Forty-five years later, I do not see any real difference between the business I do these days and the business I did back then at school. Only the scale is different.

I feel that what I learnt at DMPS kindled in me an inclination for business, which had been lying dormant in my subconscious. Deposit mobilization, capital generation, demand and supply dynamics, the margin between purchase and sale . . . are among some of the fundamental principles of business that I learnt from that thirty-minute shop at school.

The school, which believed in imparting practical knowledge without adopting a 'one size fits all' approach, brought about a 180-degree change in my life. I started to love the school environment. At home, Damodar Sir was there to tutor us. I drifted away from Kanchha and the other kids in the neighbourhood who were not so keen on studies. I threw away all my marbles and cigarette packets.

For the first time in my life, I started to focus on my studies. Instead of throwing my bag down and running out to play, my first priority on returning home would be to do my homework. My results at school improved so dramatically that I became the dux of my class.

When I passed out of the school in 1972, I was ranked among the top five in Nepal in the School Leaving Certificate examinations that year.

Two more students from my school featured among the top ten—Bishwombhar Chitrakar in the sixth position and Krishna Bahadur Napit in the seventh.

My stint at that school was the most important turning point in my life.

My marriage

Barely six months after my engagement with a girl from a business family in Patna, I changed my mind. My family was shocked.

'I will not marry that girl,' I said in front of my family. 'If I am to marry anyone, it has to be Lily or nobody else.'

What shocked them was not my decision not to marry the other girl but my insistence that I would only marry Lily.

'Lily?' father retorted. 'This is not possible.'

Lily was Sarika Sharma's nickname. Her family and those close to her called her Lily. We were old family friends. Her father, B.L. Sharma, was close to King Tribhuvan. Once the king opened a treasure chest and told him, 'You had told me that you want to visit Kashmir, didn't you? Take as much as you need.' He took out Rs 500. Sharma invited my father to go along with him.

The same cordial friendship had extended to the second generation. As her brother and I were of the same age, Lily and I were close friends. Every other day we would play *antakchhari* (a game based on songs, where one team starts a new song from the syllable that the preceding team ends their song with) at their place at Bhotebahal or at ours. As I loved to sing and had a good voice, I would steal the show.

They were four sisters, and all four were nervous when they were around me because of my strong personality. Lily, the third of the sisters, was the most timid. However, they were also fond of me as our families enjoyed a long friendship and I was a close friend of their brother too. Perhaps Lily enjoyed my company the most. So strong was the bond between our families that each would buy two sets of anything when they went shopping. Whenever my father would go shopping, he would never forget to buy something for the sisters, and their father would always remember us when buying something. Whenever our parents went abroad, they would buy similar gifts for both sets of children.

I had opened a discotheque in Kathmandu with a group of friends. It was called Copper Floor. This brought about a sea change in my life. I would come home at midnight, frequently travel abroad with my friends, wear fashionable clothes, and wore my hair long . . . all this while being a boy from a Marwari family, that too during an age of conservative thinking. My parents feared their eldest son might be slipping out of their control and, in such a situation, the best solution they could come up with was to marry me off.

They started pressing me to get married. To keep them happy, I visited many places to see potential brides. As father had trusted his best friend B.L. Sharma to find a suitable bride for me, Lily would be present at most of these functions. I always found her by my side. She was an intimate friend whom I could share my feelings with. Our formal antakchhari meetings started to turn informal.

Just when Lily and I were getting close to each other, I became engaged to the girl from Patna. She was modern, fashionable and forward-thinking. Lily's mother was present at our engagement, but for some reason I was not happy with the relationship. I felt I could not adapt to her lifestyle. Having been born into and brought up in a traditional family, I could not impose such a lifestyle on my family, even though I had opened a discotheque and given many sleepless nights to my parents. As the saying goes, gentlemen prefer blondes but marry brunettes. I was one of those men.

When I recall those days, I sometimes feel the girl from Patna too might have been just pretending to be 'forward', copying my lifestyle. Kathmandu of the mid-1970s was like Hong Kong or Bangkok in the eyes of Indians. To add to that, I was operating a discotheque, frequently flying abroad, besides dressing fashionably. Was she trying to come across as a modern, fashionable and forward-looking lady so that I would find her attractive?

Anyway, I was not comfortable with her attitude and behaviour. The more she tried to get close to me, the more

I tried to pull away. Quite some time had passed since our engagement, and she would frequently call me from Patna, but I just wanted to avoid her.

I had agreed to marry her, and now I felt trapped. I wanted to break off the engagement but was worried about the impact this would have on my family's reputation. However, I was also painfully aware that if I married just to make my family happy, I would live the rest of my life to regret it. A relationship based purely on a social contract would not have lasted long. A newly married couple are lost in themselves, as if there is no world beyond them. As time flies by, the boundaries of their world expand, and mistrust grows. The contract is breached. Moments, which once flew by when they were together, now weigh on them heavily.

Disquieting thoughts started to swamp my mind. I felt suffocated and torn by the conflict between what my head and my heart were telling me.

Lily! Her image flashed in my mind like lightning. I realized it was Lily who had been drawing me towards her, and that she was the reason I did not want to marry the girl in Patna. I looked around, and even my own room suddenly looked different. My heart felt lighter and my head clearer.

Without realizing it, I had fallen in love with Lily.

'They say that you have found another girl,' Lily, who sat next to me by chance at a movie theatre in Patan, whispered in my ear. 'Who is she?'

When I declared that I would marry Lily or no one else, it had sent a shockwave through my family. Her family had no objection, however, and I think they felt reassured at the thought of Lily marrying a young man they knew well. But my father was adamant: 'I would rather accept Lily as my daughter; this marriage is just not possible.'

The caste system was the sticking point. Though we both belonged to the Marwari community, her caste was Sharma and mine Chaudhary, and father was quite strict when it came to this matter. However, I knew him well—he was outwardly strict but soft within. I was confident that sooner or later he would accept us. However, the sword of 'marriage' dangling over my head had to be removed urgently. I eventually managed to free myself from this trap, even though it hurt my father's feelings.

I had told Lily's family, 'Don't worry. I'll talk my father into it.'

Lily, meanwhile, was oblivious to all these developments. I had not found an opportunity to discuss anything with her as she was staying away from home at a school hostel. Her family had also said nothing to her. When she came home for the winter vacation, a group of us had gone together to the cinema.

'Come on, who is this girl? Won't you tell us?' Lily again asked, trying to break my silence.

'You,' the word simply slipped out of my mouth. The darkness in the movie theatre had boosted my courage.

After my reply, Lily sat staring at the screen as though she found the movie riveting; however, I guessed that though her eyes were glued to the screen, her heart was racing and her mind was elsewhere. I suppose she must have been thinking about me.

I was so distracted I could not follow the plot of the movie. I even forgot what the movie was called.

Lily told me later that when they got home her sisters asked her, 'Did Binod babu say something to you?'

'He did,' she said. 'Why would he say that?' Her sisters told her about everything that had been happening. 'How is that possible!' she exclaimed. 'What a surprise!'

'Why were you surprised?' I asked her later, when we were out on a date at Godavari on the outskirts of the city.

'Why wouldn't I be? I'd never thought of you like that,' she said, looking at me lovingly through slanted eyes. 'How do you feel when you suddenly realize such a thing?'

'I hope you think of me like that now?' I asked romantically. She blushed.

I consider the moment we shared at Ashok Cinema as the starting point of our love, which grew deeper through phone calls and dates in the following days. We made good use of the winter vacation that year. I would feel tormented if a single day passed without us seeing each other, and Lily felt the same way. When she went back to the hostel after the vacation, I visited her many times with her brother. But it was not easy for us to meet while she was there, and eventually Lily found the situation unbearable. She became a day-student, using the pretext of a minor ailment that bothered her.

I owned a white Toyota Crown in those days and would wait at the gates of her school by the time her classes were over for the day. We would drive up to the hills of Godavari, Nagarkot and Kakani to steal private moments together, with Lily still in her school uniform. Sometimes she even skipped classes, but who cares about things like that when you are young and in love? You only want to be with the one you love all the time. We would spend hours talking, listening with rapt attention to each other. Even if the sky had fallen, we probably would not have noticed. We wished that time would stand still.

Looking at her watch in the evening, Lily would realize that she had to hurry home. Once there, she was good at making up excuses for being late, such as 'we had an extra class today', or 'we had a dance class'. I would always drop her at Tripureshwore, a few minutes' walking distance from her house. Every day, before we parted, we would exchange letters. We were not only seeing other and talking endlessly, but also writing to each other every day. And every night, we would talk on the phone too. After everybody else had gone to bed, Lily would sneak into the kitchen, and we would talk on the phone into the wee hours of the next day.

'My sisters know about us,' she told me. 'And they support us.'

Her parents supported us too, but as my father was yet to give his approval, they were under a kind of duress. I too felt the pressure. Our families were at odds with each other because of Lily and me. Our fathers, the old buddies, were no longer on speaking terms, and the two families had stopped visiting each other. However, Lily and I continued to see each other as often as we could.

No matter how hard we tried to hide our relationship, people started to notice it. The bowl-shaped Kathmandu valley was a small place in those days.

'Things can't go on like this, Binod babu,' Lily's mother told me one day. 'You need to realize that this could bring a lot of trouble to us too.'

Lily too started to say things that I found unsettling. 'Your family will never accept me. Let's go to India. We have friends there, so let's get married there and once we're married, everyone will have to accept it.'

Her suggestion pressured me even more because I did not believe in marriage without the consent of family.

'It's just a matter of days. Father will change his mind,' I tried to convince her. 'We can't exclude my family from our wedding. Everyone needs to be involved.'

I managed to convince her, but I was getting increasingly anxious about my father's intransigence.

19 April 1978

It was five days after my birthday. On my birthday, Lily and I had visited the temple of Guheshwori located behind the Pashupatinath area. Driven by some impulse, I took a trace of vermilion powder (tika), offered it to the Goddess and applied it on Lily's forehead, something that a husband does to his wife.

She was overcome with emotion. This was a sign of my commitment to her. And it worked. I felt it unburdened her soul, which was heavy with the growing pressure from her family and the uncertainty about which way my family's decision would eventually go.

Call it a mere coincidence or the grace of Goddess Guheshwori, but after that visit to the temple, we began feeling less pressured by our families. Though I do not believe in miracles, some happenings do challenge my rational mind. Within a few days, my father started to soften his stance. He invited Lily to our house and offered tika to her as his blessing. But he offered that blessing on one condition: 'If you two want to marry, you can do so. But you can't marry in Kathmandu. We would be the laughing stock of our community if your wedding took place here.'

I knew very well that he had always liked Lily, and that he actually feared facing the community, whose boundaries were hard to cross.

We decided to go to New Delhi for our wedding. The family of Jaspal Singh Sahani had made all arrangements for it. We knew the Sahani family through the sister of the girl from Patna to whom I had been engaged. Ironically, it was her relatives now solemnizing my marriage to Lily!

Jaspal used to operate a company called Supan at the time. He had won the contract for the interior decoration of the Soaltee Hotel, and used to visit Kathmandu frequently on work. With the help of his brother, Jaspal had taken Lily to India for treatment when she had once fallen ill. As he was a good friend, I used to tell him about the dispute in my family regarding my marriage. I was touched when he said, 'You are like a brother to me. Your wedding procession will start from our house.'

On 4 February 1979, we arrived in Delhi with a small group of close friends. Basant had arrived ahead of us to help with the arrangements. Lily and I were married on 7 February 1979, at the Maurya Sheraton in Delhi.

Due to Jaspal's affection and support, we never felt we were getting married far away from our country and our families. Father too arrived in Delhi at the eleventh hour to give us his blessing. We returned to Kathmandu on 9 February. By that time, we had already moved from our house at Khichapokhari to Thamel.

The day we moved into the new house also happened to be Lily's birthday.

Fatherhood

Whenever I pass over the Kupondole bridge, my eyes automatically fall on the slum behind the maternity hospital of Thapathali.

That is where my dear daughter rests.

To wait for a long time to have children is a mistake. I have always believed that once a couple is married, they should not put off starting a family. We should raise our children while we ourselves are still young.

Perhaps my daughter was also in a hurry. She did not want to stay inside her mother's womb for very long. Lily had to be rushed to the maternity hospital within a year of our marriage. She had gone into labour early, and our daughter was born prematurely, just seven months into the pregnancy. She had to be placed in an incubator. It was a torture for Lily to be separated from our child immediately after the delivery. She cried her heart out, and the tears never dried up. I was helpless. I would try to console Lily and then look at my daughter breathing softly in the incubator. May the Lord never make any father feel as helpless as I felt that day.

Those twenty-four hours were the longest of my life.

My daughter did not survive.

I laid her to rest in the cemetery behind the maternity hospital.

My family was grief-stricken. I wanted to cry at the top of my voice, but no sound would issue from my throat. My eyes were shut with sorrow, and I could not shed even a single tear. I had withered from within. I felt drained and empty.

I had always wanted a daughter. That wish was never fulfilled.

The next year, Nirvana was born on 15 March 1982. Rahul was born on 2 June 1983, even before Nirvana had turned two. The loss of our daughter was followed by the birth of our sons in rapid succession.

We waited three years for our third child. Varun was born on 13 February 1985.

All parents want to give all those things to their children they never had themselves. They want to send their children to the best schools, the ones they never attended. They want to raise their children in a way they could only dream of for themselves.

We were no exception.

Nirvana went to Rupy's and Kanti Ishwori schools in Kathmandu during the early years. Meanwhile, I was looking at well-known schools in India, from Sherwood in Nainital to Woodstock in Mussoorie. I liked Doon School at Dehradun the best. I was impressed with the standard of teaching, the environment, the culture and the facilities it offered. But it was not easy to get admission there. I had heard that even noted politicians and businessmen from India could not get their children enrolled in that school. Somebody told me that if I could enrol my son in grade one in Welham Boy's School at Dehradun, it might be then easy to transfer him to Doon after five years.

I decided to put Nirvana into Welham at any cost.

Charlie Kandhari, a very strict man, was principal of the school. I sought an appointment with him. However, even after waiting for hours outside his office, I did not get an appointment. I did not give up; it was a matter of my son's future. After my long wait, I saw the principal come out of his office, only to walk away without even looking at me. I followed him.

A white dog was trailing behind him. I followed the master and his dog.

'Mr Kandhari! Mr Kandhari!' I called out to him in a loud voice. 'I am here to meet you.'

'Yes, yes,' he replied as he walked on, not even bothering to turn around.

The more I tried to approach him, the more he moved away. I did not want to raise my voice in case that might put paid to whatever little chance I stood of getting my son into the school. I repeatedly tried to get acquainted with Charlie Kandhari, but he always avoided me.

I was at a loss to know what to do.

The Sikkimese finance minister, Chhamla Tsiring, visited Kathmandu shortly after my Dehradun visit. A close friend of mine, Captain Sudhir Rai, knew him well, and I was able to get in touch with Tsiring through him. I drove Tsiring around Kathmandu and built a good rapport with him. Then I took the opportunity to seek his help in getting my son into Welham.

'I don't have any influence there,' he said, just when I thought I had made a connection after struggling hard.

I was stunned. I thought all my efforts had been wasted. But Tsiring suggested an alternative.

'I can do one thing,' he said. 'I'll arrange a recommendation letter from Mr Kamal Nath (then Indian federal minister). Welham are sure to admit your son once they get the letter.'

He dispatched an aide to Delhi the same day. I got the recommendation letter a few days later and immediately set out for Welham.

Charlie Kandhari still did not show any inclination to admit Nirvana any time in the foreseeable future. He said all the places were taken. Then he said, 'I'll try.' At least, he did not try to avoid me, probably because he now realized that I had contacts in India despite being a Nepali.

Kandhari lived close to the school. His wife ran a beauty parlour nearby. I asked Lily to hobnob with her. She agreed. On my part, I started to cultivate Kandhari himself.

One day, Kandhari told me, 'I want to open a school in Nepal similar to Welham.'

My hard work was finally beginning to pay off. I realized that Kandhari was getting interested. I invited him to Nepal. To impress him, I invited the education minister, Keshar Bahadur Bista, to join us for dinner.

'The Panchayat Training Centre at Jiri has been vacant for years,' the minister said. 'If Welham is interested in running a school there, I could try to lease the property to you.'

I had no plans to run a school in Jiri. My only wish was to get Nirvana into Welham. However, now that the education minister had floated a proposal, I had to be seen following it up. I agreed to go to Jiri. Kandhari would not go by road. He said he did not have enough time. I chartered a helicopter to take him to Jiri. We inspected the school. He then said he wanted to use the opportunity to visit Tiger Tops, so I took him there as well.

After touring Nepal for a few days, Kandhari returned to Dehradun.

Nirvana was accepted into Welham shortly afterwards.

The school project in Jiri simply fizzled out. Kandhari did not show much interest in it and I was too busy with my own work too.

Nirvana was just six years old.

He still liked to sit on his mother's lap. He still wanted to be pampered by his grandparents. He still wanted piggybacks and shoulder-rides from his father. He was too young to follow his father to the office or to the Pashupatinath temple.

I was longing to give him the advantages I did not have as a child. It did not occur to me that I was depriving him of the happiness I had enjoyed at home with the family.

It was heart-rending to leave Nirvana behind at the school hostel. It was as painful as plucking out one's own heart and handing it over to someone else.

'Papa!' he screamed. 'Mommy! Why can't you keep me with you? Why are you leaving me here? Let me come with you!'

He was crying bitterly.

'Mommy, please don't leave me alone. Papa, I want to stay with you.'

He was pleading while his eyes welled with tears. I tried to act tough but his crying was tearing at my heart. There was a lump in my throat and I was struggling to console myself. And I had to try to cheer up Lily too.

We returned to our hotel leaving Nirvana behind, but our hearts constantly ached for him.

We wondered what such a small child would be doing at the hostel now. Did he have dinner? Maybe the warden scolded him because he spilt food on the floor. Was he still crying?

We could not stop ourselves from going back to see how he was faring. We sneaked into the hostel after dark, bribed the security guard and peeked into his room through the window. He was lying in his bed but still crying bitterly. My heart felt heavy and Lily could not even look at him. She ran away with tears in her eyes.

I too returned with a very heavy heart. My eyes were wet.

We remained tormented for a long time. Every time Nirvana came home for the holidays, he would cry and beg us not to send him back to the school. His friends and teachers told us, 'In the evenings after classes are over, he goes to a lonely corner and cries. He misses you a lot.'

Hearing that, we felt even worse.

Once, when I had gone to drop Nirvana back to school, journalist Vijay Kumar Pandey was with us. We had all stayed at the same hotel in Dehradun. The school bus was coming to pick up Nirvana and we were hurrying to get him ready. Just when the bus was due, Nirvana said he had to go to the toilet. He then would not come out, saying he needed more time. In fact, he wanted to miss the bus so that he could spend one more day with us. He missed the bus and was very happy about it, but we put him in a car and drove him to the hostel.

He played similar tricks on other occasions. While on our way to drop him at the hostel, I would hum a song by the legendary Indian singer Kishore Kumar:

> Aane wala pal, jane wala hai
> Ho sake to isme jindagi bitadun
> Pal jo ye jane wala hai
> (The approaching moment is about to pass
> I would want to live an entire life in it
> For the moment is about to pass)

The lyrics made him cry even harder.

Back at home, my mother would scold me: 'Did your father go that far away? Did we send *you* that far away?'

I was weakening emotionally, but did not lose my confidence that I was doing the right thing. I was consumed by ambition and the belief that I was giving a better future to my son. I did not listen to anyone.

A year later, it was time to send Rahul to school. That was even more challenging because Rahul had suffered from asthma since infancy. He would often have asthma attacks and we had to rush him to the hospital in the middle of the night. Timely treatment is crucial for chronic asthma sufferers.

We were now faced with a dilemma. A part of us wanted to let Rahul stay in Kathmandu but we were worried about its effect on Nirvana. What if he thought we loved his younger brother more than we did him? What we feared even more, however, was that it might affect Rahul's state of mind. Would it make Rahul less mentally strong? Nirvana was sent abroad for studies but Rahul was kept at home because of his illness. What if Rahul developed a mindset in which he saw himself as dependent and inferior?

We took a tough decision: Rahul had to learn to overcome his difficulties or he would never progress in life. You can take it as a courageous parental decision, or a cruel one.

Rahul was sent to Welham too.

After five years of trials and tribulations, it was still not easy to get Nirvana into Doon School. Contrary to my expectation, the school gave no priority whatsoever to students from Welham. What we had heard in the past was absolute nonsense. In fact, there was such strong rivalry between Charlie Kandhari of Welham and Shomie Das, Doon's principal, that the latter would not even entertain the idea of admitting a student from Welham.

Later, another friend of mine helped me get Nirvana and Rahul into Doon School. Once the two were there, we did not face any problem at all in admitting Varun later.

Academically, the three were average students, but they all turned out to be excellent in sports. Rahul, whom we had considered physically frail, turned out to be a dark horse and one of the school's sporting champions. He became captain of the football and squash teams, breaking the record as the highest goalscorer in the school's history. He was equally adept at basketball and other sports too. Rahul's stint at boarding school boosted his self-confidence, and he overcame his difficulties easily.

We were now on good terms with Shomie Das. I had planned to open a school in the past, just to impress Kandhari. This time around, however, I was serious about it. With Shomie's support, we opened Chandbagh School in Kathmandu. He became an adviser. Chandbagh refers to a garden at Doon School.

Sending children to good schools is not just about giving them a good education. It is also about their overall development and social networking. I kept this in mind while exploring options for my sons' higher education too.

After completing year ten at Doon, Nirvana went to Harrow School in north-west London. It is the institution where world-famous personalities such as Jawaharlal Nehru and Winston Churchill studied. After completing his course there, Nirvana went to Singapore Management University (Wharton Asia) to do his bachelor's in business administration. Rahul went as an exchange student to Millfield School in the UK and then to Miami University. Varun also went to Miami University, but we later transferred him to the American

University of Dubai after we decided to invest in the Emirates. After graduating, he went to Murdoch University in Australia to do a master's.

Friends from school and college tend to stay in touch and can support each other in their careers. Doon alumni hold senior positions in many important organizations across the world. Some of them are my sons' peers and this will definitely help them in the days to come. Exposure to leading educational institutions and good relations with their schoolmates, has developed self-esteem and self-confidence in my sons. I was sure from the very beginning that my sons needed both a sound academic base and a network of contacts to lay the foundation for a multinational company.

Each of my sons is looking after different aspects of the Chaudhary Group. Nirvana is based in Kathmandu, Rahul mostly stays in Singapore, and Varun is based in Dubai. My aim, to groom my sons as future leaders of the Chaudhary Group while I am still actively engaged, has been fulfilled to a certain extent. Lily has supported me in this. It was no small sacrifice on her part to send her children away to school to support my ambition. I am eternally grateful to her for that.

Now it is up to my sons to take the legacy forward.

Nonetheless, we still miss our daughter.

My Mother
She wore only cotton sarees all her life and walked around in rubber slippers. She did not allow even onion in the kitchen,

forget about non-vegetarian food! If somebody spoke in a raised voice, she would say, 'You are scaring God out of the house. Why do you talk so loudly?'

That was my mother.

She was born into a simple middle-class family in Darbhanga in the Indian state of Bihar. She had seen scarcity from close quarters, but her eyes never reflected discontent. She was illiterate but by no means lacking in wisdom.

When I started to get busy in my professional life, she would worry about my general well-being. I would be sitting in my room, focused on work, and she would come in hesitantly, fearing she might disturb me. She would sit quietly on a stool beside me and look around. She would then talk softly after gauging my mood. If she felt she had to talk to me, she would just stay in the room for a while. Sometimes, I would not even notice when she had entered or left the room.

She was very concerned about her younger sister Sudama. My aunt was not in a good financial position. Mother would do anything to make her happy. I do not ever remember mother asking for anything for herself; if she asked for anything, it was always for her sister. Her entire life revolved around addressing the needs of her sister, including the education of her son.

My mother was never robust. She was extremely thin. Yet we never saw her fall ill until she developed stomach cancer at the age of seventy.

We took her to Tata Memorial Centre in Mumbai, one of the leading cancer centres in South Asia. The doctors there told us they would have to operate on her.

When she was being taken into the operation theatre, I was standing by the door. Just before she was taken in, she slowly folded her hands to greet me. I do not know why she did that. Perhaps somebody had told her she had a very slim chance of recovery.

I was dumbstruck.

The nurses whisked her away.

We waited, pacing restlessly outside the operation theatre for eight hours. The surgery was a success.

We were ten siblings—four daughters and six sons. Except for our elder sister and three of us brothers, all the others died young.

Kusum didi was more like our guardian than a sister. We always obeyed her. I was the one she pampered the most. She and her friends would often go on tours to exotic destinations like Pokhara and Lumbini, and I would usually go with them. She was educated at Padma Kanya College. She got married to Mahesh Kumar Agrawal, who later became chairperson of the Nepal Chamber of Commerce.

My younger brother Basant and I were more friends than brothers. There is not much difference in age between us, so we grew up together. He was more into the arts than business. He was a man of poetic disposition, loving and giving. Later, he also proved himself in the field of commerce and made a big contribution to transforming the Norvic Hospital into the most modern hospital in Nepal, matching international standards.

As far as Arun, my youngest brother, is concerned, I have always treated him like my own son. I used to involve him in everything I did, grooming him as much as I groomed my own sons. He took a keen interest in business. He always wanted to prove himself and still does. He played a key role in expanding our automobile business.

All three of us had different styles of working. Our aims and goals were different. But we have always respected each other and never breached that line of propriety. That is why many wonder whether we still live as a joint family or separately. As our business started to grow, we took charge of the respective segments we were handling.

Father always believed that brothers should start to live separately before misunderstandings can drive them apart. If brothers continued to live under the same roof, pent-up anger and frustration would eventually explode, pushing them apart in such a way that they could never again come together. If they lived separately, however, giving one another breathing space, then they would continue to nurture love for one another. It is better to live apart and remain close than to live together and become estranged.

That was the reason I left our home at Thamel and moved to Ravi Bhawan.

Mother was not pleased with my decision. I took her to the new house I had bought, but she looked sad. She was very fond of her grandchildren and kept whining for ages about being away from them. Initially, I would spend only my holidays in the new house so that my parents could gradually come to terms with the fact that I was not going to be living with the extended family any more. I also accommodated guests there. Later, I started staying at the new house every Friday night.

Immediately after mother's surgery, we moved to the new house permanently. Mother conducted the housewarming rituals.

I tried hard to persuade my parents to live with us, but they would not agree to it. I then pleaded with them to stay at our place just once a week, but they would not agree to that either. Father preferred to see his sons every day at the office. Every evening, he would drop in at my office and then visit Basant and Arun before going home to Thamel.

We still visit our old house at Khichapokhari to celebrate Laxmi Puja, a ritual concerning the Goddess of wealth that is performed during Diwali, the great Hindu festival of lights. We make offerings into the old cash box and even to the measuring instruments used in the old cloth shop. The rest of the rituals take place at our family house in Thamel.

Mother's cancer relapsed.

When it comes to this disease, you remain helpless even as the person you love is emaciating and dying before your very eyes. No matter how much strength, money or facilities you have, you remain powerless.

We did everything possible. We tried Tibetan medicine. We tried Ayurveda. There was no treatment we did not seek for her. After all the systems of medicine had failed, we even resorted to rituals, but to no avail.

Mother passed away on 9 May 2000.

We took her to Aryaghat at the Pashupatinath temple.

The funeral rituals began. A large number of relatives, friends and well-wishers had gathered around the pyre where the mortal remains of my mother rested. Being the eldest son, I began conducting the rituals, guided by the priests. Our scriptures required me to take a dip in the 'holy' Bagmati river, which flows through the temple premises. I was also supposed to offer the holy water to the deceased. Just when

I bent down to collect a handful of water for the offering, the priests stopped me.

'You can't use that water. It's sewage,' one of them said. 'How can you offer such filthy water to the departed soul?'

I was stupefied that an orthodox Brahmin had asked me not to follow a ritual that was supposedly mandatory for the salvation of the soul. My mother had devoted her entire life to the worship of Lord Shiva and now I could not even offer a handful of holy water to her mortal remains! Nothing could be more shameful!

It was not that I was unaware of the sewage that flowed in the Bagmati before that day. But this sad reality really hit home only after I was barred from performing an important last rite. I did some introspection. I looked at all the well-wishers around me, the politicians, administrators, industrialists, businesspeople, social activists, journalists, artists, lawyers, and so on. All the people standing right in front of me were distinguished people in Nepali society; but here were these so-called 'dignitaries' standing on one side, while sewage, where I could not even deposit my mother's ashes, flowed on the other. I cursed myself, my society and my government.

I poured my heart out to my journalist friend Vijay Kumar Pandey.

'It would be better if you wrote about these things in such a way that it serves as an eye-opener for all,' he suggested.

I liked the idea. But how could I go about it?

'Writing just to give vent to your emotions won't serve the purpose,' he said. 'If you want to write, do it in a way that challenges the government.'

'What kind of challenge?'

'The Bagmati has become absolutely filthy. Either you clean it or, if you can't, let me do it,' Vijay said in a challenging tone. 'Can you write an open letter to the prime minister saying that?"

'I alone can't possibly clean the entire river,' I said. 'How could anyone clean the river when they keep discharging sewage into it? But if it's about improving the environment at the Aryaghat and making provision for pure water to offer to the departed, then I am ready to bear the expense.'

My entire body quivered at the thought of writing an open letter to the prime minister as I conducted the rites associated with my mother's death. The Hindu tradition does not allow indulgence in mundane matters during the formal period of grieving. It was not the time to write a letter to anyone, let alone a letter for publication in the mass media. My only duty, traditionally, was to religiously follow the last rites for my mother in seclusion.

Notwithstanding all that, I could not stop myself from writing an open letter to the prime minister after seeing the awful state of the Bagmati. I felt that if I did not immediately start a debate on the issue, my conscience would haunt me forever. Today I and my family had suffered. Countless Nepalis must have suffered in the past. If we did not act now, innumerable families would have to go through the same ordeal my family and I had to.

The article that I drafted after consulting Vijay was published on 17 May 1999 in *Kantipur* daily under the heading 'A mourner's letter to the Prime Minister'.

I knew it was impossible to instantly rid the Bagmati of pollution. However, I asked in my letter, would it not be possible to create an environment in which, at least the last rites according to the Hindu tradition could be carried out? As a citizen of the country, I made a public appeal to the prime minister to treat the water flowing through the

Aryaghat area at the very least so that it is suitable for that purpose.

I had written: 'If the line ministries or the agencies authorized by those ministries feel they are not capable of discharging the special responsibilities relating to Lord Pashupati, the venerable God of the only Hindu nation on earth, then through this letter I make a promise to the entire nation. Through my personal means and resources, and the good wishes of like-minded Nepalis, I will take the responsibility for Pashupatinath. Within six months, no son going to the Aryaghat to conduct the last rites for his mother will find himself in the position that I was.'

The article made waves across the entire country. Hundreds of people came to visit me. Thousands of people sent me letters of support. Some even encouraged me by pledging everything they owned for the cause. Innumerable people expressed solidarity. The overwhelming support boosted my confidence. I invited a South Indian architect, Raj Gopalan, to design a plan for improvement of the Aryaghat, and together we produced a Project Map.

However, I then discovered there was another project underway: the Pashupati Area Sewerage Improvement Project, led by Bidur Poudel. That project came under pressure after my article was published. Organizing a press conference, Bidur Poudel said the project was 'doing everything it takes to clean the river' and that 'the government is not weak'. The government revitalized that project by putting more than Rs 50 crore into it. We felt we should let the government try to resolve the problem before we stepped in. However, the problems dogging the Aryaghat remained unresolved.

At the same time, some people started to doubt my sincerity. Many accused me of making a promise in a fit of emotion, saying I did not keep my word. Elsewhere in the world, the government encourages resourceful people to engage in public works. In our country, however, I have had the experience of being snubbed by the government despite my willingness to do something for the nation. I did not get a chance to do my bit for the Bagmati even after making a public request to the prime minister. It was part politics, part ego on the part of the political leaders and activists, which barred me from pursuing the noble cause.

Just then, Queen Aishwarya, patron of the Pashupati Area Development Trust, sent her secretary, Sagar Timilsina, to see me. 'Her Majesty has been deeply touched by your article,' he said. 'Her Majesty is also concerned about the issue.'

He was hinting that the royal palace was planning to include us in the campaign to develop the Pashupati area. Within a few days, Basant was appointed member-secretary of the trust. He had worked for many years with the Social Welfare Council.

After Basant received the appointment letter, I told him, 'This is our obligation. Make it your first mission. If we have to extend any cooperation from our group, we will not shy away.'

Following Basant's appointment, some reforms resulted at the Pashupati and Aryaghat area. Basant has played an important role in this achievement. This gives me great satisfaction.

After our consistent efforts for the past fifteen years, we were finally able to sign an agreement, in November 2015, with the Pashupati Area Development Trust to revitalize the Pashupati Aryaghat area. The plan includes repair and renovation of Aryaghat, Batsaleshwori and Bhasmeshwor Ghats. The agreement has been signed as part of my group's corporate social responsibility commitments. A technical team of the Chaudhary Group (CG), in coordination with the trust, has conducted an extensive study of the area for the project. The pact was signed after the design drafted by the study team was approved by the Nepalese department of archaeology. Through this project, we aim to change the entire face of Aryaghat in Pashupati, which is one of the most treasured pilgrimage sites for over one billion Hindus across the world.

Even after taking my mother's life, cancer did not spare our family. Sixteen years ago, my father was diagnosed with cancer of the tongue.

We took him to Mumbai for treatment. Cancer specialist Dr Sultan Pradhan said that part of my father's tongue had to be removed. He assured us that after surgery, my father's ability to eat and speak would not be affected.

The surgery was performed, and my father seemed fine for the next eighteen months. Then the cancer relapsed. We returned to Dr Sultan, and more of my father's tongue was cut away. He started to stammer a bit, but other than that there seemed to be no problem.

The cancer came back two years later. The doctors in Kathmandu told us it had metastasized. We did not go to Mumbai this time but to Singapore and Bangkok. The doctors there drew the same conclusion. They said the tongue had to be removed. If that was the case, we thought, we should go to Mumbai where the first surgery on my father had been done. We returned to Mumbai. We visited the famous Hindu shrine, Tirupati Balaji, in the nearby state of Andhra Pradesh, to pray for my father's recovery. We also paid homage to Shankaracharya, head of the monasteries in the Advaita Vedanta tradition.

As I mentioned earlier, Lily was a devout follower of Sathya Sai Baba, a prominent Hindu guru. 'Let's seek the blessing of Sai Baba,' she suggested; so we decided to visit his religious retreat in Bangalore. No one, however, ever got a special audience with Sai Baba. All we could hope for were seats in the front row in the big hall so that his eye might fall on us. Whomever his eyes lit upon would be the ones to get blessed. Geetha Rajan, wife of K.V. Rajan, the former Indian ambassador to Nepal, had contacts at Sai Baba's temple. With her help, we got a chance to sit in the front row.

We had heard many stories about the miracles taking place at Sai Baba's temple. I could sense that my father, who was there with Lily and me, was hoping for a miracle. Sai Baba entered the hall. He blessed some of his devotees but did not even look at us. Father repeatedly leaned forward in a bid to attract Sai Baba's attention. I was silently praying for my father's prayers to be answered, but Sai Baba did not even look at us.

He left the hall without even casting a glance in our direction.

I could see my father was utterly devastated. Had Sai Baba even cast a glance at my father, I thought, that would have strengthened his willpower, and willpower, I believe, has a lot to do with overcoming cancer.

I too felt dejected but I could not restrain myself from doing something about it. I pulled my father to his feet and forced him through the door through which Sai Baba had just exited. But Sai Baba was retiring to his private rooms and his devotees stopped us from going any further.

We gave up. We stood there feeling helpless.

And then, a miracle occurred. Sai Baba suddenly stopped, turned around and looked at us. He beckoned to us to come to him, and his devotees cleared the path.

What can a human being say when faced with the divine? We were speechless. Sai Baba drew my father towards him and, with both his hands, forced him to sit. We were simply awestruck and could not utter a single word. Sai Baba took my father's hands in his own.

'What has happened?' he asked in Hindi.

Father could not speak.

Sai Baba then went into his rooms, leaving my father behind, and came out shortly afterwards with a handful of ash.

'Open your hands,' he said.

Father extended both his palms. He was looking at Sai Baba with tears in his eyes.

Sai Baba dropped the ash into my father's hands. 'Use this regularly,' he said. 'Apply it regularly.'

Tears started to roll down father's face. I too became emotional; I had a lump in my throat. We felt like devotees who, after years of meditation, had seen the face of God.

Father started to apply the ash to his face immediately.

Two days later, we returned to Mumbai to see Dr Sultan. He gave my father a thorough check-up and, after looking at all the results, said, 'Why have you come? He doesn't have any problems.'

We were amazed. We showed Dr Sultan all the test results from Kathmandu, Singapore and Bangkok confirming metastasis.

'These results are inaccurate,' Dr Sultan said. 'His tongue is absolutely clear. Go home now and put your minds at rest.'

We told him about our audience with Sai Baba but he did not believe a miracle had taken place. Others too find it hard to believe it, but it is true. From that day onwards, father has never had any problem related to his tongue, though his heart ailment does persist.

2

My Passions

Music and cinema

Legendary Bollywood star Dev Anand had come to Kathmandu for the shooting of his movie *Hare Rama Hare Krishna*. I would go to all the locations where the film was being shot—the historic Hanumandhoka area, the famous Buddhist stupa of Swoyambhunath and the Bhaktapur Durbar Square—just to catch a glimpse of him. Hundreds of people would be there watching the shooting, and I could never make my way to the front row through the crowd. Many times, I even joined the crowd of fans waiting outside the gate of Soaltee hotel where he was staying. Many of his fans would start to cry if they even so much as caught a glimpse of his profile as his car went by.

One day, we heard from the Soaltee that Dev Anand would be coming to shop at Arun Emporium.

Now that the person I was so desperate to catch a glimpse of was going to visit my shop, I had found something to boast about. He wanted to keep it a secret but I was telling all my friends about it, many of whom thought I was only joking.

Dev Anand turned up late in the evening.

We took some photos with him. He wanted to buy the Jaguar brand of socks, which were popular then. A fresh lot had just arrived and were still in our godown, so I went there and fetched five pairs in all the available colours. He carefully examined them, sniffed them and said, 'I'm looking for black ones.'

Damn! We did not have any black ones. However, I was not going to let my hero down.

'Sir, we don't have those here right now, but I'll get them for you,' I said.

'Fine,' he replied, leaving. 'Drop them at the hotel.'

As he had not told me how many pairs he wanted, I got together more than a dozen pairs from various places, packed them in a box and headed to his hotel to deliver them. When I reached the hotel, he was out on a shoot. I had to wait for hours. When he finally returned, I stood in front of him with a wide grin, hoping he would recognize me. But he did not at all, and headed straight to his room.

I tried to follow him but the hotel's security guards stopped me.

'I've come from Arun Emporium to deliver some socks that Dev Anand sir ordered,' I told them.

One of the security guards pointed to the reception desk. I said the same thing there and a receptionist rang Dev Anand. He asked me to come up to his room.

As I was climbing the stairs, my heart was pounding. Dev Anand had invited me to his room! He was expecting me! He would talk to me! I was in a state of ecstasy.

I pressed the doorbell, and Dev Anand himself opened the door.

'Have you brought the socks?' he asked.

'Yes.' I showed him the box.

'Are they black?' he asked.

'Yes,' I replied.

'Fine. Put the box over here,' he said, pointing to a rack by the door. I thought he might invite me into his suite, but he did not say anything. I was disappointed. 'Fine then, sir, I'll take my leave,' I said, stepping out.

He shut the door behind me without replying.

All my hard work had been for nothing, and Dev Anand did not even pay for the socks!

I returned to Khichapokhari from the Soaltee late at night, feeling sad and dejected. I was so downcast that even the streets looked bleak. I felt hurt. Later, I looked at it from Dev Anand's perspective. How foolish I was to expect a star like him to entertain a delivery boy like me!

As it turned out, I had many opportunities to meet Dev Anand later in my life.

I also developed an interest in songs and music.

The credit for this goes to Ryan, a vocalist in a music band called Ralpha. His real name was Narayan Prasad Shrestha. Ralpha was a very popular and revolutionary band in those days, and Ryan was a boarder in my aunt's house. He taught me music. I would play the guitar and practise songs using the notes Ryan would write for me on a piece of paper. Through him, I met Pradeep Nepal, now a senior leader of the Communist Party of Nepal (Unified-Marxist Leninist). Before devoting himself to politics full time, Pradeep had been a member of Ralpha. I also got to know Hiranya Bhojpure, Ramesh and the other members of Ralpha through Ryan.

I learnt to play the harmonium too. Harmonium Maila of Khichapokhari was my guru. He used to run a musical instruments shop in the neighbourhood, and was nicknamed Harmonium Maila because he sold harmoniums, apart from other instruments. I would visit his shop every day, either to watch him play the harmonium or to hone my own skills.

My musical journey took a new turn after I met Neer Shah, now a prominent film-maker. Neer introduced me to a musician called Shambhujeet Banskota. One day I said to him, 'Shambhujee, I want to record a song. Why don't you write one for me?' He was just beginning his career in music and was struggling, so he jumped at the chance.

It was not easy to make a recording in those days. The state-run Radio Nepal would arrange recordings, but only for established singers. They were not interested in unknown musicians. We had to hire everything, from the instruments to the backing musicians, and take them to the studio. We had to pay for the studio too. I also had to contend with some people who, knowing I was the son of a businessman, would try to fleece me.

But I was determined. I said to Shambhujee, 'This is our debut song. Let's record it and I'll meet all the expenses.'

We chose a morning slot for the recording. We had arranged for the accompanying musicians the previous day itself. I was to pick them up from their houses and take them to the studio at Radio Nepal. I had even hired a van for the purpose.

I was nineteen years old when I recorded my first song, *Maya ta jingdagi ko avinna anga ho; launu ra lagaunu aphno-*

aphno dhanga ho (Love is an integral part of life, though we fall in love in different ways).

But Radio Nepal would not play the song. They would not play any singer who had not passed a voice test. And you had to wait months to take the test. I did not give up, however. I registered for the test and kept practising my song while I waited for my turn. Eventually, I passed the test.

My song went on air, and it was played often on radio. Inspired by the success of my debut song, I soon recorded a second song, *Mera lakh lakh sapana haru* (My millions of dreams). Shambhujee composed the music, while Biswo Ballavjee wrote the lyrics. Shambhujee wrote both the lyrics and composed the music for my third song, *Ekai najarma maya basyo hai, lukichhipee heridinale* (I've fallen in love at first sight, the way she stole a look at me). It was a big hit and was later sung by other artistes too.

Annapurna (Ghimire) didi of the Annapurna Travels Group used to handle a musical troupe called Lalupate in those days. I used to receive blessings from her on the day of Bhai-tika. Annapurna didi later lived in the United States for many years. She would still call me up every Bhai-tika and for Janai Purnima.

One day, in mid-2011, Lily said to me, 'Please go to Bir Hospital as quickly as you can. Annapurna didi is there.' I had, however, taken it lightly. Only after I got to the hospital did I realize that didi was in a critical condition with kidney failure. She was only partly conscious. I was filled with emotion. I grasped her hands and, as soon as I touched her, she turned to look at me, but could not speak. She had been waiting for dialysis for three days. I immediately raised the matter with Bulanda Thapa, Bir's medical superintendent, and then called up Health Minister Rajendra Mahato to express my concern at the situation.

That evening, I received a call from the hospital. Annapurna didi had passed away.

I felt she had been fighting death until she had the chance to see me for the last time.

Annapurna didi had given me my first opportunity to sing on stage.

In view of my interest in music, she used to invite me to all her troupe's performances. During a national conference of the Lions Club held at City Hall, she asked me, 'Do you have the courage to perform live on stage?'

I replied, 'I'll do it if I get the opportunity.'

I was quite nervous in the beginning, standing with a microphone in my hand in front of hundreds of people. The clamour in the hall made me feel so scared that I thought no voice could escape from my vocal cords. But, somehow, I overcame the fear and sang well.

That was my first public performance.

The three recordings at Radio Nepal had now made me so confident I told Neer Shah, 'I have to bring out a solo album.' There were no CDs or DVDs in those days. There were only huge EPs. We had to record around half a dozen songs for that.

'Where do we go to record the songs?' I asked. 'We don't need to go as far as Bombay, do we?'

'Why would we go to Bombay? HMV has a good studio in Calcutta,' Neer said. 'We can always go there.'

He also made another suggestion: 'If you want good results with Sambhu, you'd better include Shubha Bahadur as well.'

I liked his suggestion. Shubha Bahadurjee was an expert when it came to playing, as well as arranging, music. Shambhujee had a deep knowledge of beats. They were working separately at the time, and I was the first to bring them together.

The four of us headed to Calcutta.

We stayed at the New Elgin Hotel in Calcutta. The recording took about ten days. Neer wrote four songs for me: *Euta nibhna lageko battiko prakash* (Light of a lamp that's about to go out), *Aaoo basa mero chheuma sunsan raat chha* (Come and sit beside me, it's a lonely night), *Pratikchhyaka palharu* (Moments of waiting), and *Vaishalu tarangama* (In sensuous waves).

I could not record one of the songs in Calcutta because I caught a cold. We waited for one more day, hoping my throat would clear, but it did not. We had to sync my pre-recorded voice with the new music.

An amusing incident took place in Calcutta, something we recall often in our music circle.

Neer and I had shared a room in New Elgin while Shambhu and Shubhajee shared another. Shubhajee was a man with a set routine. After his morning shower, he would put on a singlet, then emerge from the bathroom with his lower body wrapped in a towel. He would then put on his socks and boots. Only after tying his bootlaces tight would he slip into his pants.

A customs clearing agent had come to meet me at the hotel. He must have asked the receptionist for my room number and, as both the rooms were booked in my name, he first knocked on the door of the room where Shambhu and Shubhajee were staying.

Shubhajee opened the door in his singlet, towel and boots. The agent could not control his laughter. 'Wow! What a Tarzan look, brother!'

This line has become one of our great catchlines. If someone dresses oddly, or is in new clothes, we still tease him with: 'What a Tarzan look!'

After the recording of my songs at HMV, I greatly looked forward to releasing the album. I approached Ratna Recording

Corporation, which agreed to distribute the album so long as I met the costs. I agreed. To ensure a quality product, I sent the recorded songs to Victor Studios in Japan for production of the EP.

My first solo album, *Nepalese Modern Songs*, hit the market.

Raj Kapoor, the famous Indian actor, producer and director, once visited Kathmandu. I do not remember the reason for his visit, but his film *Bobby* had just been released, and the Lions Club hosted a reception in his honour at the Soaltee. The Lalupate group was performing there, and I was part of the troupe.

Raj Kapoor arrived at the hotel. His fans had gathered there in large numbers, but the security guards did not allow any of them to enter the hotel. Just as Raj Kapoor was stepping into the hotel, someone in the crowd was heard singing a track from the film in a melodious voice:

> *Hum tum ik kamare me bandh ho*
> *aur chabi kho jaye,*
> *tere nayanoki bhulbhulaiya mein*
> *Bobby kho jaye*
> (I wish you and I were locked inside a room
> and the key is lost,
> and that in the maze of your eyes
> Bobby gets lost)

Raj Kapoor suddenly paused. He turned around and looked towards the crowd. We looked in the same direction. A skinny boy who was humming the song was the centre of our attention.

The boy was Udit Narayan Jha, who went on to become one of the top singers in India.

Raj Kapoor was so impressed that he immediately asked Udit into the hotel. 'Bravo, son! God bless you!' he said, patting Udit's back.

Udit Narayan is the perfect example of a person who rises to great heights through sheer dedication and hard work. I had met him several times at Radio Nepal when I went there in connection with my voice test. I think he had already passed the test, but had yet to find a good song. He was so passionate about music that he would wait for days inside the canteen of Radio Nepal, hoping for a break. Today, he has made his mark in Bollywood.

Despite my passion for music, I could not focus on it the way Udit did. The time and energy I should have devoted to music got diverted to many other pursuits. When it comes to industry and commerce, however, I remain as passionate as Udit Narayan.

My production, *Basudev*

It was Neer Shah who came up with the idea of making *Basudev*.

I immediately accepted his proposal for a movie based on *Kattel Sirko Chotpatak* (Kattel Sir's Wound), a novel by Dhruva Chandra Gautam. It was an opportunity for Neer to prove that he had directorial skills. For me, it was a chance for a new experience completely outside the family business.

We named our company Manakamana Films. I wanted
to hire Shambhujeet Banskota as the music director. He was
yet to compose music for movies. But Neer signed on Ranjeet
Gazmer instead. Shambhujee felt slighted, and rightly so.
He had been with us through thick and thin. He was there
whenever we needed him. But when we were making our own
film, we had hired somebody else! I tried hard to persuade
Neer to sign on Shambhujee, but he would not change his
mind. 'This is our debut film, I can't take any chance,' he said.
There was no point pressing the matter after that. Neer, as
director of the movie, had made his decision.

There was an old house by the path leading to the temple
at the royal palace. The shooting of *Basudev* started in that
house. To cut costs, we used technology that could blow up the
picture shot on 16 mm. We hired equipment from Bombay.
The total cost came to about Rs 13 lakh. We also encountered
some technical problems during the shoot. To save on costs,
we had bought reels stocked by Photo Concern, a leading
studio in Nepal. We later realized that the use-by date for
some of the reels had expired. We did not want the production
costs to go up, so we reshot only those scenes that had blurred
views. As a result, the quality of the cinematography suffered
a bit. We faced other problems too. The lighting system
would break down, the cameras would not function properly,
technicians would fall ill, and so on. Somebody suggested the
project could be jinxed as we had not started the shooting at
an auspicious hour. To bolster the crew's spirits, we visited the
temple of Manakamana in Gorkha district, where the goddess
is widely believed to have the power to fulfil the wishes of her
devotees.

Film critics gave rave reviews to the movie when it
released in 1980. It is still considered one of the most realistic

and artistic movies made in Nepal. Commercially, however, it was not so successful.

The film did not give me any monetary returns, but it did give me exposure to the international film community. *Basudev* was selected under the Foreign Language Art Movie category at the Moscow Film Festival in 1983. Neer and I attended, while Shiva Shrestha represented the then state-run Royal Nepal Film Corporation. Back in those days, the Moscow Film Festival had the status of the Cannes Film Festival of today. It was there that I experienced for the first time the pride of walking on the red carpet. As soon as you step on it, you feel like a celebrity. The paparazzi followed celebrities from the moment they stepped on to the red carpet and until they reached the various function halls where the screenings were held. The cameras continually flashed, like lightning, for us too. Among the hundreds of artistes, producers, directors and technicians, I recognized only half a dozen—Smita Patil and Utpal Dutt from India, Richard Attenborough who had directed *Gandhi*, and, of course, Neer and Shiva.

The organizers had arranged to escort representatives from each country to the function halls. Before a screening, the film-makers had to stand on a dais and present a synopsis of the movie. Neer and I were invited to the stage before *Basudev* was screened. We were introduced as director and producer. Neer spoke about the movie for a few minutes. The hall broke into a thunderous applause. A girl came to the stage with roses on a platter, giving each of us one. We pinned them on our lapels and stepped down. The screening began.

The organizers would give us ten roubles at each screening for appearance as guests. We showed the movie in about half a dozen halls.

Basudev did not make much of an impact at the festival. However, we got the opportunity to meet with officials from Soviet Film, the national film-making institution of the then Soviet Union. Soviet Film had just produced an Indo-Soviet movie in collaboration with an Indian company. I thought that if we too could work out a joint venture with Soviet Film, we would be able to access to the international market. We held formal discussions with high-ranking officials from Soviet Film. I told them Nepal would provide fresh locations for Soviet movies and that the cost of production would be low. The Soviet officials liked my proposal. We signed a letter of understanding. One of their writers was to visit Nepal to write a script after deciding on a story.

Russian writer Aagisev came to Nepal within a few weeks of our return from Moscow. Neer took him to various locations in the country. They started working on a script. Aagisev returned after a few months, completing the initial draft. As per the agreement, we were to make the logistical arrangements for the movie and notify Soviet Film when that was done. However, I could not devote as much time to film-making as I did to the music.

My business interests, needs and priorities left me with little bandwidth for films.

The cinematographer of *Basudev*, Prem Upadhyay, knew the Indian actress Jaya Bhaduri well. Prem, Jaya and another Bollywood star, Danny Denzongpa, had graduated from the famous film institute in Pune in the same year. Prem opted for cinematography, while the other two chose acting.

Two years after the release of *Basudev*, Bollywood superstar Amitabh Bachchan came to Nepal for the shooting of his film *Mahaan*. Jaya came with him. This film was already attracting a lot of interest as Amitabh was playing three roles in it. Now that the film was going to be shot in Nepal, what else could film maniacs like us ask for?

I really wanted to meet Amitabh.

I told Prem, 'You told me that you know Jaya very well. Why don't you arrange a meeting with Amitabh?'

He called up Jaya right away.

They were busy shooting at Dhulikhel, and Jaya invited us to join them.

We went.

A song sequence featuring Amitabh and Waheeda Rehman was being shot. The song was *Jidhar dekhun teri tasveer nazar aati hai.*

Despite their hectic schedule, both Amitabh and Jaya paid a lot of attention to us. I praised their films. Amitabh inquired about my business. I had read a lot about him in film magazines, and that day I did get to find out first-hand what kind of person he was. I found him very affable and cordial, always smiling, always chatting; and he would make others smile too. I felt that was a sign of a true superstar—to treat everyone cordially without letting one's ego get in the way.

I invited Bachchan and Jaya to dinner at our Thamel house. They accepted the invitation without hesitation. Two days later they were at dinner with Lily and me, along with Prem and Himalaya Pandey, accompanied by their wives, and a few other friends, at Thamel.

After dinner, Amitabh read from *Madhushala*, the very popular book of poetry written by his father Dr Harivansh Rai Bachchan. He also told us his father had come to Nepal in the past to attend a literary conference; however, we could never find out the exact date or venue of the conference.

During dinner, I told him, 'I like the number that was being played in the background during the shooting.'

'Kishoreda (legendary Indian playback singer Kishore Kumar) sang that song,' he said playfully. 'Which did you like more, the song or my acting?'

'Both,' I replied. 'The song was great. But your acting made it even better.'

Amitabh laughed wholeheartedly.

'You businessmen certainly know how to make a good impression on people,' he said.

'That was no film dialogue,' I quipped. 'I meant that from the bottom of my heart.'

'Do you want to listen to that song?'

'I'd definitely love to, if you'd like to play it for me.'

'Then let's go,' Amitabh said, suddenly springing to his feet. 'Get the car.'

Jaya tried to stop him. 'Leave it for the time being. We'll send a cassette.'

But Amitabh had made up his mind. He would not listen to Jaya. I too did not want him to listen to Jaya.

'It'll only take five minutes,' he told her. 'We'll go to the hotel and come back right away.'

I got the car.

They were staying at the Everest Hotel in New Baneshwor. Amitabh asked me to wait at the reception and went upstairs. When he came down five minutes later, he was carrying a sound system with a double cassette player.

I felt a bit odd, realizing that Amitabh had taken so much trouble just because I wanted to listen to his song.

'You are carrying an entire sound system for me.'

He patted my back. 'Let's get going.'

We returned to my place.

He played the same song on one of the players and started to record it on the other:

Jidhar dekhun teri tasveer nazar aati hai
Teri surat, meri taqdeer nazar aati hai
Zinda hun mein tere liye, jeevan tera hai
Mera hai jo sab tera, ab kya mera hai
(Wherever I look, I see your face
I see your face, my fate, everywhere
I live for you, my life is yours
Whatever I have is all yours, nothing is mine now)

Amitabh gave that cassette to me before he left that night. On the cover, he had written: 'Dear Binod, Thank you for your hospitality. This is for your listening pleasure.'

The effort Amitabh took, even over a small thing like a song for someone who was just an acquaintance, made that evening unforgettable for us. I believe that this trait has been instrumental in propelling him to the pinnacle of success.

My craze for automobiles

Despite the limited resources of the family in the past, I could never restrain myself when it came to automobiles.

I was already riding a Yamaha motorbike by the time I enrolled at Saraswoti Campus at Sorhakhutte. When that

125 cc bike sped, I felt on top of the world. Very few college students had motorbikes in those days.

I would ride to college, my hair streaming in the wind. At college, I would hang around with my friends for an hour or two and then cruise to New Road. New Road was the place where youngsters would hang out and try to impress the girls. When you had a cool bike, you definitely scored!

Once I was speeding toward Bagbazaar with a friend as a pillion passenger. Just in front of Padma Kanya College, a leading girl's campus in Kathmandu, my bike collided head-on with a jeep. I was probably too preoccupied with the girls walking out of the college to notice the jeep coming from the opposite direction. My friend was hurled on top of the jeep while I, along with the bike, skidded under it. For a moment or two, a pall of silence descended on the scene. People were too afraid to even look under the jeep, fearing the worst. But I had not even passed out. As nobody came to my rescue, I slowly crawled out on my own. My clothes were dirty. I patted the dust off them. I then felt for the various parts of my body. I was completely unscathed. The bystanders were amazed to see I was perfectly fine following such a serious accident. My friend was fine too. But the bike was badly damaged.

Before that incident, I was more than happy to have a bike, not a car. Following the accident, however, I never rode a two-wheeler again.

A Fiat 124 was the first car father bought—a second-hand vehicle from a foreign project or embassy that cost Rs 18,000. I was a small boy then. The entire family was jubilant when father parked the car in front of Arun Emporium the day he bought it. However, we did not get to ride in that car even once. On the very same day, our landlord, Juddha Bahadur

Shrestha, asked father, 'Lunkaran Dasjee, where did you get that car?'

After my father told him about the great deal, Juddha Bahadurjee announced, 'You got it cheap. I was also looking for a car. I'll take that one.'

We were totally flabbergasted. However, father would never refuse anything to Juddha Bahadurjee, whom he considered his guardian. So the first car in the family slipped out of our hands before anyone but father could ride in it.

A few weeks later, my father bought another car. Again a Fiat. Second-hand.

Once I fell for a two-seater, an Austin Healey. I thought how impressed my peers would be if I owned a stylish sports car. During those days any car in Kathmandu was a rarity. People would turn their heads just to catch a glimpse of the car! I had to have it at any cost. I told my father about my wish to have the car, but he rejected it outright. I was adamant, however. I staged a hunger strike at home, subjecting my parents to emotional blackmail. After two days, mother started to pressure my father: 'Can't you fulfil your son's wish?'

Finally, I won.

That was the first car I owned. I could not resist cruising around the New Road area in that car (whose registration number was 1050) every evening, much as I had on my Yamaha bike.

As time passed, my passion for automobiles only intensified. Our family doctor, Sache Kumar Pahari, had imported an Alfa Romeo. For some reason, he did not want the car. He asked me if I wanted to buy it, which was like offering water to a thirsty person. I eventually acquired that car after much pleading with my father. I also bought a red Mercedes that Annapurna didi had selected for me. None of these cars was common in Nepal back then.

I then decided I wanted a Range Rover, the king of SUVs in those days. How was I going to get one? I did not have the money to buy one, and father certainly would not agree to buy me such an expensive car, especially after having bought me three cars already. But I could not restrain myself.

I found a way out. I used my contacts. A foreigner friend of a friend of mine was coming to Nepal from Birmingham in a Range Rover. His name was Ron. 'I'll ask Ron to buy a new Range Rover for the trip,' my friend said. 'Once he gets here, you can buy it from him. He'll sell it at a reasonable price.'

I felt as if I had won the lottery.

A few months later, Ron arrived in Nepal from Birmingham down the Silk Road. I treated him superbly so that he would like me, because I was scared he might ask such a high price for the car that I would not be able to afford it. Ron liked me and agreed to sell the car for Rs 1.5 lakh.

The price was right. But what was I going to do about the customs duty? Duty on automobiles was so high I would have had to pay around Rs 8 lakh. I went to the customs department to discuss what could be done but could not find a solution. I was racing against time. Ron was about to return home, and I could neither buy the car nor tell him that I could not buy it. I was dilly-dallying, and anxious about all my hard work going to waste.

Then I came to discover that the royal family did not have to pay customs duty on their imports. I talked to Kumar Khadga through his brother Neer Shah. Kumar had married into the royal family. But it turned out he had an annual quota on the amount of goods he could import duty-free, and that quota had been used already.

I got in touch with Helen Shah, another member of the royal family. We entered into a verbal agreement that she would buy the Range Rover for Rs 1.5 lakh, use it for a while and then sell it to me. Ron handed over the keys to Helen Shah. Now I was eager to buy the car from Helen Shah as soon as possible, but she had no interest in selling it quickly, despite the fact that there was no dearth of cars in the royal family. I never saw her in that car more than twice a year, but I had to wait for nearly four years before she finally sold it to me.

When I drove that Range Rover, I felt as if I was riding on Pegasus, the mythological flying horse. Today I have the latest Range Rover model that Nirvana gave me for my birthday, but I still have that old Range Rover too.

3

Drawing from Sports

The only person I have ever envied in my life is Suresh Gurung, one of my friends from my school days. This envy had nothing to do with studies and everything to do with sports.

He was such a great sportsman that he would master any game that interested him. Football, basketball, table tennis, squash—you name it—he was the champion. He remained a champion squash player for a long time. He worked with Nepal Airlines Corporation, the state flag carrier, for many years, and later for some private airlines. The girls at school were crazy about him, perhaps because he was such a good sportsman.

I was only an average sportsman.

Up to my college days, I was crazy about football, volleyball and table tennis. Squash was a later interest; I continued to play the game until I turned forty. I was also into bodybuilding from the time I was around fifteen. There was a gymnasium at Jyatha in my neighbourhood, and I would go there every day. Later on, I joined the American Club in Kathmandu. I stopped going there only seven years ago.

It was not easy to get into the American Club. Nepalis were not usually eligible for membership. But I always find a way to get what I want. Sandy Vogelgesang was the US ambassador to Nepal at the time, and we were well acquainted. One day I asked her, 'Could you please do me a favour?'

'What?' she asked.

'You would have to change a rule to do it for me,' I said. 'Can you change a rule for me?'

'I know you wouldn't ask for anything that I couldn't deliver,' she replied. 'If it's possible, I would even change a rule for you.'

I asked for membership of the American Club. 'You don't give membership to Nepalis. If you want to do me a favour, you'll have to change that rule. Can you do that?'

She thought for a while and said, 'I'll let you know tomorrow.'

The next day I got a reply. 'I can't change the rule for you but you can go there every day as my guest.'

Nobody had ever provided such a facility to anyone at the American Club before. I started going to the club as the ambassador's permanent guest. I continued to go there on a regular basis for twelve years, even after Sandy had completed her time in Nepal and returned home.

I still want to keep my body toned and fit, so I have built a gym at my place. When I am in Kathmandu, I begin every day with a workout under the supervision of a professional trainer. I feel a businessman, or anyone in a leadership position, needs to keep fit, even if it entails self-discipline.

As I get further engrossed in business, I find it increasingly difficult to find time for sports. These days, I play only golf.

Golf demands a strategic approach.

There are three stages to it. First, you need to understand the course, be mindful of where the undergrowth lies and where the bunkers are. It is not different from being aware of the state of the market in business. You have to have good knowledge of the competition, of the market rules and trends, and know where customer interest is heading.

The next step is to devise a strategy to strike the ball in such a way that it drops at a certain point, and take it from there to another. The ball will reach the desired point only if the right amount of energy is applied at the right angle and in the right direction. Otherwise, the ball will drop into a bunker or disappear in the undergrowth. Similar rules apply in business. We move ahead according to our assessment of the situation. The competitors make their own assessments. The one who assesses the situation best reaches the destination first.

After determining where and how to strike the ball, one has to determine which club to use. Business functions in a similar fashion. One needs to decide on the best tools—whether they are new strategies or plans to pull strings—to achieve one's goals. A businessperson needs to cultivate a wide network of contacts and be alert at all times as to the best way to use them.

Success in business, much as in golf, proceeds by these three stages.

Initially, I used to play at the Royal Nepal Golf Club next to the Kathmandu airport. I wanted to become a member of the club after I started to play at the course on a regular basis some nineteen years ago, but I was refused membership. While others had private membership for Rs1000, I was told I could get only 'corporate membership', which cost more than Rs 5 lakh a year. I understood the intention behind this discriminatory approach; they simply did not want to let me in.

There was no question about my unwillingness to pay Rs 5 lakh. I was barred from playing golf there. That incident hurt my self-esteem. I decided a fitting response to them would be to build my own golf course. I now have a nine-hole golf course inside CG Industrial Park (my industrial estate).

I have played at numerous golf courses around the world, from Scotland to Indonesia, from Thailand to India, the UAE and Mauritius. Still, I do not consider myself a serious golf player.

In business, however, I am a serious player. Here I apply all the strategies that a good player applies in golf. I bring the same zeal to my business that I brought to constructing a private golf course in CG Industrial Park.

PART II: THE ASCENT

4

The Leap

Wai Wai

The story of Wai Wai begins around thirty-five years ago.

Royal Nepal Airlines had already started flights to Thailand. Thai Airways had also started flying to Nepal. Many cartons of instant noodles could be seen trundling down the baggage belt once international flights landed in Kathmandu.

I had been looking for another product that could be made out of white flour. Pashupati Biscuits and Maha Laxmi Maida Mills were well established by then. A large portion of the white flour produced by the Maida Mills went into the making of Pashupati Biscuits. Still, the biscuit factory alone was not able to consume all the flour from the mills. 'Why don't you try producing instant noodles?' Himalaya Pandey, a friend of mine, suggested to me one day.

He was then working with Gorkha Travels, one of the leading travel and tour operators of Nepal in those days, and had noticed the large quantities of instant noodles arriving on the Bangkok–Kathmandu flights. 'Noodles are getting more popular in Nepal,' he said.

One of the reasons for the popularity of noodles was the growing number of Nepalis who were going abroad and trying out new foods. A second reason was the aggressive marketing campaigns launched in Nepal by two noodle companies. Gandaki Noodles had launched Rara while Nestlé India Limited's Maggi was being imported in huge quantities. I concluded that nothing could be more appropriate than instant noodles for the consumption of white flour. I had my own packaging plant. All I needed was the technical knowledge related to noodle production. As far as the market was concerned, Rara and Maggi had blazed the trail. I just had to blacktop it.

Himalaya Pandey and I caught a Thai Airways flight to Bangkok, following the trail of the baggage belt.

Bangkok was not new to me. I had had good contacts there since the days of starting Arun Emporium. Berli Jucker, the company that had supplied the equipment for our flour mills, had its regional headquarters in Bangkok. Through Berli Jucker, I was able to meet with noodle producers there.

There were three companies. I approached all of them, settling for Thai Preserved Foods as our technical collaborator. We did not need any additional support except to learn how to produce fully cooked instant noodles. The company was not big enough to give us any other kind of support either. It was owned by a gentleman called Kitty Pong Sri and some of his partners. He was a very creative and hard-working man but was happy with what he had. I invited him to visit Nepal to help me make my final decision, and he obliged. After spending three days exploring the streets of Kathmandu and its markets, he asked me with his eyebrows raised, 'Do you really want to start a noodles plant? The smallest lot will be 30,000 packets a day. Do you think you can ever sell this quantity in this country?' I shared with him the famous story of two salesmen going to the same market; one returning with the report that since nobody eats there is no market, and the other coming back with a completely opposite story, that since nobody eats, this is the market! That was how Wai Wai was born.

After the success of Wai Wai, we launched Mama noodles in the market. The chief executive of Thailand's President's Food, Pipat, came to see me. I thought it was about my registering the brand in Nepal but, on the contrary, he had come with a proposal for a joint venture. I told him, 'I'm ready for a joint venture, but it has to be on my terms.'

He did not accept my conditions. I felt his proposal was a ploy on his part to make my brand name subordinate to his. We could not agree on the terms. Mama forwarded another proposal through an investment bank we both dealt with. This was different from the first proposal. They wanted a joint venture in those countries where neither Wai Wai nor Mama had been introduced. They thought I should be grateful for the worldwide collaboration. But again, it would have entailed the surrendering of my brand. I rejected the offer again. In today's world, the worth of a company does not lie in its fixed assets alone. In fact, they contribute only a small part to it. A company's real worth lies in its intellectual property. That is why I have always stood firm when it comes to the brand name. Here in Nepal, we are driven by a mindset of producing goods under others' brand names, making huge profits while also paying royalty. But I chose the path of establishing my own brand. I think this strategy is the main factor that has driven the Chaudhary Group to where it is today.

Following the strategy we drew up to globalize Wai Wai, we have expanded our presence and now sell in more than thirty-five countries.

Establishing an ambitious goal for oneself can feel daunting, but one must rise to the challenge. That was how I felt when I signed the contract with Thai Food. They were, however, extremely supportive. They put me in touch with companies that manufactured plants for production of instant noodles. I bought a plant of the smallest capacity from a Taiwanese company. I installed the first plant at Saibu, Bhainsepati, in Lalitpur district. The plant could produce 30,000 packets of instant noodles in an eight-hour period. That plant is still operating in Bhainsepati. However, we have many more plants today.

In those days, there were no channels for the systematic distribution of fast-moving consumer goods (FMCGs) such as noodles and biscuits. Once the goods were produced, they were handed over to the wholesalers. I hired the late K.R. Sharma, a senior official at Nestlé India, to manage the market for Wai Wai. He worked with us for around nine years and played a pivotal role in strengthening the market, not just for Wai Wai, but for the entire Chaudhary Group.

Wai Wai hit the Nepal market in 1984. Now we needed a strong marketing campaign, and I give credit for the success of that campaign to Sharma. As part of his strategy, we produced a very popular advertisement for television featuring the model Dolly Gurung. Dolly became an overnight celebrity as a result of that ad, which was shot by *Basudev*'s cinematographer Prem Upadhyay. Wai Wai was hugely successful.

Within two years, Wai Wai had brought about a sea change in the eating habit of Nepalis. It became so popular that it virtually displaced Nestlé's Maggi from the Nepal market, making Nepal self-sufficient when it came to instant noodles. We set up our second plant at the CG Industrial Park in Nawalparasi as the demand for Wai Wai rose meteorically. We bought yet another plant that was being sold by an Indonesian instant noodles company. Today we produce approximately 1.5 million packets of Wai Wai in Nepal alone, fifty times the quantity of 30,000 packets that Kitty Pong Sri had doubted we could sell.

War of instant noodles

After the success of Wai Wai, instant noodles companies mushroomed in Nepal. They were all trying to copy us. Some of the competitors were my friends. However, they were so desperate to get a share of the market that they almost destroyed the market itself. At one point, all the other instant noodles companies formed a coalition against Wai Wai. They were not working to expand the market but to take a share of Wai Wai's by slashing prices to such an extent that they were making losses. Television channels were deluged with advertisements for instant noodles, all offering amazing prizes—from goats to cars to houses to overseas trips—to their customers.

The impact of the competition was so intense that even a well-established company like ours was jolted. Wai Wai's share of the market plummeted from 80 per cent to 40 per cent. The price difference between Wai Wai and other brands became negligible. After our competitors started to offer unbelievable discounts, the wholesalers refused to pay the minimum price we had agreed on. Minimum price is the strongest indicator of a product's place in the market. If the minimum price of your product does not vary despite your competitors' decision to slash their prices, then you know your product is firmly entrenched in the market.

Conversely, a company knows it is in trouble when the price of its products in the market falls dramatically. I passed through that phase in 2004. G.P. Shah, vice president of the Chaudhary Group, played a big role in steering Wai Wai through that crisis. During the time of the price war, he had just taken charge of the sales and marketing division of the company. It was Nirvana's decision to shift him from production to marketing, which proved to be a good move.

One day, GP, as we called him, came to me with some market news. A woman had reportedly told a retailer, 'We've had enough of Wai Wai. If we buy Mayos, we might get a diamond necklace.'

'Consumers' aspirations have changed,' GP said. 'Other companies are coming up with schemes that offer prizes, and Wai Wai consumers are feeling neglected. If we don't start giving our consumers what they want, then we'll face a tough time in the market.'

'What should we do?' I asked.

'We should offer prizes as well.'

'So should we copy them?'

'Do we have a choice?' G.P. replied. 'Mayos is offering diamond necklaces, so we should offer an entire set of diamond jewellery. Our slogan should be: "No more just a diamond necklace: now a full set of diamond jewellery."'

His idea worked. We gave sets of diamond jewellery to more than a dozen customers within a month. We came up with prizes such as houses, cars, motorcycles, laptops, desktops and many other attractive items. We were, however, not satisfied with the long-term prospects of boosting sales by offering prizes. We devised four strategies to survive the price war.

First, we decided to focus on wooing young people and making our product more suitable for children. We launched a new product called Wai Wai Quick with the flavour of chicken curry. We also started to add more nutrients such as calcium, minerals and vitamins. This brought something new to our brand.

The second strategy related to media. We started to produce informative advertisements and launched creative programmes. The Gyan Uday (Rise of Knowledge) scholarship was one of them.

Third, we pulled Wai Wai out from the cut-throat price war and launched many cheaper brands such as Gol Mol, Mama and Rin Tin, which we called 'fighter brands'. We offered many deals with those brands, such as 'buy one and get one free' and 'three packets for only Rs 20'. We launched a counter-attack against our competitors through these brands, but we never brought our premium brand Wai Wai to the battlefront.

Fourth, we changed our organizational structure. Nirvana played a pivotal role in this. In the initial days, our organization relied heavily on foreign executives and technicians. This had helped build it, but did not work in the longer term as the market started to mature. Local managers produce the best results because they not only understand the mindset of our local competitors, but can also develop marketing strategies in keeping with the broader values of Nepali society. I have an old photograph in my office at CG Industrial Park of the people in my organization. Only a few Nepali employees can be seen in it. That photograph shows how much my organization has grown, as most of our employees today are Nepali.

The four-pronged approach we devised to deal with the competition was successful. Wai Wai not only regained its initial position as the leading brand, but emerged even stronger in the market. Wai Wai and the other brands of instant noodles and snacks we produce bring an annual turnover of Rs 250 crore.

It is not that we were not successful before Wai Wai, but that brand took us to new heights, both financially and in terms of our organizational structure. An idea born at the baggage belt of Tribhuwan International Airport created the largest FMCG company in Nepal.

And the story of Wai Wai does not end here . . .

CG Industrial Park (Previously, Gangadevi Chaudhary Udyog Gram)

In 2004, there was an attempt by Maoist combatants to blow up an army vehicle at Dumkauli in Nawalparasi district. They had set off the explosion by drawing electricity from a switch at a waste processing centre inside Chaudhary Udyog Gram, which is now known as CG Industrial Park.

There had been a strange silence the day of the explosion. The only traffic along the Mahendra Highway consisted of ambulances and vehicles belonging to the security forces. A Nepal bandh (a general strike across the country) was not in place, but there appeared to be a local bandh in the area surrounding our plant. An army vehicle could be seen in the distance, its metal glinting in the sun. It was speeding madly, swaying from side to side. It came closer and closer. The sunlight reflecting from it strained our eyes.

Boom!

Flames erupted on the highway, which had been baking in the parching heat throughout the day.

Suddenly, the sky was filled with the cries of startled birds. The children who had been playing in the area began to cry. The grown-ups seemed used to it. They rushed inside their houses and latched the doors and windows. The strange and heavy silence morphed into raw fear.

Luckily, the detonation had happened five or six metres ahead of the army vehicle. The soldiers got off the vehicle, lay down on the road and opened fire on both sides of the highway. The cries of the birds grew louder. Frightened civilians tried to get a peek at what was happening through the cracks in their doors and windows. Everyone was gripped by panic. Having missed their target, the Maoist combatants had already fled. Now the soldiers focused on the Industrial Park. They stormed in and began harassing and beating up our employees. They searched every room in the facility to see if the combatants were hiding there. Some of our employees were even taken away. I had to call up a Major in the army to secure their release.

The incident took place at about 4.30 p.m. on one of the darkest days of the dark year of 2004. We knew the Maoist insurgents had forced their way into the Industrial Park to draw the electricity they needed for their ambush. But had we tipped off the army, there would certainly have been reprisals against us by the Maoists. Having not informed the army, we became their victims. We were caught between a rock and a hard place from the time the armed conflict began. Later, on 18 February 2005, the general manager of the Industrial Park was abducted by the Maoists. He was held captive for seventeen days at a time when the country was gearing up for the second People's Movement, which was also backed by the Maoists.

It was not easy to run a business at a time when the entire nation was frequently brought to a grinding halt by the armed conflict and the general strikes called by various political groups. So many times, we would hear gunfire outside the complex while we were working inside. Our staff would rush into the office, sometimes climbing in through the windows, and lock the doors behind them. Sometimes, they would sleep at the guest house on the site because going home was too dangerous. We lived in constant fear of bombings and intimidation by either the Maoists or the armed forces. There were times when our factories could not operate as we were not able to bring in the raw materials. Processed goods would remain not dispatched for days, gathering dust. To add to this, the trade unions affiliated with either the Maoists or other political parties would put forward endless, unrealistic demands. Under those circumstances, many entrepreneurs closed down their factories.

We still managed to run the Industrial Park complex, despite the fact that Nawalparasi was seen as a Maoist-controlled area in those days of insecurity, chaos and instability. The Industrial Park, which began operating in 1996, the same year the Maoists launched their People's War, actually managed to expand during the years of the conflict. However, except for the bandhs and a few incidents such as the one mentioned above, there was no strike in our plant through those turbulent days. Regardless of the tensions outside, there was no incident of vandalism or arson inside our complex. My colleagues, staff and the residents of Dumkauli made a big contribution to ensuring peace in the complex, and I am eternally grateful to them.

The creation of Special Economic Zones (SEZs) gained momentum after the rise of the Asian Tigers such as Singapore, Hong Kong and South Korea in the 1970s and 1980s. These SEZs offered all kinds of services to investors. In Nepal, every budget since the restoration of multiparty democracy in 1990 has promised Export Processing Centres and SEZs but nothing has materialized so far.

I had envisaged a similar industrial complex for ourselves with all the necessary infrastructure, such as drinking water, sewage, electricity and access roads, something which could accommodate our growth for five to six decades. In creating Gangadevi Chaudhary Udyog, I made that vision a reality.

The idea came to me in 1993. I was on a cross-country tour in connection with the FNCCI election. I realized that the swathe of land between Narayanghat and Butwal in western Nepal would be suitable for an industrial estate. The broad Mahendra Highway passes through that belt; it was less than two hours' drive from the Indian border; it was four hours away from Kathmandu and only three hours away from other big cities such as Pokhara and Birgunj.

I launched a massive search for an appropriate plot of land in the area. A former lawmaker, G.C. Mahendra, proposed Dumkauli as a suitable site. Another former member of Parliament, Hridayesh Tripathi, suggested a site at Bardaghat. I was not able to secure a deal for the Bardaghat site, so I decided to go with Mahendra's proposal. In the first phase, we acquired eighty acres of land. Then we added another fifty acres with the help of local residents. As a result, the Industrial Park complex consists of 130 acres currently. It is larger than the largest state-run industrial district at Balaju on the outskirts of Kathmandu. I selected urban planner Ajay Chaudhary—now a professor at the

Delhi School of Architecture and Design—to prepare the master plan for the complex. At that time, he was living in the United States. Everything in the Industrial Park has been carried out according to his design.

The foundation stone of the Industrial Park was laid in 1993. There were only a few scattered houses in the area. I was based at Narayanghat until the first phase of construction was over. I stayed at Chitwan Hotel in Bharatpur Heights, a facility run by Dilip Mainali, a friend from my Saraswoti Campus days. I stayed at the hotel for almost six months. Lily converted the upper floor into a bedroom and office. I would leave for Dumkauli after breakfast, Lily usually accompanying me. There was a hut just opposite the Industrial Park where we would have our afternoon meal—beaten rice, roasted soya bean, pan-fried potatoes, eggs and pickles.

I also became commercially involved in the Chitwan hotel. One day, Dilip told me, 'I can't run the hotel properly. The Nepal Industrial Development Corporation has already sent a warning letter. You have to rescue me.'

He was thinking about a partnership.

I had always wanted to be in the hospitality industry. What was more, Dilip was a close friend too. The hotel was pathetically rundown. It had to be reconstructed. I called up Kishor Pandey, the general manager of Hotel De L' Annapurna, an old friend of mine whom I knew through Kiran. We had been planning some major hotel projects in Kathmandu together; however, for various reasons those projects were not launched. We had, nevertheless, opened Bhanchha Ghar restaurant in Kathmandu together, in partnership with a few other friends. He later set up a hotel management company called Keyman. I was a partner in that as well.

Kishor and I invested in Chitwan Hotel, with Dilip remaining the local partner. We are building our CG Mall at the location of the hotel.

This was my first investment in the hospitality sector. Today, I am on a drive to open hotels and resorts across the Asia-Pacific region, setting up a multinational company for the purpose. What embarked me on that journey is a different story.

I had been inspired to construct the Industrial Park complex because of the inconvenience of operating geographically scattered factories. Once the infrastructure for the complex was ready, I realized my investment would be worth it only if I operated at least half a dozen factories on the site. I decided to seek partnerships with foreign investors, letting them utilize my infrastructure. We held discussions with Colgate-Palmolive in India, but we could not agree on the conditions for partnership. They opened their plant in Hetauda. We also held negotiations with Rajdoot Paints of India. Those negotiations too broke down, so we decided to launch our own brewery and cigarette factory. Unfortunately, they did not do well initially, only increasing the pressure on us to find a way to use the Industrial Park effectively. We decided on a second Wai Wai plant at the Industrial Park, followed by a third—the plant we bought from Indonesia—as what was being produced by the Bhainsepati plant was not enough to meet the demand. These two plants supported the Industrial Park in the early days.

We added two more plants after Wai Wai 'went viral', as one would say these days. We started to produce dozens of 'fighter brands' of instant noodles as well. We also started production of cheeseballs, chocolate wafers, Rio fruit juice, television and other electronic products. Gradually, the beverages (Nepal Ice, Haywards 5000, Real Gold) and the cigarettes (Josh, Pine, Pride) also gained momentum. Today, a dozen factories operate inside the Industrial Park complex, producing goods ranging from snacks that sell for Re 1 to television sets that sell for Rs 25,000. Around 1600 people are employed there. More than forty executives live inside the premises. Around a hundred trucks ferry goods in and out every day. Serpentine lines of hundreds of cyclists can be seen during shift changes in the morning, afternoon and evening, one group of employees heading home as the next arrives. More than 85 per cent of the employees are local residents. There are 350 women on the staff. We have formed a local, all-party committee, both for sourcing employees and for carrying out social work in the community.

The Industrial Park alone spends around Rs 70 lakh on corporate social responsibility. A year ago, we gave financial assistance of Rs 34 lakh to Samata Siksha Niketan, a school established in Kathmandu in 2001, in order to provide quality education to underprivileged children. Every year, I go to Dumkauli to hand over the Wai Wai Gyan Uday scholarships to underprivileged school students. We gave scholarships to sixty-nine students in 2010 and to 111 students in 2011. Last year, I presented a scholarship to Sita, a baby girl born to one of my employees, Harimaya Thapa, while she was at work. I said at the time that I wanted to see Sita rise to the post of chief executive of CG Industrial Park.

Offering the Wai Wai Gyan Uday scholarships is my humble effort to see dreams like that come true.

Entrepreneurs in Nepal generally complain that economic development is not possible without resolving the ongoing political problems that dog the country. Even our political leaders say the decade-long Maoist insurgency caused immeasurable harm to Nepal's economic development. This is true to a certain extent. Nonetheless, development is possible even in the midst of armed conflict and political instability if there exists the will to make it happen. CG Industrial Park is a shining example of how development is possible even in the midst of conflict.

5

Encounters with Politics

Before the restoration of multiparty democracy in Nepal in 1990, entrepreneurs like us were under double taxation. The first tax was directly and openly levied by the state, while the second was extorted from behind closed doors by those who held the reins of power.

I would like to tell a true story. An Indian industrialist wanted to set up a factory to produce hydrogenated vegetable cooking oil in Nepal. He received an appointment with a very powerful aide of Prince Dhirendra; he told the aide that his company wanted a licence to establish the factory.

'No problem,' the aide replied. 'But His Highness wants partnership in the enterprise.'

The industrialist agreed.

'Fine,' said the aide, 'then start the process.'

'But what are the terms of the partnership?'

'Do you think you're entering into partnership with some trader?' the aide scoffed. 'We're talking about His Highness.'

'So, how do we work out the partnership arrangements then?'

'Brother,' the aide said, 'you set up the plant, start production, and then His Highness will decide on your share.'

The industrialist went back to India, thoroughly intimidated.

I was not personally acquainted with that Indian industrialist and I do not know whether his factory ever opened in Nepal or not. However, this anecdote demonstrates the degree of power the royal family and their cronies exercised over Nepal's industrial and commercial sectors in those days. We would invest the capital and do all the work, and the royal palace would stake a claim for a majority of the shares. They would fix their share ratio themselves and 'grant' the remaining share to us. The prevalent ratio was 49:51—49 per cent for the real investor and 51 per cent for the Palace. Anyone who would not accept such a deal was better off packing up his bags and leaving the country. Nobody could afford to displease the Palace. You do not annoy the tiger if you want to survive in the jungle.

Whether we wanted a loan against collateral from a bank, a licence from the department of industry to import raw materials, a licence from the department of commerce to start a business or to clear goods through customs, we were subjected to a 'license raj'. I would visit all those offices every day to grease the right palms and move things along. However, the bureaucracy then was relatively honest and helpful compared with the civil service today, and was marked by an atmosphere of respect and discipline. The royal palace and those blessed by it had a huge influence on the bureaucracy. Once one had made a deal with the Palace, one did not need to worry about bureaucratic processes at the lower levels. The industrial and commercial sectors operated entirely under that system.

I later forged a long working relationship with Prince Dhirendra.

As industrial entrepreneurs, we should not oppose or support any regime on the basis of our personal biases. We need cooperation from anybody who holds the reins of power, be they royals, democrats or Maoists. Regardless of our personal ideological beliefs, we have to work in tandem with whichever regime holds power. The same applies to the bureaucracy.

In the developed world, those in the regime provide a separate space for professionals. They do not exploit them for their vested political interests, but rather create an environment conducive to professionals. For them, industrial entrepreneurs and professional manpower are crucial actors in sustaining the state. In our case, however, they are even exploited for political advantage.

We have always followed the order established by the regimes here.

1979–80

When Bishweshor Prasad Koirala returned home with the message of national reconciliation, I was busy with Copper Floor. When voices against the party-less Panchayat regime rose across the country, I was trying to pull our businesses together in the wake of my father's heart attack. During those critical times in Nepal's history, I had no involvement in politics whatsoever.

However, I found myself stuck in the web of politics and the regime after a national referendum was held in 1980 to choose between the Panchayat system and multiparty democracy.

I was only twenty-three at the time.

Prime Minister Surya Bahadur Thapa had summoned my father to meet him. Father and I went to the prime minister's residence together.

'His Majesty has declared a referendum,' the prime minister said. 'I have to ensure victory for the reformed Panchayat system at any cost.' We had a close relationship with Surya Bahadurjee. Both grandfather and father had been tenants on his land in Biratnagar since the days of Juddha Shumsher.

'What you like us to do, Mr. Prime Minister?' father asked.

'You need to support us with funding.'

We were just traders. We did not understand grand political designs and did not realize we were being used in a subtle game of regime change. We merely thought that serving a regime would open up unlimited opportunities for industrial enterprise. In any case, father could not have declined any proposal made by Surya Bahadurjee, given their long relationship. Surya Bahadurjee sought similar assistance from four or five other businessmen. Around Rs 1.5 crore was collected to fund the campaign for retention of the Panchayat regime. Some of the decisions taken by that government had been controversial and corrupt. Our motives related purely to business.

After the victory of the reformed Panchayat system, I asked Surya Bahadurjee for three favours.

The first related to National Panasonic. I told him, 'I already have the National Panasonic dealership. Now, I want to import parts and manufacture radios here in Nepal. I would like a licence to do that.'

Surya Bahadurjee agreed.

My second request related to brewing. Star Beer had had a monopoly in Nepal for a long time. I was hoping to set up a rival brewery in collaboration with an Indian company, Mohan Meakin. During several rounds of talks, they had told me that if I could get permission to initially import their beer, they would open a factory in Nepal once their brand was established in this country.

My second request was also granted. I got a licence to import beer.

My third request was for approval to establish a paper factory. I had already located a suitable plot of land. The land where our farmhouse stands today was originally intended for the paper factory. We had already hired a Chinese technical team to conduct a feasibility study. We intended to import the plant from China, and had even given a name to our enterprise—Saraswoti Pulp and Paper Mill.

Surya Bahadurjee agreed to that as well.

None of the licences I had received related to sensitive items. Nor was a referendum required to obtain such licences. However, the brewery business never got off the ground. As it turned out, under the prevailing Indian excise laws, no one could import beer from India. I tried to take the other two projects forward simultaneously but, despite some initial progress, both eventually collapsed.

Immediately after the referendum, a group of influential people got together with the intention of undermining Surya Bahadurjee. Known as the 'underground gang', the group was reportedly led by Prince Gyanendra, and comprised political opponents of Surya Bahadur such as Lokendra Bahadur Chand, Dr Prakash Chandra Lohani, Pashupati Shumsher Rana, Padma Sunder Lawati and Narayan Dutta Bhatta. They had teamed up to topple Surya Bahadurjee's government. And they used me as a pawn.

Many other entrepreneurs had funded Surya Bahadurjee's campaign in favour of the Panchayat system but only I had to pay the price for it. There was an onslaught of defamatory propaganda in the media, tying the Chaudhary Group to Surya Bahadurjee. To sustain his government, they alleged, the prime minister had given us a licence to make radios. He had sold us the paper mill licence, which was going to lead to rampant deforestation; we had bribed the Nepal Industrial Development Corporation (NIDC) to give us loans and sold the beer licence . . . on and on their allegations went. We became the subject of criticism in the Rastriya Panchayat, the Parliament of the time.

All I had wanted to do was to create a joint venture with a reputable multinational company such as National Panasonic. But the proposed factory was called a 'tinkering unit'. Holding up a sample of our radio in Parliament, supporters of the 'underground gang' belittled us: 'The government is trying to promote a factory for making *these*?'—as if our radios were toys. I was planning to establish the first paper mill in the country by bringing in Chinese technology. They alleged I was involved in rampant deforestation and in the NIDC loan scandals. I had wanted to bring another beer into the market where one brand had had a monopoly for so long. They called that a licence scam. My projects were destroyed, one after another.

What kind of system was this, I thought, where those benefiting from it the most, i.e. those in positions of power, could attempt to drag down someone who had supported the very system that gave them power? They were making me a victim of their infighting. Perhaps a bitter truth of politics is that innocent people sometimes get caught in the middle of a fight between heavyweights. I had become an easy target in the campaign to defame Surya Bahadurjee. Within just a very short span of my encounter with politics, I had been badly hurt.

Surya Bahadurjee was facing tremendous pressure to resign as prime minister. Though he knew he was helpless in the face of the plot hatched by the 'underground gang' and that he was operating under the auspices of the royal palace, he decided to bravely face a no-confidence motion rather than step down. He was backed by nineteen parliamentarians (known as the 'eighteen brothers' in those days), among them Balaram Gharti Magar, Keshar Bahadur Bista and Arjun Narsingh K.C. But this did not help him out of the situation.

Eventually, Surya Bahadurjee had to resign.

The 'underground gang' had achieved its goal. They were now free to start pursuing their own vested interests. The Lokendra Bahadur Chand government was formed, with Narayan Dutta Bhatta as minister for industries, Padma Sunder Lawati as home minister, Dr Prakash Chandra Lohani as finance minister and Pashupati Shumsher Rana as water resources minister. Less than two years earlier, Surya Bahadurjee had managed to retain the Panchayat system through the referendum. Now the new regime had not only to prove itself but also to show that dumping him had been the right thing to do. Hence, they continued to target me.

The new government allowed import of all kinds of radio sets and tape recorders under the *jhiti gunta*, or personal baggage system. Our dream of a joint venture with National Panasonic was shattered. We had to pay customs duty when importing raw materials for our factories, but the radio sets and recorders could be freely imported under the jhiti gunta. The contention that 'assembling' was nothing but 'tinkering' meant that for a long time nobody dared to run such an industry in the country. Even today, many sneer at the idea of an assembling industry. However, even in those days, many countries were fostering exactly such industries by making it cheaper to import component parts rather than finished products. This kind of industry was operating on a huge scale in neighbouring India; and many other Asian countries, including Singapore, Hong Kong, Thailand and Malaysia, had achieved significant economic growth through precisely this type of industry.

Besides radio sets and tape recorders, the government allowed free import of around three dozen other products. This brought a wave of 'sky porters' into Nepal. Smugglers would hire young people for a paltry wage and send them to Hong Kong or Bangkok, fulfilling the youths' dreams of visiting a foreign country. On their return journey, they were expected to bring in as many items as could be freely imported in their 'personal baggage'. For a long time, many young people continued to earn easy but illegal income by acting as 'sky porters'. An entire generation was duped.

Our Saraswoti Pulp and Paper Mill became the second target of the government. It revoked the loan approved by the NIDC. At the same time, the government decided to establish its own Bhrikuti Paper Factory, copying our plan even to the extent of locating the factory at Gaidakot in Nawalparasi district, only twelve kilometres from the site of my proposed factory. After preventing one of its citizens from privately investing in a factory, the government appealed for foreign investment to help open a virtually identical factory. Eventually, the government had to privatize the factory as it was poorly managed.

My plan to import beer had to be aborted too, because of India's excise duty policy. This meant my plan to open a brewery in collaboration with Mohan Meakin had to be abandoned too. Some people close to the Palace later launched Golden Eagle Beer in collaboration with the same Indian company.

While all this was happening, the FNCCI, 'the representative institution of the private sector', and its office-bearers gave me no support whatsoever. On the contrary, I was told that a delegation of the FNCCI had met with government officials to oppose the radio 'assembling' factory. They opposed an enterprise that would have generated employment and potentially changed the face of Nepal's industrial sector, choosing to support the free importation of radios instead!

Reeling under these relentless attacks from all directions, I went to meet Finance Minister Dr Prakash Chandra Lohani. Ramesh Nath Pandey, an influential politician at the time, arranged the meeting. I was not even acquainted with Dr Lohani at that point, so there was no question of any personal animosity between us. The ministry of finance was at Bagh Durbar, where the Kathmandu Metropolitan City office is now located. As soon as I entered his office, he said, 'So you are the famous Binod Chaudhary.'

I asked him the reasons behind the attacks on me.

'I don't have any personal enmity towards you,' he replied. 'You have become the victim of a political conflict. You have become a scapegoat.'

Today I enjoy a very cordial relationship with Dr Lohani.

I also called on Surya Bahadurjee at his residence to discuss a way out of the crisis. Trying to cheer me up, he said, 'This is an attempt to weaken you. However, remember one thing: overcoming these obstacles will take you to the pinnacle of success.'

This incident is largely responsible for my level of eminence in the professional sector today. Had I not been dragged into this political conflict, I might not have sought alternative ways to grow.

I was twenty-seven at the time of this incident.

Many well-intentioned people told me that I should not continue to feel resentful towards the royal palace and that I should look for a compromise. Some even suggested I should meet Lokendra Bahadur Chand and beg his forgiveness so that he might fix my problems. As Neer Shah was an old friend, some others suggested I should approach the royal palace for help through his good offices. My professional career was in a shambles at the time.

Sometimes, rescue comes from unexpected quarters. I found a saviour in the form of Prince Dhirendra.

I had met him while I was operating Copper Floor. I was well acquainted with Neer Shah and S.K. Singh in those days, and Dhirendra was a frequent visitor to our discotheque. I thought that since I knew him, perhaps if I confided in him there might be something he could do to protect me.

I went to meet Prince Dhirendra.

He was well aware of my situation. 'I know your problems inside out,' he said, as he patted my back. 'They want to destroy you.'

'What should I do, Your Highness?' I asked, putting my hands together in supplication.

'You work with me and all your problems will simply vanish,' he said. 'No one will dare touch you.'

I was awash with relief. I felt as if I had gone looking for an angel but had found God Himself instead. I proceeded exactly as he advised me.

'If you start a business with me, the whole world will know I'm your partner,' he said. 'Later on, you can work independently, but everyone will still think I have a partnership with you.'

We immediately planned to establish Apollo Steel Industries. The Golchha Group had a monopoly in steel in Nepal at that time, but we did not face any problem in getting a licence for our steel mill because Prince Dhirendra's name was associated with it. Normally, as I mentioned earlier, the royals would take 51 per cent of the shares, and the rest would go to the investor. However, Prince Dhirendra did exactly the opposite. I got the majority of shares and he kept 49 per cent.

He told me, 'I'm involved here just to help you out. You do your business. I'll take only 49 percent.'

Apollo Steel was not just another factory to me but, I hoped, an infallible means to get me out of the political mess in which I found myself. Even if I had not received a single penny from it, I would not have cared. My entire professional future was now vested in that one enterprise.

In Nepal, you do not need great ideas to become a great person. All you need to do is to hobnob with the right people. I did the same. I started an enterprise with a prince at the height of the Panchayat era. This news spread like wildfire. Suddenly, I became a distinguished industrialist. It was that easy. People changed the way they looked at me. Suddenly, I could call the shots. Even my former detractors wanted to get close to me. Everything in my business started to fall in place. I ventured into many new areas and success came my way.

Of course, Prince Dhirendra was not directly involved in everything I did that was successful, but underlying it all was his indirect involvement. His partnership with me, which removed all the obstacles in my path that had resulted from my becoming a scapegoat in a political conflict, was the main reason for my success.

Business is the most important thing to a businessman. I did what the regime politics of that hour compelled me to do. Everybody dominated me when I wanted to mind my own business. My investments and my determination came to naught. I became slightly shrewd for survival's sake. They tried to do politics with my business. I did my business on their politics. We, as entrepreneurs, have to do this to survive in the ruthless realm of politics.

In 1985, the World Bank once again decided to conduct a feasibility study of the Karnali–Chisapani hydropower project. The governments of Nepal and India agreed to evaluate the project and seal power purchase and investment agreements based on the feasibility study.

The cost of the feasibility study was about US$25 million.

Naturally, those construction companies that already had government contracts were chafing at the bit. We, however, were not involved in any such venture. During the height of the Panchayat era, the Palace, the government and the bureaucracy, in that order, steered the decision-making process. As the Government of India was also involved, it too had its measure of influence on which way the project went.

'We should also get involved in this,' Himalaya Pandey approached me with a proposal.

Himalaya's father was Sardar Bhim Bahadur Pandey, an influential policymaker and senior bureaucrat, who had also served as Nepal's ambassador to India and Germany. He had strong links to the movers and shakers in India.

'Fine,' I said, accepting his proposal. 'You start the ball rolling and I'll support you 100 per cent.'

He left his job at Gorkha Travels and became 'a man on a mission'. We set up a separate unit at our corporate office at Sanepa for the project, with Himalaya in charge.

A Canadian company called Acres International was involved in projects funded by the Canadian International Development Agency in Nepal. Its headquarters are in Ontario, but it had a resident representative in Nepal whom Himalaya knew well. Acres became our major partner in the Karnali–Chisapani project as part of a consortium that also included Lavlan SNC of Canada and Ibasco of the United States. The consortium was called Himalayan Power Consultants.

Ibaso had its headquarters in the World Trade Center in New York, which was destroyed in the 9/11 terror attack. The first and the last time I went into the twin towers was in connection with this project.

Himalayan Power tendered a bid for the Karnali–Chisapani project.

There was a marked lack of transparency in the tender process. Our bid, led by a consortium headed by the world-famous Acres, was rejected for 'technical reasons'. A consortium comprising Japan's Nippon Koei, Australia's Snowy Mountains Engineering Corporation, America's Harza and Britain's Binnie & Partners was selected instead. Most interestingly, the whole process was finalized at the World Bank's headquarters almost immediately after the tender was opened. Also, prior to the World Bank approval, the Government of India had endorsed the contract. The Indian government had also been duly informed.

We, who had been confident of winning the tender, came to know about all this much later. The Karnali–Chisapani project was not just another venture for us but a huge opportunity to establish ourselves in the field of government contracts. We had foreseen the possibility of getting these contracts on a regular basis once this project was underway. With this at the back of my mind, I decided not to give up so easily. Had our proposal or our partners been weak, I could have accepted the outcome. But despite the backing of a company like Acres, it appeared we were victims of a conspiracy hatched by our competitors.

In those days, all government ministries were divided between and controlled by the secretaries at the royal palace, who were the ones who actually called the shots in the ministries. However, these secretaries were subordinate to the king's brothers, who had divided the ministries among themselves. As a result, those in the position of secretary in the ministries were actually several rungs down in the bureaucratic hierarchy of the Panchayat system. The ministers were above them, the Palace secretaries above the ministers, and the king's brothers right at the top. Apparently, the ministers would brief the prime minister, who, in turn, briefed the monarch. The king's brothers would be briefed separately by the Palace secretaries. Though the 'Palace channel' was not formally recognized and only existed behind closed doors, it behaved like a legitimate bureaucracy. The prime minister, Surya Bahadur Thapa, described this as a system of 'dual rule'.

We decided to attempt the Palace channel. Neer Shah arranged a meeting for us with Prince Dhirendra. Not only did Dhirendra and I have a relationship of trust, but coincidentally, water resources was one of the ministries under his unofficial control.

We briefed him about Himalayan Power Consultancy and the companies associated with it. Accepting the possibility that we had been unfairly treated, he launched an independent investigation. Lal Bahadur Kadayat was the minister for water resources during the tender process. Later, the ministry was headed by Pashupati Shumsher Rana.

Prince Dhirendra summoned Pashupati Shumsher and told him that it appeared Himalayan Power had been dealt an injustice during the Karnali–Chisapani tendering process. Pashupati Shumsher tried to evade the matter, saying the decision had already been made and signed off on by both the World Bank and the Government of India.

Meanwhile, Himalayan Pandey, Neer Shah and I went to meet high-ranking officials at Acres in Ontario to tell them what had been happening. At the time, Prince Dhirendra was in New York, where his mother was undergoing medical treatment. We, along with representatives of Acres and the other companies in our consortium, went over to New York to meet him. Prince Dhirendra was impressed with our partner's capabilities, and became convinced that our consortium had not only been treated unfairly in the tendering process but that we should have won the contract too.

'I shall discuss the matter with His Majesty my brother,' he said.

After returning to Kathmandu, he told King Birendra that he believed the minister and the palace secretaries had manipulated the Karnali–Chisapani tender. King Birendra too was convinced about it and ordered Pashupati Shumsher to revoke the previous decision and 'award the tender to Himalayan Power Consultancy'. King Birendra's firm directive was that if the project was to go ahead at all, Himalayan Power must get the tender.

Prince Dhirendra sent a message to us: 'His Majesty has already issued the decree. Go and meet Pashupati.' Himalaya Pandey went to meet Pashupati Shumsher.

'How dare you ask the king to make me do this?' Pashupati Shumsher exploded at Himalaya, who still loves to tell the tale of that meeting. Furious, Pashupati Shumsher stared him in the eye and said, 'We have already written to the World Bank and the Government of India. How can we possibly revoke the decision now?'

However, despite his ranting, he had to find a way to tackle the issue to comply with the king's direct order.

In accordance with his advice, we lodged a written complaint against 'irregularities in the tender'. The ministry of water resources appointed Bechtel, an American engineering, construction and project management company, to conduct an independent review of the entire tender process. Bechtel concluded that there were anomalies in the process and that the tender should have been awarded to Himalayan Power Consultancy. The ministry forwarded Bechtel's report to the World Bank and the Government of India, based on which it was decided to award the contract for the feasibility study of the Karnali–Chisapani hydropower project to us.

The project took about five years. We also did a lot of other work such as laying the transmission line and constructing substations in collaboration with Kamani and Best & Crompton engineering companies.

This incident demonstrates how a businessperson, irrespective of his competence, has to 'do business in politics' to survive political conspiracy.

Rift with the Palace

The relationship I had established with the royal palace in 1984 through Prince Dhirendra ran into troubled waters towards mid-1989.

During my association with Prince Dhirendra, I had also established a close relationship with King Birendra and Queen Aishwarya. King Birendra gave thirteen audiences to me; he attended weddings in our family, visited the Wai Wai factory, and even invited me to the Nagarjuna Palace, discussing with me a range of subjects, including my future business plans. Everything was going well, until an incident that quickly destroyed my five-year relationship with Dhirendra.

An affair between Prince Dhirendra and a British woman was the talk of the town in those days. As a result of this affair, his relationship with his wife, Prekshya Rajya Laxmi Devi Shah, had soured. Prince Dhirendra could no longer stand living in the Palace. He decided to reject the trappings of royalty and left the country. The Palace handed over all the businesses he owned to his wife. The shares in the factories in which he had partnered with me were also transferred to her.

Before this happened, I had had a cordial relationship with Prince Dhirendra's wife. However, in the changed circumstances, she started to stake a claim on the factories without trying to understand the depth of the relationship between Prince Dhirendra and me, as well as the facts behind our partnership and the accrued benefits and obligations. She started to send her aides to me on a daily basis with lists of unrealistic demands. In the absence of Prince Dhirendra, the Palace group that had tried to ruin me during 1979–84 became active again.

In March 1989, a staffer from the royal palace came to me: 'Her Highness has summoned you to Jeevan Kunja.'

Jeevan Kunja was the palace where Prekshya lived.

Father became nervous as soon as he heard this. He was afraid something sinister was afoot. 'Relax, Father, they can't harm us,' I told him, to allay his fears.

Father and I went together to Jeevan Kunja. We were escorted into a huge drawing room. Ram Bhattarai, Dr Shyam Bahadur Pandey, Tej Prakash Shah and a few other aides of Prekshya were there already. I had thought of some of them as my friends. Prekshya had not arrived yet, and her aides whispered among themselves while we waited. Sometimes they looked in our direction, but no one spoke a word to us. If our eyes met, I would smile at them. Otherwise, I busied myself studying the portraits hanging on the walls or looked at the chandelier. Father was silent.

We were sitting opposite a huge closed door. I was secretly watching what Prekshya's aides were doing, and noticed they kept glancing towards the door. I guessed she would enter the room through that door. The door finally opened. Prekshya entered bearing a royal air. The aides immediately sprang to their feet, pressing their palms together in a gesture of respect, and bowing from the waist. We too rose, pressing our palms together. In those days, the royals did not return greetings.

Prekshya darted like lightning to the largest and grandest chair in the room. Her aides sat down after she took her seat. We too sat down.

She looked at me and said pompously, 'Binod, I have decided to give the shares of Apollo Steel to Golchha.'

Everyone in the room turned to look at me. They probably expected me to say, 'Yes, Your Highness.' But I was infuriated by what she had said. First, Prekshya had no legal basis to stake a claim on Apollo Steel. Second, she was trying to hand over the shares to someone who was not just a business competitor but also a rival at a personal level.

I remained silent for a while, struggling to control myself.

Once I had regained my cool, I said in a low voice, 'Your Highness, how can you do that?'

Prekshya and her aides stared at me, wide-eyed. They looked as though they wanted to eat me alive.

'Why can't I do that?' she asked in a reprimanding tone.

'Your Highness, I hold majority shares in this factory and I've taken a loan to cover the rest of the investment,' I replied politely and with dignity. 'How could Your Highness suddenly think anyone you wanted could be brought in?'

'What?' She rose from her chair in rage. 'You are going to disobey my order?'

Her aides rose with her. We too got up. They were trying to intimidate me using the royal customs and conventions.

'Your Highness,' I said, 'I couldn't obey your order even if I wanted to.'

'What do you mean?' She sat down again, and her aides sat down as well. We continued to stand.

'Your Highness, I took a bank loan to establish this factory. The loan is in my name.'

'So what?' She flushed with rage.

Father was scared. He was pulling at my sleeve, trying to make me stop talking, but I would not.

'I hold 51 per cent of the shares. I let His Highness Prince Dhirendra have the remainder in return for a favour. Also, you should be aware of this document which His Highness gave me.'

I pulled a piece of paper out of my pocket. It was a document drawn up at the time of establishment of Apollo Steel. On it was written: 'I have borrowed Rs 4.9 million from

Binod Chaudhary to buy 49 per cent of the shares.' It was signed by Prince Dhirendra.

'Okay,' she fumed, without even looking at the document. 'You will not obey me, right?'

'Your Highness, it's not a question of obeying or disobeying; I am just not in a position to comply. Prince Dhirendra has borrowed from me and I have also borrowed money to cover the cost of His Highness's shares. How can I include Golchha in the company until I get my money back?'

'Fine! I know what to do next.' She rose from her chair and left the room.

The aides too sprang to their feet and bowed low. Silence descended on the room. Every one stared at me as though I were a criminal. Then they too walked out of the room.

Father was so scared that he started to tremble. I took his hand and led him out of the room. We drove straight home. Father did not utter a word the whole way. He was clearly disconcerted.

'Relax, Father, they can't harm us,' I told him calmly.

I had been prepared for this development even before the meeting at Jeevan Kunja.

Immediately after the meeting, I met advocate Kusum Shrestha. Throughout the Panchayat regime, Kusum Shrestha and Ganesh Raj Sharma had fought legal battles on behalf of the Nepali Congress, the first and largest political party in Nepal. I told him everything that had happened between me and Prekshya Shah. I also showed him the receipt signed by Dhirendra.

'You have a very strong legal document there,' he said. 'Legally, nobody can touch you. Nonetheless, while the monarchy still has direct control of the country, who knows what lengths they might go to? You shouldn't wait for them to make the next move. You should go on the offensive.'

'What should I do then?'

'Send a legal notice to Prekshya Shah. Since Dhirendra has taken a loan from you against 49 per cent shares in the company, you should submit a legal request for that money to be paid back.'

Taking Kusum's advice, I sent a legal notice to Prekshya. In short, it said, that I had a document proving that Dhirendra had taken loan from me to buy a 49 per cent share in Apollo Steel. Either that loan must be repaid or the shares returned to me.

I did not receive a reply. In accordance with the provisions of the Company Act, we sent three notices. Still there was no response. The royal palace considered itself above the law in those days.

Then Kusum suggested another move. As the majority shareholder, I could call a general meeting of the shareholders with the aim of raising capital through additional investment from them. All the shareholders would have to make additional investment in proportion to the number of shares they held. The shareholding of those who failed to make the additional investment would automatically decrease. I called the general meeting, raised the level of investment to increase capital and, as Prekshya declined to make the additional investment, the proportion of her shares in the company automatically reduced.

I won the legal battle, but I feared for my physical safety. I came up with a way to tackle that too.

I approached Kishunjee, a founder member of the Nepali Congress. Father had an extremely cordial relationship with him. Kishunjee and other senior Congress leaders, including Yog Prasad Upadhyay, would visit father at our Khichapokhari home. Father used to live on the upper floor. Kishunjee would walk straight up to my father's room and sit beside him. He would then ask for paan. They had that kind of relationship. I, quite immature at the time, would wonder who this person could be. Father would later tell me, 'I would offer them paan out of respect. But, to my horror, the secret agents of the Panchayat regime would also be following them.'

I told my story to Kishunjee. He replied, 'Binod babu, hold your head up high. You don't need to worry. They can't harm you. Their days are numbered. You should support our movement wholeheartedly. You take care of us, and we'll take care of them.'

His support boosted my morale. I felt proud.

I began to support the democratic movement strongly and openly. As a result, Prekshya and her aides could not directly harm me. However, I think they succeeded in poisoning the ears of the king and the queen against me, because from the day I joined the movement, I was never again granted a royal audience.

Within a few months, the movement had spread across the country like wildfire. After the restoration of multiparty democracy in Nepal, Prekshya Shah asked advocate Sunil Panta to clear her accounts at Apollo Steel. We calculated the appropriate compensation and transferred Dhirendra's shares to my name.

Had this people's movement of 1990 not succeeded, I would have lost everything. And that is no exaggeration.

Despite my estrangement from the Palace, I remained loyal to it because I could never have achieved what I had without the support of a member of the royal family.

However, whenever I tried to restore good relations with the Palace, one or the other of staffers would block me from doing so.

I had hoped King Birendra might inaugurate the new FNCCI headquarters. I sent an invitation to the Palace but I am not sure he even saw it. The king's principal secretary, Pashupati Bhakta Maharjan, declined the invitation, saying, 'The FNCCI is about to hold an election for its office-bearers. If His Majesty accepts the invitation, then it may influence the outcome in favour of one of the contending parties.'

But I knew he was supporting one of the contending parties by not letting the king accept my invitation. That group eventually succeeded in defeating me in the election.

I faced similar impediments while organizing a large conference on socio-economic issues. It was the first conference of its kind to be held in Nepal, and we had invited dignitaries such as the President of Pakistan and the prime minister of Thailand. It would have been appropriate for the king to inaugurate the conference. But the same group that was in opposition to me did not let that happen.

Later, when I ran into Pashupati Bhaktajee, he told me, sardonically, 'You faced some difficulty again, didn't you?'

'I am all right, thanks to your grace,' I quipped.

We had published a book called *Guide to Investment in Nepal* for foreign investors. It incorporated details of Nepal's investment and revenue policies, and explored possible areas for investment. Never before had such a book been published in Nepal. We wanted the book to include in its foreword a message from the king. But his courtiers would not even allow us to present the proposal to him. 'Do you think His Majesty's role is to publish messages in books?' one of them had asked me.

This incident further demonstrated the power of the conservatives within the royal palace, and a kind of 'silent tension' has prevailed between me and the Palace ever since.

1990

There were two main reasons I took part in the people's movement of 1990. First, the incidents I have described above had made me lose all faith in the Panchayat system. The other reason was the search for self-esteem. Talking about self-esteem, the industrial entrepreneurs in Nepal were in a pitiable condition.

Chiran Shumsher Thapa headed the press secretariat at the royal palace. He was entrusted with overseeing the industrial and commercial sectors in Nepal, but he would only associate with his cronies. The only time we could possibly meet him was during his morning walks. 'Meet me at 6.30 tomorrow morning at Thapathali,' he would say. 'You walk with me exactly from that point.'

He would meet as many as eight people on his two-hour walk. The first he would meet outside the entrance to his house, and walk with him for fifteen to twenty minutes. At this point, the second would meet him, indicating that the appointment with the first person was over, and would get to walk with him up to the next point. It echoed the sycophancy that prevailed during the Rana regime.

There were a few times that I met Thapa this way, waiting for him at the Thapathali corner and walking with him until he met the next person waiting at the next point. I felt mortified meeting him like that. The humiliation was unbearable. Once he asked me to meet him at Summit Hotel in Lalitpur, which was almost his headquarters. I also visited his house a few times. People would be queuing up to meet him there. I had to wait my turn, sitting on a stool.

'You have such a cordial relationship with His Majesty. He always says nice things about you,' Tara Bahadur Thapa, a general based in the royal palace, would always tell me. 'Still, we can't change the system. Chiran looks after industry and commerce, and we have to toe the line. Why don't you meet Chiran and sort it out?'

General Thapa is my wife's relative, which was why he was so sympathetic towards me. He tried to get Chiran Shumsher to take a more positive attitude towards me but to no avail. Had I become his crony, as General Thapa hoped might happen, then I would not have had to face the problems that I did. I would have had an easy life even after the resignation of Surya Bahadurjee. Prekshya would not have been hostile towards me.

Arjun Narsingh K.C. of the Nepali Congress encouraged me to play a more active role in the people's movement. He had been my teacher at Saraswoti Campus. As a result of my association with him and my old family ties with Kishunjee, I got closer to the Congress party. I had very warm relationships with Girija Prasad Koirala, B.P. Koirala's younger brother, whom I called Girijababu, and with Ganesh Man Singh, one of the founder members of the party, whom I knew as Ganesh Manjee. I openly campaigned for the people's movement for the restoration of multiparty democracy in the country.

At that time I had already become a vice president of the FNCCI. Mahesh Lal Pradhan was the president.

The government of Marich Man Singh started to target industrial entrepreneurs like me after a number of us became actively involved in the people's movement. The finance minister, Bharat Bahadur Pradhan, summoned the FNCCI office-bearers and tried to intimidate us. The minister of state for commerce, Sharad Singh Bhandari, and the assistant minister for industry, Bimal Man Singh, were also present at the meeting.

'You were shaped by the Panchayat system. You were nurtured by the Panchayat system. How could you go against the system just because it involved some challenges?' Singh reproached us. 'This is the time to support the system, not go against it.'

We told him to his face that this was not our business, that we wanted to work in tandem with any system that was in place. We might have our personal preferences for one ideology or other, but we were not going to make enemies in the name of politics. We were not going to go against the tide.

He stormed out of the meeting, infuriated.

Within a couple of days, Vijay Shah of Jawalakhel Distillery brought the news: the Marich Man government had turned against the FNCCI because of our remarks at the meeting.

Vijay Shah was close to Sharad Singh Bhandari. Sharad Singh and Keshar Bahadur Bista would visit Vijay Shah's house almost every day. Vijay Shah was a friend of mine too. Sharad Singh told him, 'The prime minister is very angry with the FNCCI. If Binod Chaudhary and you don't issue a statement condemning the people's movement, he intends to arrest both of you under some pretext or other.'

The matter had been discussed even at a Cabinet meeting. After Vijay Shah came with this news, Mahesh Lal and I discussed the matter and arrived at the conclusion that, come what may, we could not issue a statement condemning the people's movement. Now that we had been 'exposed' as supporters of the people's movement, it was in our interests to extend our all-out support to it.

With the government sinking to the level of mulling the arrest of entrepreneurs like us, the people's movement of 1990 became a decisive battle for us. We openly went against the government. We gave our full support to the Nepali Congress and the United Left Front. One day, Sharad Singh told us, 'It's getting hard to fight the pressure from the government to detain you, please go underground.'

The assistant minister, the late Bimal Man, supported us at the time, being the son of a businessman himself and a very close friend of mine. He was very stubborn by nature. We stayed close until his last days. 'Why should they go underground?' he told Sharad Singh. 'I'll keep them at my house. Let's see who can harm them there. Let them arrest my friends if they have the guts.'

Fortunately, we never had to hide in Bimal's house. Within a few days, democracy was restored in Nepal.

We got our freedom.

At a function held at Bluestar Hotel in Kathmandu immediately after the political change of 1990, the prime minister of the interim government, Kishunjee, freely praised our family from the dais, saying, 'Wherever I went to Bihar during my exile in India, I always found Pashupati Biscuits there. My heart used to swell with pride. I used to wonder what heights our economy might have reached had there been a few more families like the Chaudharys.'

I was flattered to hear my family praised by an influential prime minister who had come to power after a long involvement in the democratic movement. I felt we had been adequately compensated for all the adversities we had faced at the hands of the authoritarian regime in the past.

My relationship with Kishunjee became even stronger. He would give me unhindered access to his private rooms at Baluwatar, the official residence of the prime minister. One day, father invited him to lunch at our place. Accepting the invitation, Kishunjee told me, 'Binod babu, come to pick me up at Baluwatar.'

I went to fetch him. He came out of his residence with his bodyguards. Once we reached the place where my car was parked, he dismissed his guards. 'I'm going to Lunkaran Dasjee's house. You don't need to come with me,' he told them. His driver had already taken out his car by then. 'You can rest today. I'll go with Binod,' he told the driver.

I had come to his residence just to guide him to our place, but instead, he was sitting beside me in the front passenger seat of my car! I was scared to drive the prime minister in my car without his bodyguards. Sensing how I felt, Kishunjee thumped my back and said, 'Don't be scared, Binod babu! Nobody can hurt me. We have great things to accomplish.'

We drove straight from Baluwatar to our house in Thamel, where he dined with us. At the dinner table, he would become serious while telling us stories of his life in exile, but then he would remember something funny and laugh heartily, making us laugh too. After dinner, I drove him back home to Baluwatar.

Kishunjee would repeatedly tell me, 'You have to be my economic advisor, Binod.'

During his tenure, the minister for tourism, Nilamber Acharya, appointed me and Padam Jyoti, a member of a distinguished business group in Nepal, to the board of directors of Royal Nepal Airlines Corporation (RNAC).

I was also part of a private sector delegation to New Delhi, to renew economic ties with India in the changed political climate. I felt that if we could meet the Indian prime minister, Chandra Shekharjee, in person, it would be a significant step in restoring economic confidence in Nepal. We contacted the Nepal embassy in New Delhi. The ambassador to India, Bindeshwori Shah, was surprised to hear our request. 'You want an appointment with the prime minister? What are you talking about?'

I understood that he was opposed to the idea of a commercial delegation meeting the prime minister. I then met Kishunjee over the matter. The saintly Kishunjee instantly solved our problem. It was as if he had waved a magic wand. He immediately wrote a letter to Chandra Shekharjee.

'Once you reach Delhi,' he said, giving me the letter as well as the name and telephone number of Chandra Shekarjee's personal assistant, 'dial this number and say you have a letter from Krishna Prasad Bhattarai and need to meet the prime minister.'

'What about the embassy?' I asked.

'Forget the embassy. Go straight to Chandra Shekharjee and tell him I've sent you.'

As soon as I reached Delhi, I dialled the number Kishunjee had given me. I introduced myself to Chandra

Shekharjee's personal assistant and told him what had brought me to Delhi. As soon as he heard Kishunjee's name, he fixed up an appointment for us with the Indian prime minister. I handed Kishunjee's letter to Chandra Shekharjee as soon as I met him.

This was the first-ever meeting between any private sector delegation from Nepal and an Indian prime minister. Kishunjee's affection for me and his unique modus operandi made it possible.

Girija Babu and I

One of my assistants came rushing breathlessly into my office. 'Girija Babu is here. He wants to meet you.'

I had just come to Biratnagar to take charge of operations at Pashupati Biscuits, and I was living there. At my assistant's announcement, I ran out of my office to greet Girija Prasad Koirala. An old jeep with a canvas top was parked outside. The dust kicked up by its tyres was yet to settle.

I walked closer to the jeep. A lean man stepped out, flanked by a handful of people.

That was the first time I met Girija Prasad Koirala. Before that, I had only heard about him. He stepped into my office. 'We have a good relationship with your father,' he said. 'When I heard that you have come here, I decided to come and meet you.'

I could only nod.

'We have been receiving a lot of support from Lunkaran Dasjee. We expect the same from you,' Girija Babu said, revealing the real reason for his visit. 'The time has arrived for the people's movement. You have to support the party.'

He left after fifteen minutes.

After the general election in 1992, Girija Prasad Koirala became the prime minister. His party secured a clear majority. I was a close aide all through his first term in office. When it came to issues relating to industry, commerce and other aspects of the economy, he trusted me more than he did either the finance minister or the chairperson of the National Planning Commission. I do not know why he trusted me so much. We worked together on a number of issues related to economic reform. A group within the party which was, I must assume, jealous of my closeness to Girija Babu, started to lobby against me and went on to poison his ears.

I was included as a private sector representative in the official delegation accompanying Girija Babu on his first visit to India as prime minister. Senior industrialists such as Hulas Chand Golchha, Mohan Gopal Khetan and Banbari Lal Mittal were also in the delegation, but I was the leader. Umbrella organizations from India's business sector, such as the Federation of Indian Chambers of Commerce and Industry (FICCI), the Confederation of Indian Industries (CII) and the Associate Chambers of Commerce and Industry of India (ASSOCHAM), had organized a joint reception in honour of Girija Babu. I had taken the initiative to bring these three rival organizations together. To achieve that, I had reached out to Indian entrepreneurs whom I knew personally, well ahead of Girija Babu's visit. Girija Babu had also entrusted me with the responsibility of drafting his speech.

He told me, 'I will say what I have to say from a personal perspective. However, you should prepare a draft incorporating what the private sector wants to hear.'

I drafted a speech to the best of my ability and forwarded the draft to Dr David Abraham, a prominent American professor who was then living in Nepal. After incorporating his suggestions, I went to show the final draft to Girija Babu.

Many of his aides were upset over his decision to let an outsider draft his speech. They had been poisoning his mind against me. He did not even so much as glance at the draft, but instead asked me to show it to one of his aides. I felt hurt. The aide read out a few lines and grimaced. 'How can the prime minister make such a flowery speech?' he said.

'Do as you please,' I replied and left.

I believe this marked the beginning of the distance that developed between Girija Babu and me.

I subsequently did accompany Girija Babu on his official visits to Israel, Finland, Egypt and Germany. He still entrusted me with preparing the list of private sector representatives to be included in the official delegation. I tended to include the younger generation of entrepreneurs, such as Pradeep Kumar Shrestha, Shashi Agrawal and Bijay Kumar Dugar. Another group of businesspersons did not like my choice of delegates. They formed another delegation with the help of my detractors in the party. As a result, the delegation now consisted of two distinct groups of entrepreneurs, each huddling together and away from the other. If Girija Babu had to discuss a matter or if he needed the views of the private sector, he would turn to me. My group was still the official representative of the private sector.

Later on, two incidents led to increasing discomfort between Girija Babu and me. The first was the RNAC scandal and the second the investment board row, which not only hurt my self-esteem but also left me feeling humiliated.

After these two incidents, I distanced myself from the Congress party.

The RNAC scandal

Kishunjee had appointed me to the board of directors of the RNAC. I was still holding that post when Girija Babu was elected prime minister for the first time in 1992.

As a director at the RNAC, I had serious differences with Girija Babu on two issues. One of them was the sale of the RNAC's aircraft.

The corporation had two Boeing 727s, one brought in 1972 and the other in 1984. In 1993, the corporation decided to sell both aircraft, citing 'a directive from the Prime Minister'. The corporation wanted to get rid of them under the pretext that the aircraft were too old. In fact, the corporation was eyeing the commission it could make from the sale. The aircraft were not in such a bad shape that they could not fly. All they needed were some basic repairs.

I opposed the decision from day one. In my capacity as a director of the board, I conducted an independent study and handed over the recommendations in the form of a report to the corporation's management. The corporation could have earned more than Rs 50 crore million in profit if both the aircraft plied on routes of three to four hours' duration, such as from Kathmandu to cities like Mumbai, Kolkata, Delhi and Bangkok. However, nobody was interested in my report.

Eventually, the corporation decided to dispose of both the aircraft for the price they would have fetched had they been scrap. If I am not mistaken, the corporation received less than Rs 11 crore million from the deal. What is more, one of the Boeings is still flying in Tanzania, which vindicates my position.

Another reason for the misunderstanding between Girija Babu and me was the Dhamija scam. Girija Babu's German son-in-law and his brother were directly involved in the case.

I still vividly recall that meeting of the RNAC's board of directors. The board meetings were generally convened between quarter to five and half past five in the evening so that the secretaries from the line ministries could attend after their regular office hours. The first thing they would do was to eat chicken cutlets. I was not interested in waiting for up to forty-five minutes while they ate, so I would arrive for the meetings at around 6 p.m.

One day I arrived for the meeting at 6 p.m. to find them all impatiently waiting for me.

'What's up?' I asked, as I took my seat. 'I can sense there's a serious issue on the agenda.'

'No, no, nothing like that, Binodjee,' one of them said awkwardly. 'We were just waiting for you.'

'So what's the matter?'

'We've already taken care of it. We just wanted your presence.'

'Come on, tell me, what have you done?' I asked.

'Nothing special,' one of them said. 'We're going to replace the General Sales Agent for Europe. We don't need to discuss this at length now. It's already settled.'

I was shocked. I could sense that they were trying to keep me in dark about some big scandal. I was already wary about the RNAC's following the Boeing scandal.

'Why was it necessary to remove the existing GSA and appoint a new one?' I asked. 'I deserve to know.'

They looked at each other.

'We have received a letter from Dirgharajjee,' one of them said, producing a sheet of paper. Dirgharaj Koirala was one of Girija Babu's advisors.

'What letter? Let me see it,' I stretched out my hand for it.

The letter asked the board to 'settle the issue of the appointment of the GSA for the Europe sector as soon as possible'.

Earlier, the board had received a proposal from the prime minister, which was actually a directive, to appoint Fair Limited, a company operated by Dinesh Dhamija, as the GSA for the Europe sector. The proposal did not include any information on Fair Limited's track record. In those days, RNAC used to sell tickets worth roughly US$110 million in Europe. I felt that such a huge trade should not be handed over on an ad hoc basis to an unknown company.

'Does the prime minister's office have the right to appoint a GSA?' I had asked the board.

'No, we take the decision,' one of them said. 'But we have to abide by their directive.'

'Don't give me that crap,' I snapped at them. 'If the PM's office thinks it has the authority to make that decision, then it should come here and make it. However, if the board of directors has the authority, then it has to independently assess the performance of the existing GSA. We need to have solid reasons, such as the net worth and institutional capacity of the proposed GSA, to prove that it's better than the existing one.'

All of them were dumbstruck.

'So, what should we do then?'

'Let's set up a panel to investigate the matter. They will go to Europe to assess the status of both companies and recommend one to us.'

But that board of directors did not have the guts to take such a decision, one that would have bulldozed the prime minister's directive.

The meeting was adjourned.

They never convened the next meeting. After a month, the board was dissolved. Members of the new board met at the prime minister's residence at Baluwatar to appoint the GSA.

This incident not only dragged Girija Babu, a towering figure in the democratic movement, into financial irregularities but also shortened his political tenure. The Public Accounts Committee of the House of Representatives launched an investigation and released a report implicating the prime minister in the scandal. This report could not be tabled in Parliament. The country was thrown into midterm polls.

The case became so controversial that passions ran high even after the elections. The minority government led by the Communist Party of Nepal (Unified Marxist-Leninist) scrapped the Dhamija agreement. It also formed a judicial probe panel led by Supreme Court Justice Min Bahadur Rayamajhi. However, the panel could not establish beyond doubt that there had been financial irregularities in the case. Nobody came forward to testify that the prime minister had issued a directive to the RNAC to appoint Fair Limited as the GSA.

Meanwhile, the Commission for the Investigation of Abuse of Authority (CIAA) also set up a special committee to look into the case. The committee summoned me for my statement. I went. I met the tourism secretary, Mohan Raj Sharma, and RNAC's general manager, Bobby Shah, outside the CIAA building. They were just leaving after having had their statements recorded. I went to the chairperson's office.

'We have summoned only you because of the legal compulsion to summon everyone related to the case,' he said. 'We know very well that you had tried to stop them from taking this decision.'

I felt proud that day. I had done the right thing, even though I was in the minority.

The CIAA, however, absolved Girija Babu of any wrongdoing, stating it could not prove that the former prime minister had ordered the appointment of the RNAC's GSA for Europe. The commission also concluded that it was 'natural' and 'a legal responsibility' of a prime minister to direct any institution and its officials to expedite a job.

Investment Promotion Council row

The coalition government of the Nepali Congress, the Rastriya Prajatantra Party and the Nepal Sadbhavana Party constituted an Investment Promotion Council under the chairmanship of the prime minister on 2 April 1998.

I was appointed vice chairperson of the council.

Surya Bahadurjee was the prime minister then. We consulted Girija Babu about the council. His attitude was positive; he was impressed with the progress made in Sri Lanka, where a similar institution had been created. Despite the civil war in Sri Lanka, this board was credited with helping the country achieve better economic progress than other South Asian countries. He said all the parties and the government in

Sri Lanka had given top priority to the recommendations of that board.

'We, too, have been considering establishing a board of investment for years,' he told Surya Bahadurjee. 'If you establish it, I will continue it after I become prime minister again.'

The top leaders of the two parties in the ruling coalition agreed that I would be appointed vice chairman of the council. Congress leader Arjun Narsingh K.C. was a witness.

Surya Bahadurjee kept his promise. On 7 April 1998, I received a letter confirming that the Cabinet had decided to appoint me as vice chairperson of the Private Sector Investment Promotion Council led by the prime minister. The other members of the council consisted of representatives of each of the four national-level political parties, the chief secretary of the Government of Nepal, the governor of the Nepal Rastra Bank (the central bank) and the vice chairperson of the National Planning Commission. Representing the private sector were members Ananda Raj Mulmi, Mahesh Lal Pradhan, Padma Jyoti, Diwakar Golchha, Prabhakar Shumsher Rana and Anup Shumsher Rana.

The structure of the council, as we envisioned it, was modelled on similar boards in Singapore, Thailand, Malaysia and Sri Lanka. It would have its own secretariat inside the prime minister's office. The proposed aims of the council included creation of an investment-friendly environment in the country, harmonization of the views of the political parties on business matters for achieving economic growth, wooing foreign investment and providing an effective 'one-stop shop' for investors by coordinating with the line ministries.

However, Surya Bahadurjee had to resign as prime minister only four days after the formation of the council.

In accordance with an understanding between the coalition partners, Girija Babu replaced him. Now the onus lay on Girija Babu to institutionalize the council. He had promised the council continuity during the consultations that Surya Bahadurjee and I had with him. However, within a few days of Girija Babu's taking over as prime minister, rumours were rife that the government was considering establishment of another agency in place of the council. None of the members of the council were told what was going on. Even I, the vice chairperson of the council, was kept in the dark. The government neither invited us to assume office nor consulted us about the future of the council.

On 16 July 1998, the government announced the formation of the Industry, Commerce and Trade Consultancy Group. I was asked to be a member of it. This consultancy group was different from the council we had envisaged. The autonomous council's mandate was to bring about a convergence of views among the political parties on issues relating to economic prosperity and investment promotion, in line with the internationally accepted concept of a 'board of investment'. This consultancy group, in contrast, was nothing more than a group of five to six advisors to the prime minister, representing the government as well as non-government sectors. It had no role at the policy-making level to determine the economic course the country should take; neither were its powers and responsibilities clearly established. We were well aware of the pathetic status of dozens of non-empowered councils related to environment, tourism, imports and employment promotion. Agencies that do not have clearly defined powers, responsibilities and organizational structures are useless. That was the reason we had envisioned a board that was empowered as well as autonomous. However, Girija Babu had rejected that vision and created, instead, just another useless agency.

This made me lose confidence in Girija Babu. The idea of accepting a position, which came to me by the grace of the Girija Babu-led government, and would, at the end of the day, achieve nothing, offended my pride and my sense of honour. I wrote a letter to the prime minister telling him I could not accept membership of the new agency. I even published the letter in the newspapers about it. Many of my friends advised me not to decline the offer made by an important person like Girija Babu or, at least, not to publicize my letter.

I would not listen to anyone. I rejected the appointment.

The 'board of investment' concept was scrapped in a political environment in which the goal of national economic growth was sacrificed for the sake of vested interests. Today, we can see the price the country is paying for that.

Proximity to the UML

Around fifteen years ago, the CPN-UML was trying to win the confidence of the private sector, much in the way the Maoists did more recently once they were in power.

We, as industrial entrepreneurs, were wary of the UML in those days. The reason, of course, was the word 'communist' attached to its name, and the pejorative terms such as 'brokers', 'bourgeois' and 'capitalists' they used when speaking about the private sector. We were haunted by the fear that the UML would want to nationalize all industry and that we would have to fight yet another autocratic system.

Shortly after they came into the open as a political party, the UML leaders succeeded in creating a strong power base. The powerful speeches and charismatic image of the general secretary of the party, Madan Bhandari, was primarily responsible for UML's rise in popularity in such a short period of time. Nevertheless, the UML had to allay the fears of the private sector in order to secure its political future.

In April 1992, the country was gripped by election fever. It was in that context that I attended a seminar organized by the UML at Bluestar Hotel or entrepreneurs from the industrial sector.

'Local industrialists like you have risen to great heights by utilizing local resources, labour, capital, and through your sheer industriousness. I don't have words to express my admiration,' Madan Bhandari said. 'The country's economic future rests in your hands.'

Following his speech, we were allowed to address the seminar. I took the microphone and said, 'Comrade, at the outset, you need to change your approach to the private sector if you want collaboration with us. On the one hand, you address us as local industrialists and say the progress of the country rests in our hands. You praise us for industrializing Nepal by utilizing labour, capital and the resources of the country. On the other hand, however, in your written material, you describe us using terms with pejorative connotations, such as "brokers", "bourgeois" and "capitalists". First of all, you need to remove all those terms that mock or belittle us from your written material. Then we can talk about collaboration.

'Comrade, what is the meaning of the word "broker" in the present day? What does "bourgeois" mean? Who is a "capitalist"? We are all brokers. We make products by utilizing the labour force, and bring them to our customers. We are, therefore, brokers between the workers and the customers. We invest capital and earn capital, hence we are capitalists. Therefore, the way things are presented in your written material does not provide an honest picture of the private sector. You can't win our confidence that way.

'Comrade, no matter what you say in a public forum, we view what you put in writing as a reflection of your true position. Therefore, there has to be uniformity between what you say and what you write. So long as your official documentation continues to use pejorative terms in relation to the private sector, we will continue to harbour distrust and apprehension.'

After the seminar, comrade Bhandari took me aside and said, 'I am very impressed with the way you express yourself. You have expressed your views in an extremely effective manner.'

Before we left, he told me, 'We'll meet soon.'

However, I was never to meet him again.

Following the mid-term polls of 1994, the UML formed a minority government led by its chairperson Manmohan Adhikari. I was the chairperson of the FNCCI at the time. The UML forming the government was akin to the Maoists forming the government after the Constituent Assembly elections of 2008. Immediately after the government was formed, the BBC called me from London seeking my reaction.

'Now that a communist government has taken over power in Nepal, how do you think you'll be able to function?'

I replied honestly: 'I think you are trying to imply that the industrial sector in Nepal will be now nationalized and that people in private business are ready to flee the country with their capital. Some industrial entrepreneurs here have similar fears. But the fears are completely unfounded.

'Times have changed. This is not the age of the Soviet Union. Russia itself has transformed into a socialist state. China, too, has adopted a mixture of socialism and capitalism. Hence, I don't see any reason to panic just because a communist government has been formed. I fully back this government and I call upon the business community also to support this government.

'This change is the need of the hour. The people had given a clear mandate to the Nepali Congress to run a stable government in the country for five years. That government collapsed within three years due to the intra-party strife. The Congress party itself is responsible for the position it is in today. Therefore, we, the business community, must assimilate this change and be prepared to cooperate with the government. We need to initiate dialogue with the party which has come to power for the first time, on the fundamental problems dogging the industrial and commercial sectors of the country and suggest ways to derive optimum benefits while addressing these problems.'

This was a clear endorsement of the government, which was not sure whether the private sector would cooperate with it or not. Since I was chairperson of the FNCCI, my expression of support for the government was instrumental in shaping the view of the entire private sector. The UML leaders openly praised me for taking that position. This played an important role in bringing me closer to the UML.

I used to meet with Hari Pandey of Gandaki Noodles while I was vice chairperson of the FNCCI. He played a big role in my election to the post of chairperson. Coincidentally, he was an active leader of the UML and went on to hold the key ministerial portfolios of industry and water resources. I called him up and said, 'I have given a clean chit to this government from the private sector. Now your leaders should work to win our confidence.'

'You tell us what this government needs to do,' he said.

'I will organize a reception in honour of the members of the new Cabinet,' I said. 'You should use it as an opportunity to bring about a fundamental change in the attitude of the private sector towards a government with a communist background. Give the private sector the message that the UML has jettisoned its traditional bias against it and has adopted timely and relevant economic policies. Then a new relationship based on mutual trust can be nurtured.'

'What does the private sector want to hear?'

'Your ministers should publicly state that they are committed to an open market economy and that the government will not back away from economic liberalization. Bring in programmes that bring the benefits of an open market and economic reform to the grass-roots level.'

'You start your preparations. I will take the initiative inside the party,' he said, approving my proposal.

After that, I took part in many discussions with the UML. I had a role in drafting the party's economic policy. The communist terminology and approach that the UML had been using with respect to the private sector were amended. While I was collaborating with the UML, I had no plans to affiliate myself with the party. As a representative of the private sector, all I wanted was cooperation with the ruling party. My other aim was to get the UML to commit to the private sector, on economic liberalization and foreign investment.

We did not have to wait long to see if the UML would keep its promises.

On 29 December 1994, the UML government tabled its first half-yearly budget in the House of Representatives. This was the first-ever budget presented by a communist government in the history of Nepal. It being so, it introduced some powerful social programmes. But it also included liberalization and promotion of the private sector to dispel any doubts remaining in the business community about its commitment to its promises.

First, it introduced a programme called *Aphno Gaun Aphai Banaau*—Build Your Village Yourself. As the programme was clearly set out in the budget, people could hold their elected representatives directly accountable for the use of the money earmarked for the programme. For the first time, villagers got a chance to see huge amounts of money. This programme became so popular that it is still being emulated. Though the slogan has changed, people at the grassroots village development committee level have been getting up to Rs 30 lakh a year—the amount disbursed depending on the population—towards development. Another popular initiative was pension for the elderly. The budget announced a pension of Rs 100 to all citizens of the country who were over the age of seventy-five. Today this pension has increased to Rs 500. I think the programme was an attempt to honour those who had served the country for a long time.

As far as the industrial sector, including the private sector, was concerned, the UML designed a package for the protection of national industries. Twenty-six industries were identified as 'sick' and a policy formulated to protect them. The budget slashed import tax and, most importantly, removed tax on property. This was the main reason I openly lauded the budget. During the interim government led by Kishunjee, the finance minister, Devendra Raj Pandey, had introduced a property tax, which was out of step with the efforts being made to promote a liberal economic system following the political change of 1990. We opposed it from the very beginning, but neither the interim government nor the elected government led by Girija Babu amended it. This tax did not raise even Rs 3 crore a year. It, in fact, discouraged the transfer of capital to investment at a time when there was a liquidity crisis in the country.

We briefed the new finance minister, Bharat Mohan Adhikari, about this. We made him realize that the property tax was an unnecessary burden on the private sector and unfavourable for promotion of internal investment. Agreeing with the private sector, he scrapped the property tax. I welcomed the decision on behalf of the FNCCI. I also met Bharat Mohanjee in person and said, 'We thought the Nepali Congress championed the cause of the private sector but it went on to impose a property tax on us. On the other hand, we were apprehensive about you as a communist but you have removed the property tax.'

I have enjoyed a cordial relationship with Bharat Mohanjee ever since.

Following my dispute with the Nepali Congress regarding the investment board, I openly sought to become closer to the UML. That was the beginning of my direct and active involvement in politics. This happened at a time when the big business houses were hesitant to associate themselves with a communist party. Businessmen were supposed to be associated only with the Nepali Congress or the royalists.

The UML suggested I have a seat in the Upper House of Parliament after the general election in 1999. 'All political parties have secured some points towards seats in the Upper House,' the UML leadership told me. 'However, we can't appoint a person to the House on the basis of our points alone. If you talk to the Rastriya Prajatantra Party, and the Sadbhavana Party, and they agree to add their points to ours, then we can get a seat in the House. You come forward and we will support you.'

I liked this proposal. I discussed it with the top UML leaders such as Madhav Kumar Nepal, K.P. Oli and Ishwore Pokharel. Oli called up Pashupati Shumsher Rana of the RPP in my presence to propose my name.

'If you agree on Binod Chaudhary, then we will support his nomination,' he told Rana over the phone.

In those days, Pashupati Shumsherjee and Surya Bahadurjee had not parted ways. There was no possibility of Surya Bahadurjee rejecting my nomination. It was possible to clinch a seat in the Upper House with support from just the UML and the RPP, but I still wanted to include the Sadbhavana Party. I talked to Badri Mandal and Hridayesh Tripathy of the Sadbhavana Party. They agreed with me.

I could see a vista of political opportunities opening up in front of me. I was taking a plunge into politics despite the fact that I was basically a non-political person. I thought I could make a bigger contribution to the nation by playing a part in politics rather than staying out of it. I was very upbeat as I waited to be nominated to the Upper House.

As the day for formation of the Parliament drew closer, I felt that the parties that had promised a seat to me in the

House were trying to avoid me. I then heard that the RPP leaders, Kamal Thapa and Dr Prakash Chandra Lohani, were negotiating for the very seat that had been promised to me by the UML. Soon it was confirmed that the UML had decided to give the seat to an RPP leader from Makwanpur district. I could not believe my ears. The UML itself had approached me. It had promised that seat to me. How could it possibly break its promise? However, anything is possible in politics.

I could not get in touch with the UML leadership, so I telephoned Surya Bahadurjee.

'What is this?' I asked him. 'How could you do this to me after agreeing to appoint me to the House?'

Instead of answering my question, he said, 'Just hang on a minute. We're facing a problem on a national scale here. We're struggling to keep the party together. Don't just think about yourself.'

I did not like his response.

'This is not just about me, Surya Bahadurjee,' I snapped. 'You are the ones who pulled me into this and now I'll look like a fool if you bring in another person at the eleventh hour.'

The rest of the conversation was nothing but obfuscation of the truth on his part.

A few days later, I went to the UML headquarters. There I discovered they were holding a standing committee meeting. I barged into the meeting room without even sending a message beforehand. All the top guns were there. They looked at me with their eyes wide open. As soon as I entered the room, I said, 'What is this? You took me to such a point that you have utterly humiliated me by dropping me. If you had some other plans, why did you drag me into this mess?'

UML General Secretary Madhav Nepaljee tried to pacify me. 'It's nothing like that. This is part of a broader issue. It's not aimed at putting you in a difficult position. Please don't take it personally.'

'Mr General Secretary,' I replied, 'I am not talking only about myself. You were the ones who had assured me that my nomination was guaranteed. If you had any doubts whatsoever, then you should not have proposed my name. Now my reputation is at stake.'

Having said that, I turned my back to them and left the room. They tried to stop me, but I did not care.

Later on, Pradip Nepaljee came to see me. 'We will give you Nawalparasi constituency-1,' he said. 'Your industrial park is located there and you've made a huge contribution to the place. Taking that into consideration, we have coordinated with the RPP for the other seat. If we give that seat to the RPP so that they can bring in one of their men from Makwanpur, then in return, they'll allow us in Dang.'

The crux of his agreement was that this was part of his party's broader alliance with the RPP. But I was not convinced. I felt the UML could not be trusted to keep its promises.

This episode was a huge blow to me, shattering again my association with the political world. In a way, it poisoned my relationship with the UML too. I started to reduce my involvement in the party's activities and diverted my attention to expanding my business interests at home and abroad. I also concentrated my energies on the institutional development of the Confederation of Nepalese Industries (CNI). All this proved to be a blessing in disguise in terms of my professional life. Had I become more actively involved in politics, especially at that time, I could not have focused on the expansion of the Chaudhary Group at the international level.

There are a few striking similarities between business and politics. In neither area can you afford to pursue personal vendettas or hold grudges. You might be in cut-throat competition with someone today, but tomorrow you might find yourself having to collaborate with the very same party. Both businesspersons and politicians recognize that reality. The most important thing is to wait and be alert to opportunities.

Even while keeping my distance from the UML, I was still thinking of entering politics. I was always toying with the idea that I might do it if an opportunity arose and the time was right. My philosophy is that people should, if they can, assume a role in public life at some point in their life. My expansion of the Chaudhary Group, this book, and my political journey . . . they have all been guided by that philosophy.

My own experiences have played a crucial part in pushing me into active politics. I worked with the FNCCI for six to seven years, and I was involved with the CNI too. My association with these organizations taught me that everything, at the end of the day, is related to politics. No matter how powerful the organization you lead and how serious the issue you raise, you have to depend on political leaders for the execution of your plans.

The Constituent Assembly election paved the path for building a new Nepal. I felt it was high time that I joined politics. The private sector was intimidated by the dominance of the Maoists in the Constituent Assembly. The Maoists had come up with radical nationalist slogans to 'nationalize the properties of broker capitalists' and to 'rein in foreign investment'. The Maoists' People's War itself was founded on these radical beliefs. If they succeeded in putting their ideology into practice, the country would suffer irrevocable setbacks, with the potential to morph into another Soviet Union. Some of us from the private sector would often discuss this problem. We believed we had to take on some kind of direct role in politics to stop the Maoists from imposing their radical ideas on the Constituent Assembly. It was not possible for us to exert a restraining influence by standing outside the political sphere, especially at a time when the issue of drafting a new constitution was being raised. We concluded that we had to step into the field of politics using our existing connections with the political parties.

I faced no dilemma. I had, to some extent, worked with all the political parties. A number of them wanted to nominate me to the Constituent Assembly, but I felt most comfortable allying with the UML, despite the events of the past. There was no point in opening old wounds. If you have some pent-up grievance, instead of carrying it around it is better to let it go. That was what I chose to do. I re-established contact with the UML. Bharat Mohanjee and Bishnu Poudeljee helped me do that.

Besides me, the businessmen who had allied themselves with the UML included Tek Chandra Pokharel, Vijay Shah, Radhesh Pant and Shyam Pandey. We forwarded to the party a list of people we thought would be appropriate nominees to the Constituent Assembly. The party then asked us to select two candidates from the list. We discussed this amongst ourselves and agreed to recommend Tek Chandra and myself. The party made both our names public. However, Tek Chandra was ultimately dropped from the final list of nominees.

Having failed to get any of my friends from the business world into the Constituent Assembly, I lost a lot of my enthusiasm to take part in it myself. I told the party leaders, 'You couldn't even give me half the slots I wanted. Therefore, do as you please. You must have many party workers. If you face pressure from them, do feel free to remove my name from the list.'

The party argued that it had recommended only my name from the private sector, as part of the political understanding to include every sector in the Constituent Assembly. My friends too encouraged me to accept the nomination. I eventually became a member of the Constituent Assembly, representing the party that I had once distrusted.

The very next day of my appointment, there was some irritation within the party over my remark that 'nobody can make Binod Chaudhary a communist'. What I actually wanted to demonstrate was that the UML was not a radical communist party and that I too could not afford to adhere to a communist ideology in the twenty-first century. Much like the Communist Party of China, the UML had embraced economic liberalism, the best example of this being the coexistence of both trade unionists and a businessman like me within the party.

I know very well that politics cannot survive in the absence of an economic agenda. I have a good understanding of not only commercial and economic issues but of politics too. There are similarities in running a party, or even a state, and running a company. You need managerial skill for each and I have that capability. However, neither I nor my family expect any leverage from our involvement in politics, hoping that one of us will make it to the helm of power one day. I have joined politics to give of myself and not to extract for myself. I do not want to link my professional dreams to politics. Now I want to link politics with tangible plans; I want to link it to outcomes; I want to link it to the will to contribute something, to accomplish something.

There is another similarity between politics and business. In neither profession can you reach your destination solely on the basis of your thoughts, capabilities and efforts. Your success hinges on the environment around you, on whether your colleagues share your dream or not.

I could pave the way for my professional growth even when the environment was not conducive. My colleagues always stood by me. That is why I am successful in my profession today.

My political journey is a different tale. I have innumerable memories related to the unceremonious demise of the Constituent Assembly, and the dirty games I saw in the run-up to that, the complications that surfaced during the drafting of the Constitution, and the true colours of our political leaders. I shall definitely reveal them someday.

The royal palace massacre

'Binod Babu! Binod Babu!'

I was jolted out of my slumber by someone knocking hard on my bedroom door. At first, I thought the knocking was a dream, and I closed my eyes again.

'Binod Babu! Binod Babu!' I heard the same insistent voice.

I hurried out of bed and looked at the clock. It was four in the morning. And someone was indeed repeatedly knocking on my door and calling out my name. It was no dream.

I opened the door, rubbing my eyes. Our cook was standing there.

'What is it?' I asked irritably.

'Basant Babu is on the telephone,' he replied quickly.

As soon as I heard that Basant was calling me up at that hour, I started to panic. My eyes, which had been heavy with sleep only a moment before, were now dilated with fear. God, something terrible must have happened!

I raced into the next room where the telephone stood and picked up the receiver with a shaking hand.

'Hello . . .'

'Hello, Brother,' Basant sounded scared. 'It's very bad news.'

I went weak. My lips felt parched. My hair stood on end.

'The crown prince reportedly went mad. He gunned down the entire royal family before turning the gun on himself,' he said quickly.

I had thought something terrible must have happened to someone in my family. The realization that my loved ones were safe and sound gave me some degree of relief. However, my brain was still spinning. I could not believe my ears. Basant was speaking so quickly that it was hard to follow him.

'What are you talking about?' I asked.

'It's true, Brother. I've been receiving a lot of calls.'

'Did he actually go mad?'

'That's what all of them are saying.'

'Who's all of them?'

'It's being reported by the BBC and the CNN,' he said, clearly convinced that the reports were true.

'Why did he suddenly go mad?'

'I don't know. I'm trying to get a handle on what happened.'

'Call someone from the Palace.'

'I've tried that already but no one answers,' he said.

I was at CG Industrial Park in Nawalparasi district on that night of 1 June 2001. We had been at a meeting to evaluate the company's performance. The meeting went on late into the night and was adjourned to the next morning, so I was staying there overnight.

The only information Basant could provide about the incident at the Palace was that all the members of the royal family had been killed. He was very nervous, and that was making me nervous too. I called up a few people. They answered the phone immediately, as if they had been sitting with their hands resting on the receiver. All of them said the same thing—such a thing had indeed happened, but none had a clue as to how or why it had happened.

I tuned in to the BBC. It was broadcasting international news. I read the breaking news scrolling across the screen but there was no mention of anything related to Nepal. Nonetheless, with so many people awake and in a state of agitation so early in the morning, I knew something terrible must have happened. I woke up all my colleagues and asked them to call up their contacts. They all returned with the same news—a massacre had taken place at the royal palace. None of the royal family was alive.

At first, we suspected the Maoists. Could they have attacked the royal palace?

The Maoist insurgency was at its peak at the time. The Maoists had demonstrated their strength by launching a deadly attack on Dunai, the headquarters of Dolpa district. Police posts across the country were vulnerable to Maoist attacks, and politicians were approaching the unanimous conclusion that the police alone were no match for the Maoists. The case for mobilizing the armed forces was growing.

I, for one, never gave any weight to the theory that the Maoists were responsible for what happened at the Palace. 'Even if something terrible has taken place there,' I said, 'the

Maoists don't have the capability to successfully undertake a raid on the royal palace.'

Who else could be behind it then? Could it be a foreign power?

'How could a foreign power bring in its troops to directly attack the Palace?' I snapped. 'Nobody other than a member of the royal household would have the access required to pull off such a thing.'

'What if a member of the royal family had been used by an external agency or force?' One of my aides posed the question, and everybody fell silent.

Confirmation of the news soon arrived. The BBC, in its breaking news, reported that about a dozen members of Nepal's royal family, including the king and the queen, had been massacred.

Though the reason remained shrouded in mystery, this report dispelled all doubt about the incident itself.

I ordered a car to take me back to Kathmandu immediately.

We left Nawalparasi at quarter to six in the morning. Owing to heavy rains during the night, the road was wet and slippery, so we could not drive quickly despite the urgency of the situation. We moved ahead slowly. By the time we reached Pulchowk intersection at Narayanghat, people had started to gather in groups on the road, all talking about the massacre.

There were no vehicles on the road except a few trishaws, but the streets were filled with people. News of the royal palace massacre had already spread like wildfire.

The further we drove towards Kathmandu, the larger the crowds we saw. There were very few vehicles coming from Kathmandu. The highway was virtually deserted. At Malekhu, just a couple of hours away from Kathmandu, we were stopped by an angry mob.

'How can you be driving around when our king has died,' a young man with sturdy arms and bloodshot eyes asked us.

I introduced myself and said, 'We're hurrying back to Kathmandu precisely because of that.'

He lowered his voice.

'Brother, what's the real story?'

'I don't know,' I said. 'All I've heard is that everyone in the royal family has been killed.'

He let out a long sigh of despair and asked his friends to clear the way to let us pass.

Local residents tried to stop us at a few other places along the highway, but I managed to negotiate our way into Kathmandu. Ordinary people were grief-stricken at what had happened to the royal family. Some of them were weeping while others were infuriated, alleging the whole thing must be a serious conspiracy.

Kathmandu was even more chaotic. Only a few shops were open. People had gathered in large numbers on the streets, all talking about the killings. The entire city was abuzz with the news. One could sense, despite the charged atmosphere, that people still had boundless faith in and love for the royal family.

1 June 2001 passed, plunging the entire country into despair.

Many were the associations the people of Nepal lost that tragic day, which has gone down as Black Friday in Nepal's recent history. Ordinary people lost their beloved king. Many grieved for Queen Aishwarya; others shed their tears for Crown Prince Dipendra or for Princess Shruti and Prince Niranjan. But few remembered another royal who also died that night: Prince Dhirendra.

For me, that dark night marked my separation from Dhirendra.

I had been one of the witnesses to his moment of truth.

Neer Shah and I were in London on a business trip. Prince Dhirendra happened to be in the city at the same time, and his aide was with him too. We went to meet Dhirendra. One evening, the four of us were walking around in the city when it suddenly started to rain heavily. Dhirendra pointed to a sign at a dark corner a little down the road. It said: White Haze Bar.

We entered the bar. An array of lights splashed across our faces.

That was where we met Sherlie.

Dhirendra was so attracted to her that he ordered Dom Pérignon, the most expensive champagne in the bar. It cost £150 a bottle in those days. Before one bottle was finished, Dhirendra would order another. Between nine at night and three in the morning, we had finished more than twelve bottles of Dom Pérignon.

We became the centre of attention in that bar. Naturally, Sherlie was intrigued. She was also attracted to Dhirendra.

Eventually, Prince Dhirendra gave up his position and royal status for his love for that lady.

As I have mentioned earlier, he played a pivotal role in shaping my career. Had I not his support in my hour of crisis, I might still have continued life in some profession or other, but I would probably not be in a position to write this memoir.

Prince Dhirendra was considered to be rebellious and the defiant one among the three sons of King Mahendra. He renounced the 'prince' title to marry Shirley. He was the dearest to me. He would stand by a person he liked until the end. He would tell me time and again, 'I don't care what they do to me, but I am always ready to lay down my life for my elder brother.' His elder brother was, of course, King Birendra. Even after relinquishing his royal status and setting in London, I never felt Dhirendra's trust and love for his brother ever wavered.

I met him once more in London. He used to live just outside the downtown area. I got in touch with him and we spent a day together.

What I can infer from my formal and informal interactions with Dhirendra is that he was actively involved as a contact person for the king during both the Panchayat era and the years of the Maoist insurgency. During the Panchayat era, he believed the king should establish a dialogue with the political parties. Because of that belief, he acted as a facilitator between the king and the party leaders. A group within the Palace never forgave him for that, and eventually that same group was instrumental in driving him away.

He had already lost his royal status when he was working to establish contact between the Palace and the Maoists during the insurgency. This gave him the space to maintain continuous contact with the Maoists. He was able to move around more freely. I have seen him visit some dangerous places without a single bodyguard. He visited many parts of the country and even travelled abroad to meet politicians at all levels. By maintaining a low profile, he managed to escape attention.

His initiatives could have brought about something positive . . . if only the royal palace massacre had not taken place.

Gyanendra and the 1 February royal takeover

My relationship with the former King Gyanendra—even when he was Prince Gyanendra—was limited to formalities.

Some of my good friends were close to him. They used to tell me about his likes and dislikes, including his view of me. Once General Tara Bahadur Thapa told me that he had said to Gyanendra, 'Your Highness, you should have more dealings with Binod Chaudhary. He's a very useful person.'

Gyanendra had replied, 'Yes, I know him. He's a completely ruthless and shrewd businessman.'

In my opinion, to be called shrewd is a compliment for a businessman. Shrewdness can be viewed both positively and negatively. At times, circumstances compel a businessman to take ruthless decisions. A businessman has to make decisions with his head more often than with his heart and has to be ruthless if a situation demands it. A business house can be ruthless in its dealings with its competition while at the same time doing good for the greater society. Sometimes, you have to be ruthless even to yourself to achieve a positive outcome.

Even though there was no partnership between Gyanendra and me, nonetheless, I welcomed his move to assume full control of the state on 1 February 2005. I was prepared to give him the benefit of the doubt.

I had hosted a small reception at my place to bid farewell to a foreign ambassador. Close friends and colleagues had been invited. The atmosphere at the gathering changed after we heard King Gyanendra's address to the nation broadcast on television. Some of my guests said the king had done the right thing. Most of them concluded that it was a welcome development in that it would bring a degree of 'stability' to the nation and that politicians should 'learn a lesson' from it.

Owing to their constant wrangling, the political parties had not just failed to form a stable government but had also failed to solve the Maoist problem. We saw a faint ray of hope in the king's declaration that he would at least try to do something for the country. We hoped that, besides addressing the festering political crisis, his efforts would also give impetus to the sluggish economy.

As a businessperson, I have closely followed developments in the economies of South East Asia. I was hopeful that Gyanendra, through his active, hands-on rule, might bring about socio-economic and political transformation in the country much as Mahathir Mohamad had done in Malaysia and Lee Kuan Yew in Singapore.

Some of my friends who were close to him would tell me, 'Gyanendra understands how the world works. He will be able to lead the country in the direction it should go.'

Gyanendra was also a successful businessman himself. His Soaltee hotel was among the best in the country. Surya Tobacco, Bhotekoshi hydropower project, Telco and Spripadi were some of the other high-profile companies with which he was associated. These companies were not free from controversy, however. His detractors said that Gyanendra had harassed the previous Telco agent U.G. Jain so badly in order to get the agency for himself that Jain had to leave Nepal. He has also been accused of ruining the profitable state-run Janakpur Cigarette Factory so that he could launch Surya Nepal as a joint venture with the ITC.

I do not take such controversies very seriously. To a certain extent, politics and business are like warfare. We choose our weapons and our tactics to match those of our competitors. Nobody is going to sympathize with the losers here. Only the winners count. As a businessman, Gyanendra did what he had to do. We thought that if he could demonstrate similar capabilities on the political front, he would be able to silence his detractors.

We discussed the possible strategies Gyanendra might use until late into that night.

'Binod, I hear the relationship between you and Gyanendra is strained. I hope it won't affect you,' a friend of mine said. His remark made me suddenly feel unsettled.

Every negative situation I had weathered between 1980 and 1990 began to run through my head. To what extent had Gyanendra been involved in the efforts of certain people in the Palace to undermine me during those years? I felt more and more uneasy. Now I did not have Dhirendra to support me; Kishunjee was not in a position to help me either. I then thought about my reputation, not just at the national level but internationally as well. This boosted my confidence somewhat. Nobody at the helm of power could mete out injustice to a person of my stature. I convinced myself and my friends of this: 'As a clever political player with a big vision and, now, huge responsibilities, surely he wouldn't waste his time on petty quarrels and personal vendettas.'

My friends were convinced.

I was convinced too. .

We all know the fallout of Gyanendra's direct rule.

6

World Leaders and I

I am an extrovert by nature, and a forward-thinking person, perhaps the reason I have always been ahead of my times. These qualities also lay behind my leadership of the FNCCI as its president at a young age. The federation provides its members with a platform to establish direct links with business leaders across the world. However, not everyone knows how to use a platform like that as a launch pad to the global business stage. They eventually get stuck on the platform itself.

Among the sweeping reforms carried out at the FNCCI under my leadership, one was to provide for direct participation of the private sector in policy-making bodies. This was done through the Economic Liberalization Project assisted by the USAID. At the same time, I also wanted to expand the linkages and international exposure of the FNCCI. I was sure it could never fully exploit business opportunities by limiting its association to the Punjab and Haryana Chambers of Commerce and Industry! Here, I was also fortunate in that the country was transformed into a multiparty democracy and had embraced economic liberalization just as I took over the reins at the FNCCI. I was the vice president of the FNCCI when Krishna Prasad Bhattarai headed the interim government following the restoration of democracy in the country in 1990. Bhattarai even offered me a position as his economic advisor. He brought me on the board of directors of key public enterprises such as the RNAC and the Nepal Electricity Authority.

When Girija Prasad Koirala took over, I enjoyed a relationship of mutual respect with him too. I was part of Koirala's delegation during his first official visit to India. I was the keynote speaker from our side during a reception jointly organized by the CII and the ASSOCHAM in Koirala's honour. I worked on expanding the FNCCI's relations with these associations in India. During Deputy Prime Minister Madhav Kumar Nepal's visit to India, I signed a partnership agreement with the CII. The FNCCI suddenly broke out of its shell and woke up to the possibilities of global engagement. In this context, I could also expand my own business linkages and explore opportunities across the world.

At the age of just thirty-six, I found myself interacting with not just leading businessmen in the region and beyond, but also with top political leaders, economists and philanthropists. It has been my destiny to interact with people who are usually one generation senior to me. From the day I stepped into the world of business, I had to mix with my father's contemporaries.

I became a founding member of the South Asian Association for Regional Cooperation (SAARC) Chamber of Commerce and Industry, which was established almost at the same time as SAARC itself. As a founding member, I was part of the drive to develop the SAARC Chamber into a catalyst for regional economic integration, with a view to creating a South Asian economic union modelled on ASEAN and the European Union. We established the first secretariat of the SAARC Chamber in Islamabad. Two schools of thought emerged in the process of creating these outfits. The representatives of the bigger member states wanted to put more emphasis on opening up markets for themselves throughout the region, while we from the smaller member states wanted some kind of support or preferential arrangement before fully opening up our markets for free trade. What is the advantage of an economic union that benefits only the bigger parties? Moreover, the markets in some of the world's smallest and poorest countries were already quite open for a big player like India. Due to these differences, the entire SAARC Chamber and, as a matter of fact, the entire SAARC process, remained a non-starter. However, we again see a flicker of hope for the economic integration of South Asia since Narendra Modi became prime minister of India, as we did during the short stint of I.K. Gujral as India's prime minister.

I did not find my experience with SAARC very encouraging, but our partnership with the CII led me to the World Economic Forum (WEF). When the CII invited me to the WEF Summit in India, I got the opportunity to closely interact with people such as Professor Klaus Schwab, who had founded the WEF, and Dr Collect Mathur. The WEF leaders were quite impressed with my vision and my eagerness to take Nepal's business to the world. Within a few weeks of the summit, they nominated me to the coveted list of Global Leaders for Tomorrow. Benazir Bhutto of Pakistan and Salman Khurshid of India were among those nominated to the list. There has been no looking back since then. I have been invited to all the Davos functions and activities since that first summit I attended in 1986. Over the years, my relationship with the FNCCI and the CII has become even more solid. I convinced the CII to set up an office at the FNCCI. By 1996, when Nepal and India were reviewing their trade treaty, the CII was actually lobbying for us in Delhi.

To sum up, the initiatives I took while with the FNCCI and, later, the CNI that I founded, took those bodies, and in the process my own professional network, to new heights in terms of linkages, exposure and opportunities. This period also saw me coming into contact and, in some cases, developing personal relationships with many of the world leaders, which, in turn, shaped me into an emerging global leader.

Hussain Muhammad Ershad

Hussain Muhammad Ershad came to Nepal in an official capacity. My Bangladeshi friend Mintoo urged him to visit me at my place in Kathmandu, and Ershad readily agreed. Mintoo had told him I was a good friend of Bangladesh. As a result, Ershad did not think twice about visiting my house even though we were not acquainted at all. This speaks volumes about his humility. Let us not forget that we are talking about the same inspirational leader who, as President of Bangladesh, played a major role in transforming that country's economy by developing infrastructure and creating a basic institutional framework of governance. He is probably the most revered leader in Bangladesh since Sheikh Mujibur Rahman.

During our conversation, Ershad not only shared his vision for South Asia but also told me about his one-on-one talks with other leaders in the region, including King Birendra. He told me that he and Birendra had played a crucial role in establishing SAARC. Ershad has always strived to create synergy among the countries of South Asia to transform the region for the benefit of the third of humanity that lives here.

He even told me that he and a few like-minded regional leaders had actually mooted the SAARC process so as 'to work around India as a group, rather than as each country separately'.

From that day on, I became a great admirer of Ershad's. We soon became close friends, so close that he would free himself from his official engagements as soon as possible and take me out with him to dinner to meet important people from different walks of life. I admire him not just for his humility or his marvellous vision for South Asia but also for his disciplined manner, his simple way of dressing and the ease with which he carries himself. He is simply a great human being. He does not work by design; he does not do anything for personal gain. He is also a great disciplinarian.

I recall an incident that shows what a marvellous human being Ershad is. Once, when I invited him to attend an economic summit I was organizing in Nepal, I also invited him to my place for lunch. He was very busy with the summit as well as with other meetings. Still, he turned up. He not only came to lunch but brought a set of jewellery as a gift for Lily. We later found out that despite the demands on his time, he had personally gone to a jewellery shop at the Soaltee where he was staying and bought the set from there. What etiquette, what thoughtfulness! He always goes the extra mile in any relationship.

However, as expected, many of my detractors here in Nepal and elsewhere have spread rumours over the years that I have been cultivating Ershad because of some vested interests.

Notwithstanding all this, he and I have become like family to each other. In fact, I call him dada—'elder brother'. Even today, he will immediately drop everything to give time to me, should I need it. Would a statesman of Ershad's stature and integrity become close friends with me had I tried to cash in on my relationship with him? I have never tried to exploit this relationship for any interests of my own. Pure mutual admiration is the basis of our relationship. Ershad is among the three close friends I have in Bangladesh. The other two are Mahbubur Rahman, chairperson of National Bank, and Abdul Awal Mintoo, whom I have mentioned earlier, a noted entrepreneur and a director of the same bank. So I had good connections in Bangladesh even before I met Ershad.

My admiration for Ershad has never diminished, not when he no longer had the seat of power, not when he was sentenced to jail. Our relationship has been purely personal. It was never a business association where one calculated gains or risks. When we met, we would discuss ways to create regional synergy and achieve collective progress in South Asia. He always encourages me to become politically active: 'Your country needs a dynamic leader like you in order to transform itself. We are here to help you in every possible way. I would personally campaign for you. Just say the word.'

Ershad is altruistic to such an extent that he holds that a true leader should not shy away from even laying down his or her life for the greater good of the nation. It is no wonder that he is among the leaders who have helped shape my world view. If I ever decide to enter the political fray again, I am confident that Ershad would be there to advise me. And I for one would certainly take his advice too. I do not care if he is called a dictator, and some people criticize me for supporting him. Ershad may have been a dictator, but he was a benevolent one—a dictator who stood for the people, for their progress and their prosperity.

Sri Lankan statesmen

I first visited Sri Lanka more than three decades ago. Nava Raj Ghimire of Annapurna Travels came up with the suggestion that as the airport in Calcutta was congested and it was very difficult to get enough cargo space for our consignments, we might explore the possibility of trans-shipping our goods from Singapore and other destinations through Sri Lanka. In those days, planes from Sri Lanka to Nepal were flying with underutilized cargo space. It was a brilliant idea. I left for Sri Lanka shortly afterwards and immediately fell in love with the country. But fate had other ideas for me. The idea of trans-shipping goods through Sri Lanka never became a reality, and I had to wait for many more years until I could return to that beautiful country, during the course of a joint venture with the Taj Group.

To get to the main point, I came across Tilak de Zoysa, a well-known Sri Lankan entrepreneur or, rather, an intellectual, at an international seminar (CACCI). I was instantly drawn to him. He was of sharp mind, and yet a thorough gentleman. Anybody who talked to him for just a quarter of an hour was likely to be won over, heart and mind. We became good friends. Our friendship grew deeper after my visit to Sri Lanka, where we worked on our joint venture with the Taj Group. We also met at various forums, including the WEF. Tilak became my link to Sri Lankan political and business leaders.

I met with Prime Minister Ranil Wickremasinghe through Prof. G.L. Peiris shortly after the turn of the new millennium. My meeting with Prof. Peiris was arranged by the Bangladeshi ambassador to Sri Lanka, Ashraf-ud-Doula, who was also a veteran of the Bangladeshi war of independence. Ashraf is another person I admire a lot. He lost one of his legs after an injury sustained during the war and walks with the aid of crutches. But he has absolutely no hang-ups about this, and is as confident as any man can be. Although I was a Nepali entrepreneur and he the Bangladeshi ambassador to Sri Lanka, he did not hesitate to introduce me to the Sri Lankan leadership for the mutual benefit of our countries.

I was impressed with Prof. Peiris, a Rhodes Scholar at Oxford, vice chancellor of the Colombo University and a former minister for external affairs. Though I was only an entrepreneur from Nepal, he took no time in taking me to meet the prime minister! This showed how much Prof. Peiris and, as a matter of fact, Wickremasinghe too, cared for their country. Anyway, I became close to both Prof. Peiris and Prime Minister Wickremasinghe over time. Wickremasinghe and Mrs Wickremasinghe even attended my son's wedding that took place in Goa, together with Prof. Peiris.

I admired Wickremasinghe also for giving hope to Sri Lanka by sealing a peace deal with the Liberation Tigers of Tamil Eelam (LTTE), even though he was prime minister for a comparatively short time, between 2001 and 2004. His line of thought was that the government should try to bring the LTTE into the mainstream to end the festering civil war through negotiations rather than through use of force. He wanted to devolve more power and autonomy to the Tamil-controlled parts of the country, which was why he signed the peace accord with the LTTE. Things started to transform overnight. Japan coordinated an aid group meeting, which pledged assistance of US$55 billion. The Sri Lankan stock exchange gained 300 points immediately. Foreign direct investment (FDI) started to pour in and interest rates and inflation dropped from double digits to single digit. Non-resident Sri Lankans started to return to the country, to also pursue investment. However, within a few years, all hopes of peace and prosperity were dashed when Wickremasinghe was defeated in the elections. The forces that stood to benefit from prolonging the civil war, including the LTTE itself, conspired to defeat him,

Sri Lanka fell back into a bloody civil war.

Over the years, I have worked with Ranil Wickremasinghe and Prof. Peiris, sharing with them ideas for addressing the many socio-economic and political problems common to Nepal and Sri Lanka. Prof. Peiris has been very helpful in this regard. I have hardly met a better orator, and even fewer who have his razor-sharp memory. In a meeting of, say, 150 persons, Prof. Peiris can not only recognize at least 100, but also remember their names and vividly recall conversations and events related to those people from past meetings. He also has an amazing memory for dates, even those concerning events that happened fifty years ago.

The manner of Wickremasinghe's defeat and Sri Lanka's recollapse into war taught me that, despite forces tirelessly working for peace, there are other and sometimes more powerful forces that will go to any lengths to prolong war and unrest for the sake of their own vested interests. Here, I would also like to add emphatically that some countries presenting themselves as champions of human rights and democracy are actually warmongers themselves. While claiming to promote democracy, human rights and the inclusion of marginalized peoples, they foment unrest in different parts of the world.

Hence, it would not be an exaggeration to say that for some rich and powerful countries, there are no set standards for democracy and human rights. Standards apply according to convenience.

The crisis in Sri Lanka was festering as too many groups with vested interests were involved. There were some international lobbyists who would not let Sri Lanka resolve its problems, on the lame pretext of human rights or other issues. In other words, it was virtually impossible to resolve the problem through negotiated settlement. Sri Lanka required a bold leader to resolve this crisis once and for all. This necessity gave birth to a daring leader such as Mahinda Rajapaksa, who had that courage to eliminate this problem at any cost. So how did he go about it? He placed his most trustworthy people in his core team. He asked one of his brothers, Gotabhaya Rajapaksa, to take charge of the defence portfolio. Another major challenge was economic development. He appointed another brother of his, Basil Rajapaksa, to build the economy. He also had other dedicated and talented people such as Prof. Peiris in his team. He then stepped up efforts to solve this problem militarily. The rest is history.

It was unfortunate that a leader like Rajapaksa could not contain the aspirations of his loyalists and supporters in creating a new dynasty in Sri Lanka. This feeling began to take root quickly, and a new polarization started to take place in the country.

Otherwise, as Lee Kuan Yew had rightly noted, if there is any country in South Asia that has the potential to become a bigger and better economy than Singapore, it is Sri Lanka. Rajapaksa was so determined to make this happen that he was willing to risk his career and life to settle this festering problem, no matter what. I have seen very few leaders with his courage; he unflinchingly took on a section of the international community comprising some of the most developed and powerful western countries, as well as the media during and after the war.

It was Prof. Peiris who introduced me to Rajapaksa on one of my business trips to Sri Lanka. Prof. Peiris, by that time, had joined Rajapaksa's party and had also taken on the position of foreign minister in the government. 'Come, you must meet our President,' he told me, just before driving me to the presidential palace. God knows what he had told Rajapaksa about me, because the President received me as if the entire economy of Sri Lanka hinged on my decision to invest there, as if he were meeting the world's top businessman. It was his way of expressing gratitude to a foreign entrepreneur—that too, from a country like Nepal—who was willing to invest in Sri Lanka when the local entrepreneurs had all but written off their own country. 'Sri Lanka is indebted to you. We can never repay what you have done for Sri Lanka. As long as we are here, we will do everything possible to support you,' he told me. He still says this to me whenever we meet. This is how he won my heart, and more of my investment! We have already invested in eighteen hotels in different parts of Sri Lanka and are having discussions with the authorities to obtain necessary approvals for the construction of a big cement plant as well. We have the blessings of the new government for this project, which will reduce the import of cement into the country and save approximately US$400 million per annum, in foreign exchange.

There has been a ruckus over human right issues in Sri Lanka. The United Nations itself has joined the chorus. An embargo has been imposed on the country. India, under pressure from Tamil politicians, voted against Sri Lanka in

Geneva. As a friend of Sri Lanka, we have lobbied in a very big way in India against any move aimed at hurting the island nation.

What the wider world is overlooking is that Sri Lankan leaders had little option but to seek a military solution to the civil war, given that attempts to put in place a negotiated peace settlement had led to the downfall of Prime Minister Ranil Wickremasinghe. We should also not forget that the LTTE supremo Prabhakaran had consciously resorted to the tactic of using human shields to protect himself. Innocent people were bound to be killed because of this strategy. Also, were the LTTE rebels not responsible for killing innocent people in Sri Lanka? Was it really human rights abuse on the part of Rajapaksa to try to eliminate the problem for good instead of letting the bloodbath go on year after year? After friends of Sri Lanka like us lobbied the Indian authorities on behalf of Sri Lanka, the second round of voting in Geneva did not see India voting against Sri Lanka. I have also worked with various media groups to counter propaganda against Sri Lanka.

I have recently addressed the House of Lords in the United Kingdom in favour of Sri Lanka. I told them that though I am not a Sri Lankan, I have witnessed Sri Lanka when it was deeply disturbed by what some call 'insurgency' and others, 'terrorism'. 'My job is not to interpret what is right or what is wrong. I certainly have a job to talk about what I have seen. Sri Lanka had sunk to such a level that nobody wanted to go and live there, forget do business. It had become practically difficult for the Sri Lankans themselves to stay and do business there. I have also seen how things have shaped up over the recent years. Hence, those who stand for sustainable peace, those who stand for prosperity and a congenial environment for people to live in and do business, should support Sri Lanka.' My speech surprised the British lawmakers. But what I told them had to do with my conviction—it was not a move to appease the Sri Lankans.

Having witnessed how international opinion is divided on the matter of insurgency—some supporting it, others supporting those who are trying to contain it, and still others rooting for democracy—I have often said that it is unreasonable to keep hostage a country and its people at large. Sanctions and embargos on trouble-ridden countries have often made the lives of their ordinary people, who have little to do with politics, very difficult.

In 2013, I was invited by the Government of Sri Lanka to speak at the Commonwealth Business Forum held in Colombo in conjunction with the Commonwealth Heads of Government Meeting. I spoke eloquently, largely on the theme of regional cooperation, receiving thunderous applause from the representatives of more than sixty countries. Rahul Bajaj was moderator at the forum, and the chief executive officer of Infosys, Rajesh Krishnamurthy, was among the business leaders who took part.

Call it my destiny or my nature, but I become deeply absorbed in the affairs of any country in which I invest. I become passionately interested in its politics, its society and its economy; what is more, I become emotionally involved too. I start to 'own' the problems and prospects of that country and become its passionate advocate. That is probably the reason leaders of these countries start to reciprocate my goodwill.

The polarization against Rajapaksa, which started taking place in the country in the latter part of 2013, gathered momentum with his decision to contest a third term and the announcement of snap elections. Civil society leaders, human rights activities and trade unions rallied round to form a common front. They proposed a joint opposition to Rajapaksa, and fielded a common candidate, which resulted in Maithripala Sirisena contesting the presidential elections and being elected President in January 2015.

With the formation of a 'national government' under the leadership of President Maithripala Sirisena and Prime Minister Wickremasinghe, the prospects of a permanent solution to the north-east conflict has become a reality and Sri Lanka is beginning to earn the confidence of the international community. This is a positive development, which augurs well for Sri Lanka, in its endeavour to become a developed country and achieve a more stable and stronger economy. Premier Wickremasinghe has always demonstrated his willingness to go that extra mile in order to improve relations with neighbouring countries, and his magnanimity was quite evident during the aftermath of the earthquake in Nepal.

He met me in his office, summoned all the senior officials, including the army commander and made arrangements to provide relief and other assistance to Nepal immediately. It was heart-warming to see the spontaneous cooperation and support forthcoming from the prime minister, as a true friend of Nepal.

I am happy that, despite all odds, the Sri Lankan economy has been transforming over the recent years. FDI is improving, and tourism is growing meteorically. Today Sri Lanka's per capita income stands at US$4000. If you can be totally dispassionate, you will realize that what has been happening in Sri Lanka over the recent years is a transformation under its courageous and visionary leaders who have the courage to pursue the long-term interests of the country at the cost of paying a huge short-term price.

Narendra Modi

In 2011, the FICCI invited me to be a guest speaker at one of its programmes in Gandhinagar, the state capital of Gujarat in India. Narendra Modi, then chief minister of Gujarat, was the chief guest. All the FICCI executives were present. They introduced me to Modi as the president of CNI and a representative of Nepal's business community. That was the first time I met Modi. He had carved out a global reputation for Gujarat as a distinctive part of India, the way the Government of Kerala had for that state in tourism. Modi's Vibrant Gujarat campaign has achieved miracles.

As the guest speaker, I talked about India–Nepal relations, both the opportunities and the challenges, from the perspective of a businessman. I said that Nepal was waiting for a leader like Modi to take the country to a completely new level, based on its tremendous natural resources. The idea was to spark Modi's interest to turn his attention towards Nepal. To motivate him further, I also spoke with emphasis on the deep-rooted cultural and religious ties between the two immediate neighbours. I went on to urge Modi to play a role in transforming Nepal into a prosperous country. At the forum itself, I invited him to Nepal to attend a conference being organized by the CNI. I could see that what I had said had struck a chord with Modi. As soon as I concluded my speech and sat down beside him, he said, 'Now that you have invited me to Nepal, I shall definitely come.'

The story of Jeet Bahadur

'But you have to do me a favour,' he added. I was somewhat taken aback, but assured him I would do whatever was possible to help a great leader like himself.

'There is a Nepali boy by the name of Jeet Bahadur whom I've raised,' he said. 'He's like a son to me. He has been separated from his parents since he came to India as a child. I want you to find them for me.'

'You're such an influential politician and the chief minister of Gujarat. Why don't you use the formal government channels? They will find them in no time,' I replied.

'No,' said Modi. 'The government cannot accomplish this. Only someone like you can help me.'

I presumed he had already tried to find the boy's parents using the formal channels but with no success.

'Of course, sir,' I said. However, he gave me no further details, and I did not ask for any either. I did not take his request too seriously.

I then went to Delhi for an engagement before flying back to Kathmandu. I thought the first thing I would do was to send a formal invitation to Modi on behalf of the CNI. However, when I checked my email, I was surprised to see that Modi had not only formally accepted my invitation to visit Nepal but had also again sought my assistance in tracing Jeet Bahadur Magar's family. This time, he had provided all available information about the boy and his family. I immediately embarked on the search.

There were three useful facts we knew about Jeet: his father's name, his village name, which Jeet remembered as 'Kawasaki' (though the actual village turned out to be Giribari, which is a little distance away from a village called Kawasoti), and that the boy had six toes on one foot.

With these three threads of information, we left no stone unturned in our search for Jeet's family. By an incredible stroke of good fortune—for us and, of course, for Jeet—we had been promoting potato farming at Giribari to feed our potato chip factory. All the farmers from Giribari have a connection with us. We assigned one of my most effective team members, Ram Chandra Dhital, to coordinate the work of finding Jeet's family. By passing the word among the farmers in the districts around Kawasoti, we found out, within only thirty hours of our inquiry, that Jeet's father had already passed away and that his mother had remarried. His older brother, who had taken Jeet to India with him, had given up his dream of finding a better future in India and had returned home.

The story of Jeet—in fact, the story of many Nepalis like him—is all too real and all too tragic. This is the story of Nepalis who migrate to India and other places in a desperate attempt to escape poverty and hunger. Jeet's brother had moved to Delhi with Jeet in a bid to support his family, particularly his younger siblings. Although Jeet was only eight years old at the time, he and his brother found odd jobs in the old quarter of Delhi. After two years, their employer said he could no longer afford to pay Jeet but would send the boy to Rajasthan to work as a domestic help at his in-laws'. I could just imagine how frightened the boy must have been and how bitter his brother must have felt. However, having no other choice, Jeet went to Rajasthan all by himself at the tender age of ten.

Jeet began his new job in Rajasthan at the house of his master—and I say 'master' because Jeet was like a slave. That house became his entire world. He did not even know what Indian state he lived in, let alone the name of the town. One day, unable to endure the hardships inflicted on him any longer, he ran away. He actually wanted to return to Delhi but did not know how to go about it. After wandering the streets for hours, hungry and exhausted, he somehow made it to the nearest railway station. There he boarded the first train he saw, but it was headed in the opposite direction, towards Mumbai. I guess he had entered one of those crowded general compartments. Seeing a frightened foreign child, the other commuters started to bully him. Then the ticket inspector arrived. As Jeet had no ticket, he was told to get off the train. Just then, a woman who worked at a bank in Baroda intervened. 'Please don't do that to the child,' she said. 'If you force him off at some small station, he might fall victim to one of those gangs that force children into begging. They might pluck out his eyes. Please, at least, let him travel to the next big city.' The boy was allowed to travel to the next big station, which happened to be Baroda.

It is remarkable to note the twists and turns in Jeet's life. At Baroda, the compassionate woman who had intervened on his behalf decided to take Jeet Bahadur home with her. After sheltering him at her place for a month or two, she took him to a camp run by the Rashtriya Swayamsevak Sangh (RSS), a right-wing Hindu nationalist volunteer group, which engages in charitable and educational activities across India. This is an organization also often charged with trying to fan communal tensions. Narendra Modi happened to be the coordinator of that camp.

Modi then took on the responsibility of raising Jeet as his own child. Let there be no doubt: Modi never used Jeet as a domestic help or for any other kind of job. When Jeet was brought to the camp, Modi first asked the boy what he wanted to do. Jeet said he wanted to study. Modi made all arrangements to provide Jeet with an education. Modi was impressed with Jeet's sharpness, and the way the boy learnt

Gujarati in no time. But what clearly got Modi smitten was the boy's honesty. Once, Modi asked him if he wanted anything. The boy said he was interested in archery. Modi then bought him a huge electronic archery set, the sort professional archers use. But Jeet refused to accept the gift, saying all he needed was an ordinary bow and arrow. Modi loved him even more after that, and there was no looking back for Jeet after that.

Eventually, we did manage to put Jeet Bahadur back in touch with his family but he always remained Modi's son. Prime Minister Modi brought the boy with him to Nepal during his official visit in 2014.

As regards my plan to invite Chief Minister Modi to attend the CNI conference in 2011, I faced resistance in Nepal from the very beginning. As we had to observe the correct protocol for Modi's visit, I approached the prime minister, then Dr Baburam Bhattarai, as well as officials in the foreign ministry. I started to sense resistance, though it was never overt. Then, one day, the prime minister called up the CNI vice president, Narendra Basnet, urging him to convince me that this was not the right time to invite Narendra Modi to Nepal.

'Please make Binod realize that inviting Modi to Nepal at this time could affect the entire process of drafting the Constitution,' Dr Bhattarai said to Basnet. 'Modi being here could be enough, in itself, to trigger a heated debate about Hinduism, which we do not want at this point.'

This is what Narendra Basnet told me. But Dr Bhattarai did not say anything to me about this. The Indian ambassador to Nepal, Jayant Prasad, told me that the ministry of external affairs in India could not endorse Modi's visit to Nepal unless the Government of Nepal also agreed to it. But, because of its unnecessary apprehensions, the Government of Nepal was not convinced that Modi was being invited not as a Hindu leader but as the leader of the Vibrant Gujarat movement, and that his visit would have opened a lot of vistas for bringing Indian investment into Nepal. But there were so many blocks laid on our path that we had to drop the plan altogether. I felt very bad. Even Modi felt bad.

'What happened to your plan, Binodjee?' Modi asked me over the phone. 'Is there any problem?'

I briefly explained the situation and urged him to take the initiative from his side.

'No,' said Modi. 'I, too, can't discuss this matter with our government.'

The Government of India was led by the Congress, which allegedly had a track record of restraining foreign trips by chief ministers of states ruled by the Bharatiya Janata Party (BJP).

However, this could not dent my relationship with Narendra Modi. In fact, our relationship has further strengthened over the years. Modi expressed his deeply felt gratitude after I reunited the boy with his family. Through Jeet I got personally linked to Modi, but I have never exploited this relationship to advance any of my business interests. I am convinced that if I were ever to seek Modi's favour, it would be for matters related to Nepal's development.

Someone else who brought me closer to Modi was Sri Sri Ravi Shankar, who founded The Art of Living Foundation. I'm a person who believes in karma, but I don't blindly follow religious orthodoxy. It only takes me five minutes to complete my daily prayers. I am also not one of those orthodox Hindus

who dismiss other faiths. I bow my head in reverence when I
see a Buddhist temple, a church or a mosque. Nonetheless, I
have to say that I am extremely influenced by ancient Hindu
philosophy and culture. I am not superstitious but I firmly
believe in the law of karma. If your days are bad then bad
things happen to you so that even if you say something good,
you could offend your listener because of a judgemental error
on his part.

Digvijaya Singh

I have worked closely with politicians from all the major
parties in India. I have had deep interactions with Digvijaya
Singh. As an entrepreneur from a country that depends so
heavily on India for business, I have, over the years, pushed
for the leaders of Nepal and India to establish informal,
one-on-one relationships. However, in my experience, the
leaders of India's Congress party have become significantly
less politically engaged with Nepal over the years, especially
when Pranab Mukherjee was finance minister. As I knew him
very well, I tried to convince him that the Congress leadership
should have closer ties with the leadership in Nepal, and he
did introduce me to many influential people. However, India's
non-political actors gradually became the decisive force in
India's dealings with Nepal. There are many books explaining
how that kind of engagement has impeded both economic
and political development in Nepal, so I do not want to go
into it here. Nonetheless, I continue to enjoy the support and
encouragement of the Indian authorities, including political

leaders, in expanding my business interests in India. Ashok Gehlot is one of them.

As part of my goal to make Wai Wai the only company in India with a pan-India presence, I have been setting up Wai Wai plants in many different parts of India. In the food manufacturing industry, fast and efficient distribution in catchment areas, as well as costs, is very important. While I was planning to set up another Wai Wai plant in western India, I learned that the ministry of food processing industries had come up with a scheme under which the Government of India would provide a subsidy of Rs 50 crore to anyone who established a 'food park'. A food park is a concept that aims at establishing direct linkages from farms to processing, and ultimately to the consumer market. Ramdev Patanjali Ayurveda Limited had set up food parks in a few states under this scheme. I decided to build one in Rajasthan, choosing that state because it was well integrated with the rest of the country, with access to the massive Delhi–Maharashtra corridor, which links Delhi, Gujarat, Rajasthan and Maharashtra.

We identified a partner for the food park project in Rajasthan and selected a 100-acre plot. However, just three days before applications closed, our partner had to pull out of the project, placing it in jeopardy. Coincidentally, just at that time, I and a few family friends were on a week-long trip on Royal Rajasthan on Wheels, a luxury tourist train. When the train reached Jaipur, Varun and other members of the team involved in the food park project, who were still in Rajasthan, were there to meet me. It was then that I suddenly thought of Ashok Gehlot, the chief minister of Rajasthan, with whom I was well acquainted. I sought an appointment with him, and he immediately took time out to see me. After I told him about the story of my food park project, he immediately called up a leading real estate development company called ARG and asked them to help me out.

That very evening, I handed over the matter of the food park to my team and the ARG, and left to continue my train journey. Within three days, we were able to apply for the food park, which is now under construction. This is a shining example of the level of commitment of Indian leaders towards their state. Politicians in many other parts of the region, including Nepal, need to emulate this. I feel indebted to the great politicians and statesmen from the different political parties of India who have, over the years, given their selfless support to me to help create business and employment in many parts of the country and helped me expand my business. I have found some governments in India friendlier than many other governments towards foreign as well as domestic investors. Insofar as the political parties in India are concerned, none of them is unfriendly to investors like us.

I recently made the acquaintance of Vasundhara Raje Scindiajee, the chief minister of Rajasthan, during the wedding of my second son Rahul. She had already heard about us and the wedding. I found her to be sharp and entrepreneurial. She was very keen about what we were doing under the food park project. It did not take her long to grasp that the food park we were setting up in Ajmer was going to be a game changer in linking the Rajasthan farmers to the market. Under this venture, we would establish not only the core operational facilities in Ajmer with over Rs 120 crore of investment in a one-acre plot of land, but also twelve other regional processing units in twelve districts of Rajasthan. These units would be available to the local farmers for processing their goods for direct sale in the market, helping them fetch better value for their produce. Scindiajee wanted to be personally involved

and summoned a meeting of her key officials, promising
everything that was needed for the facilities.

Dr Mahathir bin Mohamad

I have already talked about the grand success of the FNCCI-
organized economic summit that was attended by some of the
great leaders of Asia, such as Hussain Muhammad Ershad,
Farooq Leghari and Anand Panyarachun. I had always been
fascinated by the rise of the Asian Tigers under leaders like
Dr Mahathir bin Mohamad of Malaysia and Lee Kuan Yew
of Singapore. I came up with the idea of inviting Mahathir
Mohamad to help us prepare and carry out substantial
homework on governance and administration for Nepal's
transformation. I preferred Mahathir because it was under
his leadership that a country, which was in no better shape
than Nepal, actually metamorphosed into a leading regional
economy. Though some criticize him, calling him a dictator,
nobody disputes that Dr Mahathir was *the* person who not
only transformed Malaysia economically but, in the process,
also played a pivotal role in shaping the ASEAN economic
block.

It was not difficult for me to bring Mahathir to Nepal.
His son is a friend of Iku Mohamed, our close family friend
Yusuf Mohamad's son. Iku is a leading animator in Japan, and
is also highly sought after in Hollywood. It was not that I was
unacquainted with Mahathir, having met him several times in
the past. But I chose to approach him through Iku.

'I need a favour from you,' I told Iku. 'You have to help me get in touch with Dr Mahathir Mohamad.'

'No problem,' he replied. 'We'll go to Malaysia and meet him together.'

Iku himself was planning to write a book on Mahathir in Japanese.

He fixed up an appointment for me with Mahathir, and I immediately flew to Malaysia for the meeting. Mahathir had recently stepped down as prime minister and was recuperating from a surgery. We had a long discussion on a range of issues. I was impressed with his knowledge of Nepal, and with his understanding of the legacy of the Gurkhas scattered all across South Asia and South East Asia. He explained how he helped integrate Nepalis into Malaysia, given that we had played such an important role in shaping the country. He and his spouse had never been to Nepal and were both keen to visit.

By the end of that first meeting, Mahathir had agreed, in principle, to visit Nepal. 'Please provide me with information on the socio-economic issues as well as the political situation in Nepal, and I'll try to come up with some meaningful observations,' he said.

He also asked Iku to arrange meetings for me with the top business and industrial leaders in Malaysia. This shows Mahathir's leadership skill. Though he was no longer the prime minister of Malaysia, he was very eager to leverage every opportunity that came his way to the benefit of his country. Iku took me to Ananda Krishnan, a Sri Lankan raised in Malaysia, who went on to become one of the biggest businessmen in that country and one of the richest men in the world. Mahathir is very close to Ananda Krishnan and has his office on the top floor of one of the Petronas Twin Towers, which was jointly built by Krishnan and a Malaysian oil giant. Krishnan owns a number of big companies in the sectors of oil, gas, satellites, media, telecommunications and gaming. My friend Mintoo had introduced me to Krishnan before Iku had taken me to him. Mintoo was his business partner in a bid for a gas field in Bangladesh around twenty-five years ago. At that time, I had wanted to get Ananda Krishnan to invest in the power sector in Nepal through his company Powertek, a leading power generation company in Asia.

Mahathir also introduced me to some of his senior staff. His senior assistant, Dr C.A.C. Badriah was the contact person for Mahathir's visit. I began preparations for his visit as soon as I returned to Nepal. As the day of the visit drew near, his advance team arrived in Nepal. Mahathir had also informed Nepal's ambassador to Malaysia about this visit. The stage was set, and everything appeared in place for it. Unfortunately, unforeseen and dramatic events were to call off the visit.

On 1 September 2004, the very day Mahathir was due to land in Nepal, a deadly riot erupted in Kathmandu. An angry mob attacked many buildings protesting what they saw as the government's failure to save twelve Nepali hostages in Iraq who were executed by an Islamic militant group. The violence spread like wildfire. While this was happening, I was at Hyatt Hotel in Kathmandu, overseeing arrangements for Mahathir's stay.

'*Tun* Mahathir has left for the airport from his residence,' beeped a message on my cellphone. Tun is the highest honorific title in Malaysia.

My heart began to race. I started calling up top security officials to get their views on the situation. I called up the home minister, the chief of army staff and the inspector general of police, among other authorities, but nobody could provide me concrete assurance that Mahathir would be safe. Nobody seemed to be taking charge to contain the situation.

'Now the Tun is ready to take off for Kathmandu in his private aircraft,' beeped another message. Here, it may be noted that Mahathir did not even want us to arrange a chartered flight for him.

In a last-ditch effort to salvage the visit, I got in touch with every person who could possibly help us. I was now thinking about airlifting Mahathir to the Hyatt from Kathmandu airport as soon as he landed in Nepal.

'Let's not take any chances, Binodjee. The situation is still pretty volatile,' a senior army official told me over the phone, which effectively ended my months of effort to bring Mahathir to Nepal.

With a very heavy heart, I called up Mahathir.

'What's happened?' Mahathir asked.

'You know how emotional Nepali people are,' I told him. 'The situation in Iraq has provoked huge public outrage here. I don't want to take any chances with your security and safety. And our government has also urged me to suggest postponement of the visit.'

'No problem, Binod,' Mahathir replied. 'I've been through things like this before. Don't worry. Relax, and focus on planning another visit sometime in the future.'

Later, one of his aides told me that once it was clear his visit to Nepal was not on, Mahathir rescheduled his travel plans and headed to another destination directly from Kathmandu.

These events, in fact, brought me closer to Mahathir. I went to Malaysia to call on him and personally apologize for the incident. I met him in his office in the Petronas Twin Towers.

'I shall definitely come to Nepal. You just make fresh arrangements for my visit,' he told me.

When at last he visited Nepal, in March 2014, he invited my family to tea. Though I had wanted to invite him to my place for lunch, his hectic schedule did not allow it. But his invitation to my family was a huge honour for me. These days, I am in close contact with both Mahathir and his son.

7

My Guru: Sri Sri Ravi Shankar

Around seven years ago, Kavita Khanna, a very dear family friend and wife of the legendary Bollywood star Vinod Khanna, called me up with a rather strange proposition. I had become friendly with Kavita through Vinod, who is a close friend of mine.

'Binod, I want you to meet Sri Sri Ravi Shankarjee,' Kavita told me.

'Sure, sure,' I replied. But I was not really interested, and put off the plan to meet Guruji.

However, Kavita did not give up. She repeatedly made appointments for me to meet Guruji, but I never found the time to keep those appointments. It was partly because of my hectic schedule and partly because I simply did not feel a strong urge to meet him.

'I can see you're never going to be free on the dates we fix for you to meet Guruji,' Kavita said one day. 'So you tell me what dates you'll be in Delhi and available.'

I gave her a list of dates.

'Fine,' she said. 'I'll come from Mumbai on one of these dates and we'll go and meet Guruji together.'

Although I felt no particular urge to meet Sri Sri Ravi Shankar, I had no objection to meeting him either. I had not personally met him, but I knew him to be a great spiritual leader.

One morning, Kavita took me to meet him. He was sitting on a sofa and his disciples were seated cross-legged on a carpet in front of him. In the Hindu tradition of master and disciple, the Guru always sits at a higher level than the disciples. However, as I walked into the hall where Guruji was sitting, this escaped my mind. I walked straight to him, bowed and sat on a sofa beside him. He talked to me about Nepal. After an hour, some of his female disciples started to lay breakfast on a table in front of him.

'Serve this man first of all,' Guruji told them, smiling.

They served breakfast to me as well as Guruji. We began to eat. In retrospect, I wonder if Guruji's disciples were annoyed with me for not showing enough respect to him. But I am sure Guruji did not mind at all. He is beyond such mundane things.

Over breakfast, we continued to talk about the state of affairs in Nepal. Guruji was particularly interested in the Maoist insurgency, which was at its height at the time, and I could sense that his interest was born out of compassion.

'I'll come to Nepal soon,' Guruji told me just before I left.

He struck me then as an intelligent and compassionate person. Soon afterwards, I felt myself being drawn to him by some unknown force or attraction. Perhaps it was because of his strong positive aura, but thoughts of Guruji kept coming up in my mind.

After a week or so, Kavita called me up again.

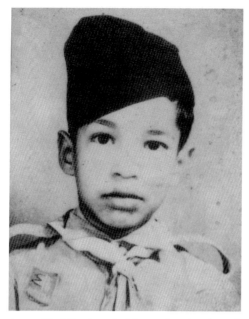

As a student of Juddhodaya Public High School, Kathmandu.

With father, mother and brothers in Haridwar.

Greeting Mother Teresa in New Delhi.

With late king Birendra Bir Bikram Shah and
late queen Aishwarya Rajya Laxmi Devi Shah.

With Annapurna didi and (L–R) Arun, Basant and Kiran.

At Tiger Tops resort, Chitwan, with Sarika and the boys.

On a trek in Dolpa.

Playing golf, with Mt Everest in the backdrop.

Listening to Bill Gates at a *Forbes* conference in New York.

With (L–R) Muhammad Yunus, former president of Nepal, Ram Baran Yadav, and former CNI president, Narendra Basnyat.

Meeting Indian Prime Minister Narendra Modi in Kathmandu.

In the presence of Gurudev Sri Sri Ravi Shankar, along
with Sarika and Nirvana.

At the launch of Nepal Social Business, in partnership with Lions Clubs International, in Canada.

At a school in Kavre which was built by the Chaudhary Group as part of its earthquake rehabilitation efforts.

Alongside sons, (L–R) Rahul, Nirvana and Varun.

Family. Top from left: Rahul, Nirvana and Varun.
Bottom from left: Surabhi (Rahul's wife), Sarika and
Ashrayata (Nirvana's wife).

'Guruji wants to come to Kathmandu,' she said. 'And he has asked me to get in touch with you to plan his visit.'

I began immediate plans for his visit. I met Sashi Raj Pandey and Bimal Kedia, who were associated with Guruji's ashrams in Nepal. I arranged for the army parade ground to be available for a yoga session. In short, I did all the groundwork for his visit. I went to meet him at the airport when he arrived, and stayed with him for the three days of his visit.

A number of questions rose in my mind as I observed the level of reverence given to him and the sway he held over thousands of his followers. Why were these people, including some noted intellectuals and influential personalities, so devoted to this man for what appeared to be purely altruistic reasons? I could also sense that Guruji's only motivation was a wish to help human beings overcome suffering. Why? And why were his disciples unconditionally surrendering themselves to him?

'Please tell me what is this all about,' I implored Vinod Khanna, who was among his devotees. Vinod had suddenly given up acting and turned to spiritual matters when he was at the peak of his Bollywood career.

Vinod told me the long and fascinating story of his spiritual journey—about how he had been drawn to Osho initially and had then found Guruji.

'Look, Binod, if you are lucky and also mentally prepared to find a master, then you'll find one,' he said in the end. 'A master is someone in whom you have unlimited faith and into whose hands you are ready to submit yourself unconditionally.

'Don't think that because you're an accomplished person, you don't need a master,' Vinod added. 'Everybody needs a master, and who knows, you're probably being drawn to your master already.'

His words served as a moment of enlightenment for me.

I suddenly felt there was a huge vacuum in my life. There were many issues that I found perplexing—personal, professional, socio-economic—and which I could not share with anyone, and on which there was no one who could offer me unconditional guidance. I did not know anyone whose judgement was not coloured by a vested interest, conflict of interest, or some other limitation.

I then realized that I had already found my master. I became a devotee of Guruji and found I could freely discuss any issue or share my personal happiness and sorrow with him while he guided me with unconditional love, as a parent guides a child. I felt there was nobody in the world who loved and protected me more than Guruji. Gradually, my wife and children were also drawn to him. Soon, I found myself always longing to be with Guruji.

Guruji once took me with him on a two-week tour of Latin America. Brazil, Argentina, Uruguay and Paraguay were among the countries we visited. There I saw how Guruji transformed people's lives. His powerful breathing technique called *Sudarshan Kriya* leads to life-changing experiences. I saw notorious criminals who were behind bars, drug addicts and even diehard atheists completely transformed by Guruji. I saw leading academics, artists, film stars, industrialists and politicians in those predominantly Christian countries submitting themselves to Guruji. Why? The answer is, the more you achieve in the material world, the more empty and conflicted you can feel inside. Eventually, you find yourself lonely and miserable. That is why we all need a master to guide us and to free us. In the broader sense, Guruji wants to restore *Sanatan Dharma*, the ageless universal religion, to the world. He says Sanatan Dharma leads to compassion and transforms passion into dispassion.

Over the years, my devotion to Guruji intensified more and more, so much so that I no longer had the appetite to pursue my worldly ambitions.

'Guruji,' I once said to him, 'I have achieved a lot in life. I wanted to build a business empire and I have done that. I have also tried my hand at politics. Now I'm tired. My children have grown up and they can take charge of things. I want to let go of this baggage and be with you all the time.'

I thought I could be of some help in further spreading Guruji's message and growing his organization, whose reach already extended to 153 countries.

But Guruji declined my request, even though he knew that a person of my calibre and influence working full-time for him would definitely have helped expand his organizational base.

'Both India and Nepal will witness major transformation in the days to come,' Guruji said. 'You still have an important role to play.'

But this did not stop me from finding every occasion I could to be with him. I meet him in the ashram whenever the occasion permits, particularly during Navaratras, and also travel with him to many different parts of the world. My family and I are overwhelmed with his affection for us. He is the single living force that directs our lives.

Over the last several years, I feel that we have seen a qualitative change in our lives, both personally and in terms of business; and my son Nirvana feels this way too. An unseen force is constantly helping us through our problems. My organization has grown manifold—in depth as well as reach—in many more countries. Non-performing businesses have started to perform. And all this is happening somehow, without too much pain and anxiety on our part. Unforeseen complications or problems created by unhealthy competition is a part of life, particularly in the Third World. These complications and problems give you a unique opportunity to solve them. With positive thinking coupled with positive action, you can solve them forever. Such power comes through the grace of the master.

I once asked the same question to both the owner of Kent, Mahesh Gupta from Delhi, who is very dedicated to the Art of Living Foundation, and to Guruji, as well as to Ajay Mirg from Bhopal. Their experiences were similar to mine. Under Guruji's larger umbrella, they have seen unprecedented spiritual and business growth.

I often feel, subconsciously, that Guruji is telling his disciples: '*Tum mera kaam karo mein tumhara karunga*' (You do my work and I'll take care of you).

Call it destiny, Narendra Modi had also become very close to Guruji over time, and Guruji has now become a strong cord that binds me and Modi together.

8

Professional Battles

When I was around ten, I was frequently visiting Pashupatinath temple with my father. He would always meet a sage who roamed around the temple premises wearing a cap made of beads. One day this sage suddenly grabbed one of my hands, pulled out a piece of paper from his bag and gave it to me. 'Recite this every day,' he told me.

A few Sanskrit mantras were written on that piece of paper. Later, I realized that it was a hymn to Lord Shiva. I have been reciting that mantra every day ever since, both in the morning as soon as I wake up and at night just before I go to bed. I would not claim that daily worship of Lord Shiva has brought miracles into my life but it has definitely strengthened my will. It has given me the power of mind to overcome all sorts of difficulties in life.

Whenever there are obstacles in my way and my destination starts to blur, I seek solitude. I close my eyes and take a few long breaths. I feel calmer. I recite the mantra the sage gave me. It boosts my confidence and helps me focus.

Only by focusing the mind can you identify the root cause of a problem, and once you have identified the root cause, half the battle is won.

Nabil Bank

G.C. Srivastava, a management consultant at Nepal Arab Bank Limited, was the first to let me know that 50 per cent of the shares of the bank were up for sale. He told me, 'The sheikhs now want to pull out their investments from the bank. They have asked us to dispose of their shares within a year. If you are interested, I can arrange a meeting with the relevant people.'

This was in 1994. The first ever joint-venture bank had been operating in Nepal for almost a decade. Emirates Bank International of the UAE had been handling its management. I liked Srivastava's proposal. If I were to open a new bank, it would have taken me many years to establish one of the reputation of Nepal Arab Bank. Taking over this bank would save me time and energy.

I told him, 'I'll buy it. You take it forward.'

Nepal Arab Bank was established by the Galadhari Brothers Group, a reputed business group from the United Arab Emirates (UAE). They initially wanted to open a bank in India, but when that did not work out, they opened banks targeting the Indian market in the four neighbouring countries of India—Nepal, Bangladesh, Sri Lanka and Pakistan—simultaneously. Later on, there was a misunderstanding between the rulers of the UAE and the Galadhari Brothers. The ruling sheikhs went on to nationalize all the undertakings of the Galadharis. Nepal Arab Bank Limited came under the UAE government ownership. The largest bank in the UAE, Emirates Bank International, started to handle its management. The executives of Emirates Bank were shocked when they saw the balance sheet of Nepal Arab Bank. At a time when their companies across the world were earning billions of dollars in profits, it was natural that the sheikhs were not impressed by the bank's meagre turnover of US $2–$3 million in Nepal. One of the executives snapped at the Nepal Arab Bank officials, 'What is this? Why does this company perform so badly?'

Srivastava and other executives tried to explain the situation to them but the Emirates Bank executives would not listen. Asking them to withdraw their investments within a year, one of them added, 'If you can't sell the shares of this bank, go and throw them in the Dubai creek. Just don't bring them back to me.'

I went to meet Graham Twelis, an officer at Emirates Bank in Dubai. He took me to the bank's chief executive officer, David Berry.

'I will buy 30 per cent of the shares in the first phase,' I said. 'Please help me operate the bank for the time being and I guarantee you I'll buy the remaining 20 per cent as well.'

Berry was initially hesitant but finally agreed. A sale of even 30 per cent of the bank's shares was a big deal. I got a few business partners on board. Girija Prasad Koirala was Nepal's prime minister at the time. Another Nepali Congress leader, Mahesh Acharya, was the finance minister, while Hari Shankar Tripathy was the governor of Nepal Rastra Bank and Satendra Pyara Shrestha his deputy.

I sought and quickly obtained permission from the central bank to buy 30 per cent of the promoter's shares in Nepal Arab Bank.

I sealed the agreement with Emirates Bank at the Oberoi hotel in Delhi. I made only two demands: that I should be on the board of directors and that the CEO should be appointed on my recommendation. They agreed. D.C. Khanna was appointed CEO of the bank on my recommendation.

Just when things were going smoothly, I came upon a legal hurdle. The Galadharis had placed a strange clause in the company registration documents, saying no Nepali citizen could buy more than half per cent stake in the company. Due to this clause, Nepal Arab Bank, which was formed as a joint-venture undertaking, had no Nepali promoter. Some business interests in Nepal had lobbied for the joint-venture undertaking, expecting a partnership. The Galadharis had exploited these interests in getting the bank opened, but had inserted that clause to prevent anyone from claiming a stake in the bank after it was established. This was disclosed to me later by the Bangladeshi lawyer Rafibul Islam, who had handled the legal formalities associated with setting up the bank.

I met him many times while buying the promoter's shares. After we came to know each other well, he revealed he had met in Switzerland an influential person from the Palace to land a separate deal on behalf the Galadharis for the licence to open the bank. The means used by Rafibul Islam to obtain a licence for the bank were questionable; however, Nepal Arab Bank, on its part, had ended the government's monopoly in the banking sector.

I asked him how the clause in the company registration documents that now stood in my way could be changed.

'The provision can be removed by convening the annual general meeting of the bank before the promoter's shares are transferred,' he advised.

When a meeting of the bank's board of directors was convened to call for the AGM, Shambhu Poudel and Gajananda Agrawal, who represented the ordinary shareholders, opposed my plan. They argued that if that provision was removed, then the bank would eventually fall entirely into the hands of a business house. Yet they had not perceived any such threat when the Galadharis owned the bank; neither had anybody cared about the provision when Emirates Bank International took over. Now, however, when a fellow countryman was trying to run the bank, the clause had become an issue. These shareholders boycotted the meeting. Nonetheless, the board endorsed the proposal to amend the documents to pave way for the share transfer. However, Shambhu Poudel fought a case against that decision all the way to the Supreme Court, which issued an interim order to stop the process.

Eventually, word spread that Emirates Bank was eager to withdraw from Nepal and sell off its shares. Many players were suddenly interested. They started to pull strings at the central bank and the finance ministry. Some started to lobby for transfer of Nepal Arab Bank shares to Beema Sansthan, a state-run corporation that had a monopoly in the insurance sector. Meanwhile, D.C. Khanna had to step down as CEO as his year-long tenure had ended. Suresh Kadadkar, who succeeded him, started to negotiate with another group that was interested in buying the shares.

I approached him and asked him point-blank, 'How could you start negotiating with another party despite the agreement with me?'

'We have already given you more than enough time,' he said. 'Other potential buyers are pressuring us. If you can't settle the matter soon, we would be compelled to sell the shares to some other party.'

I was speechless.

Shortly after that, I had to leave for Delhi to attend a meeting of the World Economic Forum. There I met the chairperson of National Bank of Bangladesh, Mahbubur Rahman. He and I were vice chairpersons of the SAARC Chamber of Commerce and Industry during its first term. Though he represented Bangladesh and I Nepal, we developed a very good relationship. And, of course, I knew Abdul Awal Mintoo, another director of that bank, extremely well.

I told Rahman about the hurdles I had been facing in trying to buy the promoter's shares in Nepal Arab Bank.

'I can't buy the shares just because I'm a Nepali citizen. A clause in the company's registration document itself has to be amended. However, you could buy the shares on behalf of National Bank of Bangladesh. I'll help you do that. You can transfer the shares to me the day the clause is amended.'

'I can do that,' he replied, 'But on one condition.'

I became a bit apprehensive when I heard that but he grabbed both my hands and said, 'I won't buy just 30 per cent, I'll buy 50 per cent of the shares.'

As soon as I returned to Kathmandu, I started renegotiating with Emirates Bank International along the lines Rahman and I had discussed. The Emirates Bank officials did not have any problem with National Bank of Bangladesh buying 50 per cent of the shares. I established direct contact between the two banks, and they sealed the deal.

To proceed with the deal, National Bank had to get permission from Nepal Rastra Bank, where Satyendra Pyara

Shrestha had succeeded Tripathy as governor. The necessary licence was obtained. Finally, Emirates Bank International withdrew from Nepal Arab Bank, selling the promoter's shares to National Bank of Bangladesh in mid-1995.

Those who had been trying to make the situation difficult for me were dumbstruck when National Bank of Bangladesh took over Nepal Arab Bank. Defeated but defiant, they alleged I had circumvented the law to gain control of the bank by using the Bangladeshi bank. They started a propaganda campaign against me in the media. Governor Shrestha was also dragged into the controversy, as they charged him with giving permission to the Bangladeshi bank without the endorsement of the council of ministers. However, there was no legal impediment to a foreign bank transferring its promoter's shares to another foreign bank. I was not guilty of breaching any law since my gentleman's agreement with Rahman and Mintoo was legally irreproachable.

A few years later, some internal dispute erupted among the partners in National Bank of Bangladesh, requiring intervention by the Bangladeshi central bank. At that point, National Bank decided to pull out of Nepal Arab Bank. Mahbubur Rahman and Abdul Awal Mintoo transferred the 50 per cent stake they had bought from the promoter to NB International, one of their undertakings. After this, Nepal Arab Bank was formally transformed into Nabil Bank.

Another link between Nabil Bank and our family is that we hold around 5 per cent of the public shares. This plays an important role in the election of the public director of the bank. NB International still holds the majority shares of Nabil Bank. Rahman, Mintoo and I still stand by our gentleman's agreement.

My detractors' allegation that I circumvented the law is not completely untrue. The 'system' in the country had compelled me to take the circuitous path. The writ filed by Shambu Poudel was eventually quashed by the Supreme Court, which ruled that the hurdles thrown in my path were without legal basis and that I had a legal right to buy the promoter's shares in the bank. But it took five years for that decision to come. Had I waited for the verdict, somebody else would have taken over the bank, which might not then have emerged as one of the country's leading commercial banks.

Nepal Arab Bank is one of those success stories that makes me feel proud. Today it is one of the most profitable banks in Nepal. Shambhu Poudel's and Gajananda Agrawal's sons are still directors of the bank, and I have good relations with them. My battle with them ended the day the Supreme Court ruled in my favour.

Butwal Power Company

The government first called for bids for a 75 per cent stake in Butwal Power Company (BPC) in 1998. Bidders had to file both technical and financial proposals. Although twenty-five companies bought the tender forms, only two submitted their proposals. One of them was a consortium that included the Chaudhary Group and a British-American power company called Independent Power Corporation (IPC). Another bidder was Interkraft Private Limited Nepal, a consortium comprising a Norwegian company and Nepali business figures such as

Padma Jyoti, Pradip Kumar Shrestha, Balram Pradhan and Gyanendra Lal Pradhan who were involved with Interkraft Nepal.

Our technical proposal was judged superior to that of Interkraft's, being awarded ninety-two points in comparison with their seventy-six. The financial proposals of both parties were opened in July 1999. We bid Rs 109.09 per unit share, which translated into Rs 68.65 crore. Interkraft bid Rs 90 per unit share, which amounted to Rs 57 crore.

Based on their technical and financial proposals, the government should have transferred 75 per cent of the BPC's shares to the IPC. Not only that, Interkraft had also submitted an alternative proposal with some preconditions such as renewal of a power purchase agreement with the Nepal Electricity Authority that was about to terminate, and a contract to construct a dam for the Melamchi drinking water project. This, despite the fact that the privatization cell of the ministry of finance, while inviting bids, had clearly stated that the bidder could not include any preconditions. In spite of all this, Interkraft was chosen over the IPC, whose proposal was not accepted. The government even asked for another financial proposal from Interkraft going against internationally accepted norms.

We lodged a complaint with the government, stating that its conduct in the matter was against international tender practices. We insisted that the government evaluate the financial proposals that had been first submitted. The government treated our letter as though it were mere wastepaper.

In its second financial proposal, Interkraft bid Rs 72 crore, which was slightly higher than our bid. However, again, its proposal was flawed. Unlike us, Interkraft wanted to buy the shares in instalments. If the amount was calculated in US dollars at the prevailing foreign exchange rate, their bid was lower than ours. But the government, turning a blind eye to all this, was set to accept their proposal. We went all out against it.

The government was compelled to scrap the tender process and start again.

The next call for bids was made a year later. Again, though six companies had bought the tender forms, it was only the IPC and Interkraft that submitted the required technical and financial proposals.

The technical proposals were opened on 14 February 2001. Six months later, the government sent a letter notifying us that our proposal had been rejected, on the grounds that we had not attached a covering letter and that the bank guarantee that should have been attached to the financial proposal, was attached to the technical proposal instead, and vice versa. It should be remembered here that our technical proposal was approved, fetching very good marks in the initial tender process. This showed that the government, and particularly the ministry of finance, deliberately wanted to bar the Chaudhary Group from participating in the privatization of the BPC.

On 17 August 2001, the ministry of finance returned our financial proposal without even opening it. It had opened only Interkraft's proposal. We marched into the ministry of finance immediately and opened our sealed proposal in front of everyone there. We had bid Rs 82 crore—Rs 9 crore more than Interkraft had.

The controversy attracted a lot of media attention. The finance minister himself admitted that the amount pledged by Interkraft was too low. The government then cancelled the second tender, saying the bids were too low.

It was only when the shares were tendered a third time that Interkraft offered more than we did. We proposed Rs 86 crore while they quoted Rs 95 crore. This time too they said they would make the payment in instalments. Taking into account the exchange rate of the US dollar, this effectively reduced their bid to Rs 90 crore, only Rs 4 crore more than ours.

Finally, Interkraft did get the BPC.

Considering the complex machinations by which this happened, I believe the government wanted to award the tender to Interkraft from the very beginning. This explains why the first two tenders, which we should have won, were scrapped. And once Interkraft came up with a better proposal, the government immediately endorsed it. What kind of a referee is this, I wondered—a government that shows a red flag whenever I win and a green flag as soon as I lose!

The presence of a Norwegian company in the Interkraft Nepal consortium was a plus point for them. The BPC benefited from Norwegian finance and technical assistance. On the other hand, it was our mistake to quote only Rs 86 crore in the third tender. Interkraft, which had raised its bid from Rs 57 crore in the first tender to Rs 73 crore in the second, had studied our proposal carefully, bidding Rs 95 crore in the third tender as a result. To be honest, we never imagined Interkraft would be successful in winning the tender. Perhaps I should have changed my strategy after realizing that the government and the members of the privatization cell were opposed to us and that the BPC would benefit from Norwegian assistance. I should have looked for ways to get the government to favour us, and should have also looked for a Norwegian company to partner with. By the time all this occurred to me, it was too late.

To me, the privatization of the BPC was not merely a matter of obtaining shares in a hydropower company. I had imagined it as a strategic springboard for my long-term involvement in the energy sector. I had even chalked out a plan for proceeding in that direction.

The failure to win the BPC tender was a huge blow to the Chaudhary Group and to our dreams of participating in the power sector.

My experience with the Modi Khola hydropower project was just as bitter.

I had obtained the licence to develop the Modi Khola project in the course of the first Investment Summit. An American company was our chief rival. The then influential US ambassador to Nepal, Julia Chang Bloch, had tried hard to get the contract for the American company. However, the minister for industry, Ram Krishna Tamrakar, and the head of the department of foreign investment, Narendra Basnyat, favoured me.

I got the licence.

This would be the first private sector investment in any hydropower project in Nepal. A number of laws had to be enacted to make this possible. The first-ever Power Purchase Agreement (PPA) was prepared by the director general of the Nepal Electricity Authority, Ajit Narayan Singh Thapa. It was a risky proposition to bring foreign investors into the hydropower sector, which demands huge capital, at a time when the laws governing the sector were not fully developed.

I was negotiating with potential foreign partners. Talks with the Canadian company Ontario Hydro were at an advanced stage. In the meantime, the Arun III Hydropower Project, which was to be funded primarily by the World Bank, was scrapped. The government of the time wrote to the bank saying it did not want the Arun III project to proceed. However, to demonstrate that it was capable of developing a project on its own, the government withdrew my licence for Modi Khola, purportedly because it was going to undertake the project by itself. A foundation stone was laid by UML leader Pradip Nepal, who was the water resources minister. To this day, however, there is no sign of the project.

The Modi Khola project was our second failure in the hydropower sector.

Following these two major setbacks, we decided to stay away from the sector for the time being. However, I had always felt that if I wanted to take up a long-term project in Nepal, it had to be in the hydropower sector.

I started scouting for another opportunity.

The Maoist insurgency was flaring up. The US government directed all American companies involved in infrastructure projects in Nepal to pull out. Hazra Engineering, an American partner in the Bhote Koshi hydropower project, decided to sell its shares. We lobbied, with the help of our previous partner Independent Power Corporation (IPC), for the shares but were thwarted in this attempt too. Prabhakar Shumsher Rana, who was the Nepali investor in the project, wanted to buy those shares himself, a natural step for him as he was already an investor.

In 2006, after a long hiatus, we again started to explore opportunities in the hydropower sector. Nirvana took the initiative. This time we decided to develop a project from scratch instead of obtaining shares in a project developed by others. We went ahead with proposals to independently develop the 84-megawatt Madi Seti project and the 400-megawatt Doodh Koshi project in partnership with an American power company, the AES.

Despite the acute power crisis in the country, the authorities concerned were still not interested in encouraging potential investors like us. On the contrary, they continued to discourage us by creating unnecessary hurdles in our path. They created numerous obstacles for us in obtaining the survey licence for the Madi Seti project. When they ran out of excuses, they decided to grant the licence by downgrading the project to 24 megawatts. Accordingly, we spent Rs 50 lakh on preparing the detailed project report, only to be told that there was another change and that the project would be one of 84 megawatts after all, and that it must be a reservoir-based and not the run-of-river type.

As far as the Doodh Koshi project is concerned, the government remains undecided despite our repeated assurance to it that we are capable of developing the entire project with our own capital and that we can generate electricity from the project within four years. Many governments have come and gone since we applied for the licence for that project, but not one of them has been prepared to take a decision on it. During the tenure of the government led by Jhala Nath Khanal, Water Resources Minister Gokarna Bista, a very popular and dynamic leader, recommended that we be granted the licence. But even his suggestion fell on deaf ears, drowned out by the vested interests of crafty groups both within and outside the government.

This is a glaring example of how thoughtless our political leaders can be, even when the country is reeling under load-shedding extending to fourteen hours a day.

The politicians and the government, however, are not entirely responsible for this sorry state of affairs. The bureaucracy is equally responsible. The civil servants involved in the hydropower sector have woven such a web around themselves that no entrepreneur who wants to invest in the sector can be free from their influence. Even the politicians have not been able to get past the bureaucratic stranglehold despite attempts made by some good leaders such as Bista. If the bureaucratic walls could be taken down, this country—the second richest in the world in terms of hydropower potential— would not have faced the power crisis it does today.

I have faced hurdles created by the 'system'—the intertwined network of politicians, bureaucrats and other players—in every sector I have attempted to enter. However, my destiny has also shaped me such in such a way that I never give up on any project I start, regardless of the kind of obstacles the system might impose. I will continue to fight the system. Even if I fall down, I pick myself up and forge ahead.

The defeats I suffered in relation to the hydropower sector only served to motivate me further.

As I continued to explore possible opportunities in the sector, I came in touch with Guru Neupane, promoter of Siddhikali Power Company. I decided to invest in two of his hydropower projects—Upper Trishuli and Chameliya. I was weary of fighting the bureaucracy in trying to start a project of my own, and saw no other choice but to seek an opportunity to engage in projects being developed by others. The PPA for the 84-megawatt Upper Trishuli is now in the process of being signed, and the detailed feasibility report for Chameliya is under preparation.

Meanwhile, we continued to look for other experienced partners in the power sector. Through Guru Neupane's initiative, we re-established contacts with Coastal Energy, an Indian power developer, which had expressed willingness to work with us in the past. It has developed many hydropower projects from Arunachal Pradesh to Sikkim in north-eastern India. We sought an equal partnership with Coastal Energy.

Some years earlier, Coastal Energy had sent us a proposal through Anil Sahu, one of our contacts in the Indian state of Meghalaya. Sahu had brought Coastal Energy's main promoter, S. Surendra, to our New Delhi office. However, he had not sought an appointment with me and I was unable to meet him even though I was in the office. Had we met that day, we could have taken our engagement in the hydropower sector to the next level.

To me, this shows that we get what is destined to be ours only at a time determined by fate.

In the meantime, another important development took place. Yogendra Shrestha, promoter of Nepal Share Markets, went missing as soon as news of his involvement in 'financial irregularities' in the company became public. To recover the money lost due to the 'irregularities', the central bank decided to auction the promoter's stake in Himal Hydro, one of the companies affiliated to Nepal Share Markets. Like the BPC, Himal Hydro was a company set up by the United Mission to Nepal (UMN) to develop the hydropower sector in the country. Nepal Share Markets held 68 per cent of the shares of the company, which had started the process of acquiring land to develop two projects, one of a capacity 60 megawatts and the other of 20 megawatts.

We decided to buy the 68 per cent stake in Himal Hydro. Our bid for it was the highest.

At one point, following our defeat in the protracted battle for the BPC, the Chaudhary Group was wondering about its future in the hydropower sector. Today, a number of projects of a total capacity of 200 megawatts is under development by our group.

The lesson we learnt was that the BPC saga had actually proved a blessing in disguise.

Mahalaxmi Sugar Mills

This project made for the biggest professional battle of my life. The trouble began on 8 April 2002.

On that day, the state-run Rastriya Banijya Bank wrote a letter to the Credit Information Bureau advising that my father, my spouse Sarika and I be blacklisted for defaulting on the loan taken for Mahalaxmi Sugar Mills.

We received a drop copy of the letter by fax. Following the letter, the bureau blacklisted all three of us.

I was shocked when I saw the letter because I had settled all my debts regarding the mills two years earlier. How could they link me to the company now?

My association with Mahalaxmi Sugar Mills began around 1990, when a number of sugar mills were opening in Nepal. Om Prakash Kanaudiya, who was then the chairperson of the Association of Commerce and Industry of Krishnanagar, showed me a 134-acre plot at ward number 1 of Jawahari Village Development Committee of Kapilvastu district. Prince Dhirendra had bought this land for a sugar mill, which he had named Puja Sugar Mills. However, the project was dropped for some reason and the land was lying vacant. 'India's Birla Group has also conducted a feasibility study to open mills here,' Kanaudiya told me.

'Why didn't you go for it then?' I asked him.

'We can't do it on our own,' he said. 'You contribute the bulk of the capital. We'll chip in. You can leave the rest to me.'

We moved ahead with the project. Under a joint financing scheme, with the Nepal Industrial Development Corporation, Employees Provident Fund, Himalayan Bank Limited and Nepal Bank Limited as principal lenders, a loan was issued to us of Rs 30.17 crore, which also included loan capitalization.

The sugar mills began production in 1997 but we never got much by way of practical support from Kanaudiya. He passed away soon after the mills came into operation. However, his son Birendra Kanaudiya, who was affiliated with the Nepali Congress and even held the post of assistant minister for water resources at one point, stepped into a management role.

After Birendra Kanaudiya took over the management, matters became uneasy. Whenever we sent one of our representatives to the mills, he would chase them away with the help of local goons. The institutions that had loaned money to us became aware of the tension between Kanaudiya and me. On 3 July 1998, a joint meeting of the lending institutions decided that 'the company promoters, Binod Chaudhary and Birendra Kanaudiya, shall accept each other's shares in the company, and duly notify us of the same'.

This decision made it possible for one of us to sell our stake to the other and to dissociate himself from the company. I welcomed the move and handed over all the responsibilities and liabilities of the mills to Kanaudiya, settling my stake in the mills for just Rs 4.85 crore, although I had invested Rs 12 crore. We signed the share transfer agreement on 15 October 1999, after which I and all others affiliated with the Chaudhary

Group resigned from the mills' board of directors. Our resignations were accepted at a board meeting on 11 February 2000. We also duly notified the Company Registrar's Office of this.

It is no wonder I was stunned when Rastriya Banijya Bank suddenly blacklisted us two years after we had severed ties with the mills.

What actually happened was that after we notified the Company Registrar's Office about our dissociation from Mahalaxmi Sugar Mills, the office had written to Birendra Kanaudiya seeking verification of this development. However, Kanaudiya never sent a response. As a result, our name was not formally removed from the list of the mills' promoters, leading to our blacklisting by Rastriya Banijya Bank, which, separately, was quite well aware that we were no longer associated with the company. After we sold our shares, all the five banks that had loaned funds for the mills had signed a new agreement with Kanaudiya transferring the management of the mills to an entity called Rohit Group. How could the banks then publicly humiliate us by associating us with the mills' loan defaulters? These banks also sought a proposal from Kanaudiya to restructure their loan to the company, which had now ballooned to Rs 80 crore, including interest. After recovering some money from Kanaudiya in early 2004, the banks went on to restructure the loan on the condition that he repay more money within a year's time. The lenders had also agreed to let him take over the management.

It may also be noted here that on 6 December 1999, the bankers had decided to conduct a field study to get the real picture of the financial health of the mills. Their report on December 27 in the same year stated that 'Kanaudiya has worked hard to bring the company to its present level . . . and the future of the company looks bright if it continues in this way.' It was based on this report that Rastriya Banijya Bank issued a no-objection letter on 7 January 2000 so that Birendra Kanaudiya could take loans from other banks and financial institutions. This letter automatically deactivated the liquidity guarantee I had given to the project.

I filed a petition in the Supreme Court, saying we had been illegally blacklisted. Kanaudiya too issued a public notice in the *Kantipur* daily on 28 September 2004, declaring that the Chaudhary Group was not associated with the mills. It was on 18 January 2006 that the Supreme Court ruled in our favour.

Nepal Rastra Bank, the Credit Information Bureau and the five banks that had issued the loan, then filed a writ at the apex court, appealing for a review of the verdict. That court again ruled in our favour, stating there were no flaws in the earlier verdict. With my legal position further consolidated, I approached the Credit Information Bureau, urging it to remove our names from their blacklist. They said that could not be done until they received a copy of the court's verdict So I produced my copy. The bureau then removed our names from the blacklist on their website, saying it would be some time before they could erase it from their records.

Still, this battle was not over for me.

Some parliamentarians called into question the verdict of the court, raising the possibility that the Supreme Court judge who had handled our case might be impeached. I had to testify before the parliamentary Public Accounts Committee, as if I were a criminal. Chitra Bahadur K.C., leader of a fringe leftist party, was chairperson of that powerful committee. However, the chairperson of the Nepal Bar Association, Shambhu Thapa, and many senior advocates, including

Radheshyam Adhikari and Madhav Baskota, none of whom I knew personally or professionally, not only supported the court's verdict but questioned the committee's legal right to review it.

'The Public Accounts Committee is not the authority to review the verdict of the Supreme Court,' Thapa told the parliamentarians. 'If the verdict is flawed, then the judiciary alone can rectify it. Your work is to draft laws. Nonetheless, even if you draft a new law, it cannot affect the court's verdict since the new law can address only those cases that do not predate it. If the parliamentary committee is to review the verdicts made by the Supreme Court, then what would be the significance of the court?"

With the legal eagles vehemently opposed to such involvement, the committee decided not to review the verdict.

So in the end, I won that battle.

9

The Politics at FNCCI

I originally chose not to join the Federation of Nepalese Chambers of Commerce and Industry. I had many doubts about the modus operandi and background of this institution. Though our companies were affiliated with the FNCCI, I did not even attend its annual general meetings.

Mahesh Lal Pradhan wanted to pull me into the FNCCI during its elections in 1988. Mahesh Lal was running for the position of the FNCCI president against Maniharsha Jyoti of the Jyoti Group. Maniharshajee was backed by leading business families such as the Golchhas, the Dugars and the Madanlal Chiranjeelals. Mahesh Lal wanted to woo younger entrepreneurs to challenge them. However, he was not trying to mobilize younger people with a long-term vision to transform the federation; to him, it was only a strategy to win the election.

I discussed the matter with my confidants like Vijay Shah, Kishore Khanal and Dr Gopal Shrestha. We concluded that we had to become insiders in the federation to reform it, and that opting out would not serve our professional interests. As the people who had been dominating the federation were supporting the other side, we gave our full support to Mahesh Lal and canvassed for him at different chapters of the federation across the country. Sensing the popular mood in favour of Mahesh Lal, Maniharshajee decided to pull out of the race.

The seats reserved for the associate sector of the FNCCI were always divided up among the old and established business houses. A newcomer never got a seat. I should have got an executive post in the federation under Mahesh Lal's leadership, going by the gentleman's agreement between us. But, despite winning the election, he could not bring himself to challenge the tycoons who dominated the federation. His behaviour defeated the very cause for which we had got involved in FNCCI politics in the first place. I think he did not want to further annoy the Golchha, Dugar and MC groups following his victory over their favoured candidate.

Tolaram Dugar and Madan Lal Agrawal were very active in the federation in those days. They tried to reassure me, saying I had just joined the federation and that they were currently struggling to incorporate all the older members, and would include me after the next election.

I was disappointed that Mahesh Lal did not fully support me. He was the one who had urged me to join the federation and I had blindly supported him without weighing the pros and cons of doing so. I had even canvassed votes for him. But now that the election was over, it appeared he was trying to avoid me.

'I'm not going to give up,' I said to Dugar and Agrawal directly. 'If someone has to quit, then you quit, or we can always go to elections again. I'm prepared to fight it out even if I get only one vote because I assume you have the power to easily defeat me.'

It was not the first time a member of our family had been the target of these people's injustice. Father had asked Basant to file his candidacy for a post in the federation in a previous election, considering that I showed no interest in FNCCI politics. These people had persuaded Basant to relinquish his plans, making him the same promise they made me now. I was not going to let my family be taken advantage of in order to suit their convenience.

I still vividly recall that balcony at Blue Star Hotel where eleven candidates were assembled to claim ten executive posts in the federation. Everyone was trying to persuade me to give up. Had I withdrawn, the election itself could have been avoided. But I was adamant. Exasperated, Madan Lal Agrawal headed to Mahesh Agrawal of Mahashakti Soap and Chemical Industries, and snatched away his application form from his hands. Mahesh could not oppose his own uncle, after all.

Now there were ten candidates for ten positions and I became an associate member of the FNCCI. Mahesh Lal was nowhere to be seen while all this unfolded.

I was so encouraged by this psychological victory that I decided to file my candidacy for the position of vice president at the federation in the same year. My forceful entry into the executive committee had shaken the institution. When I declared my intention to contest for the post of vice president under the associate sector, it sent shockwaves across the federation. I was putting forward my name for the vice presidency at a time when even many of the founding members could only dream of doing such a thing. Hulas Chand Golchha had been groomed for the post, but I decided to go ahead to challenge him. Some members made fun of me for daring to challenge a senior and distinguished businessman like Golchha, and I'll admit it felt somewhat odd to oppose a man who was my father's peer. But I ignored them.

I asked Mahesh Lal to support my candidacy. I even tried to pressure him, but he would not give me his support. 'As I was elected unanimously to the post of president, I can't take sides,' he told me. 'You have to fight this battle on your own.'

I was left with no other choice than to form a new group immediately, which was a daunting challenge for a person who had just entered the federation. Surya Prasad Pradhan from Butwal, who later became a lawmaker, strongly backed me. Vijay Shah, Kishor Khanal and Dr Gopal Shrestha were there, of course, to back me in the associate sector.

Having failed to convince me to give up my candidacy, many members started to lobby against me. The immediate past president of the federation, Pashupati Giri, went all out against me. He met every member of the executive committee to lobby against me. I too intensified my own lobbying to counter him. Gradually, the tide started to turn in my favour. My opponents realized that Hulas Chand Golchha might not have the easy victory they had expected. They now devised a new strategy—to work out an amicable solution with me. Sometimes Hulas Chand would hold one-on-one parleys with me, and sometimes the entire executive committee would urge me to settle for a deal. Mahesh Lal was in a fix. He could not support Hulas Chand since he belonged to the rival faction. I had backed him during his election, but he could not support me in return as that would annoy all the big business houses.

This was probably the first instance in the history of the federation when the election of the associate vice president attracted more attention than the election of the president itself. Suddenly, I became the centre of attention in the umbrella body incorporating the country's foremost industrial entrepreneurs, and this attention worked in my favour. I had already registered a strong presence in the federation. It then suddenly occurred to me that if I pressed ahead with my candidacy, I might actually emerge victorious, but also stood to lose many friends in the process. That was unavoidable in politics—it would always be two steps forward sometimes, and one step back at other times. I withdrew my candidacy. I settled instead for the position of chairperson of the influential industrial committee of the federation. This was the most powerful position in the federation after that of vice president. So it was that I succeeded in rising to a very important position within the federation in a very short span of time. And, despite all the opposition I faced in the past, I never let that affect my behaviour as vice president. I played an active role in the federation, harbouring no hard feelings or biases against anyone.

In 1990, Mahesh Lal Pradhan again filed his candidacy for the post of president at FNCCI. Laxmi Das Manandhar was his rival. Manandhar was backed by the powerful Salt Trading Group comprising the Dixit and Hem Bahadur Malla families. We had a good relationship with Laxmi Das Manandhar and Hem Bahadur Malla, and had been shareholders in Salt Trading since father's days. However, I still supported Mahesh Lal, and Laxmi Das lost the election.

Dr Gopal Shrestha had, however, supported Laxmi Das and was against our faction. However, once the election was over, he supported me in every way. He even joined the Chaudhary Group later on. Sadly, he is no longer with us.

In the next election, I directly filed my candidacy for the post of vice president. One of the leading businessmen of the country, Mohan Gopal Khetan, was my rival. Perhaps he thought Mahesh Lal might persuade me to pull out of the race, but I was intransigent. Eventually, Khetan was compelled to withdraw from the race and I was elected vice president of the FNCCI unopposed.

During my term in that position, Padma Jyoti of the Jyoti Group was the ex officio vice president of the federation in the capacity of being the president of the employers' council from the associate sector.

From the time I joined the FNCCI, I was actively engaged in trying to empower its district chapters. These chapters, spread all over the country, had only a ceremonial role in the federation. Though the office-bearers at the secretariat could easy solve their business problems, it was not so easy for those in the districts to do so. The Agro Enterprise Centre and the Economic Liberalization Project supported by the USAID helped me push this cause forward. The donors actually wanted to mobilize resources for the project centrally, but I came up with a plan for the institutional development of enterprises at the district level. This helped open new chapters of the federation in the districts and empower the existing ones. It also led to the modernization of the office buildings of the federation secretariat and the district chapters.

Another important achievement during my term was an amendment to the federation's statute. I wanted an amendment that powered the chapters in the election of the federation president and other office-bearers. For that, the chapters needed to provide at least 50 per cent of the voters.

But members from the associate sector did not agree with this proposal, fearing it would end their pivotal role in federation politics. Nevertheless, we managed to secure this arrangement with the help of some like-minded friends and colleagues. That was the first time the secretariat had delegated significant powers to its district chapters. This ended the decisive role of the associate members in the elections. The district chapters could now call the shots in the federation.

Yet another reform we introduced in the federation related to the way we went about our issues and demands. We started to be more aggressive in our approach, whether it was in dealing with the government or otherwise lobbying for our agenda. The federation even took to the streets to oppose unfair levies such as the sports and toll taxes. The media started to air our opinions. Mahesh Lal's leadership was helpful in bringing about these reforms. He did not stop my aggressive campaigns, possibly because he wanted someone to do the work of reformation at the federation while he, as president, could take the credit. These reforms, as well as changes brought about by economic liberalization and the growing role of the private sector, raised the size and status of the FNCCI. I won many friends and supporters across the country for actively campaigning for these reforms. The strong bonds I had developed with many district chapters of the federation also made me a natural candidate for the position of president by the time of the upcoming elections in 1993. But my detractors hardly wanted to see me elected unopposed. They tried to field Padma Jyoti against me. However, he declined as his father Maniharshajee had just passed away. Hulas Chand Golchha then stepped forward to challenge me. Mahesh Lal and a few others pressured me until the eleventh hour, both directly and indirectly, to withdraw my candidacy.

Election fever started to grip the federation. I visited the districts. Besides my friends such as Nirak K.C., Bipin Malla, Shashi Agrawal, Vijay Shah and Kishor Khanal, the Newar community outside the Kathmandu valley, especially Ananda Raj Mulmi, Dr Gopal Shrestha, Ashok Palikhe, Chakor Man Shakya and Rajendra Pradhan, also supported me. The Nepal Chamber of Commerce even declared me as its official candidate. The Western Chamber of Industry and Commerce, encouraged by the Pokhara chapter, also backed me strongly. However, I did not have to campaign for very long. Hulas Chand then withdrew his candidacy, citing health reasons.

I was elected unopposed as the president of the FNCCI.

I again applied for the top post in the federation in 1996. This time Padma Jyoti stood against me.

Sometimes your success becomes your enemy. The more bricks I added to the structure of the federation, the more organized my detractors became. A new equation emerged against me in this election.

The federation office had moved from a rented apartment at Tripureshwore to its own four-storeyed building at Teku. I had worked hard to mobilize funds from many sources for the construction of the new building. Everybody supported me then. The FNCCI, which had been limited to collaboration with the Punjab, Haryana and Delhi (PHD) Chamber of Commerce and Industry, now entered into partnerships with the national-level industry organizations of India. We sealed a partnership accord with the Confederation of Indian Industries and worked with them in the run-up to the signing of the Nepal–India Trade Treaty in 1996. The draft of the treaty was prepared before the end of my tenure.

The FNCCI became an integral part of the delegations accompanying Nepal's head of state on foreign visits, and featured on the itinerary of visiting foreign heads of state. The federation was now treated as an authorized interpreter of documents issued by the state. Foreign donors were drawn to the federation. All these reforms suddenly made the position of the FNCCI president even more desirable. Nobody realized how much hard work lay behind my achievements. My colleagues now wanted to grab my chair, by hook or by crook. They teamed up to prepare a list of future federation presidents. For the first time in the history of the federation, the members campaigned against its own president, arguing that no individual should hold the top position for more than one term.

Even those whom I thought were very close to me were against me in the election. The likes of Neer Shah, Vijay Shah and Kishor Khanal, who had always stood up for me in the past, supported the rival camp. Suraj Baidya, a friend, publicly campaigned for Padma Jyoti while Mahesh Lal planned his election strategy behind closed doors.

The election fever was unprecedented. It was not just the entrepreneurs, the media and the political parties too were actively involved in it for the first time in the federation's history. The CPN-UML supported Jyoti. The Nepali Congress was divided, though its influential leader Arjun Nursing K.C. backed me. The election set a bad precedent at the FNCCI, as the political parties have played a decisive role in all its elections ever since. The parties even issued a directive to their supporters in the district chapters to vote only for those candidates whom the parties had formally endorsed. I do not entirely blame the politicians for this. They, naturally, will exploit entrepreneurs to achieve their goals. Far more deplorable is that support for federation candidates is traded for money in some of the economically backward districts.

By 1996, the entire private sector was divided, politically as well as communally.

Despite the stiff competition, most of the members of my faction were elected. I too was hopeful of reclaiming the top post. On the day the election result was to be announced, I left home in the morning fully prepared to reassume the position of president. The AGM was being held at Blue Star Hotel. As my car entered the gates of the hotel, some of my friends signalled to me to stop.

'What is the matter?' I asked, rolling down the window.

'Please don't go into the hotel now,' one of them said. Pointing to Hotel Sita, a few blocks away, he added, 'Let's go there first.'

My heart sank. I reversed the car, which was halfway across the Blue Star entrance, and headed to Hotel Sita, where our election office was located. As soon as I stepped out, some of my friends led me by hand into the office. They were holding an emergency meeting.

I had lost the election.

'Binod Babu, you must go now to Blue Star Hotel,' someone said. When I heard this, I was actually shaking.

According to the federation's statute, the outgoing president must welcome the president-elect in person; he must personally remove the federation pin from the lapel of his coat and pin it on the president-elect's coat. Any defeat is painful, but marking one's own defeat in this way was especially painful.

Following this defeat, I started searching for a candidate for the next election who could transform my defeat into a victory.

Ananda Raj Mulmi was the strong leader of the Pokhara chapter of the federation. He had backed me during my unopposed election to the presidency in the past. I thought that if I could make him president, it would serve two purposes: the Kathmandu businessmen's plot to defeat me in order to share the top post among themselves on a rotational basis would be foiled; and the leadership of the federation would be handed over for the first time to an entrepreneur from outside the capital.

I proposed Mulmi as our official candidate. Chiranjivi Nidhi Tiwari was pitted against Mulmi and had the support of tycoons like Padma Jyoti, Mahesh Lal Pradhan, Pradip Kumar Shrestha, Suraj Baidya, the Golchhas and Madanlal Chiranjeelal. On the other hand, my friends who had backed Padma Jyoti, had returned to my camp. Those disgruntled with the federation leadership too backed us. We had set up our publicity office at the same venue—Hotel Sita. We relentlessly canvassed for Mulmi across the country. I always stood beside him throughout the campaign.

Mulmi won the election.

I now wanted to keep myself away from the politics of organizations representing the private sector. However, politics kept following me. The creation of the Confederation of Nepalese Industries was the next step.

Founding the CNI
The formation of the CNI traces back to the Nepal–India Trade Treaty.

The treaty, which was signed in 1996, triggered a wave of industrialization in Nepal as it exempted certain goods produced in Nepal from customs duty. Many joint venture companies with well-known corporations were established. Exports to India rose meteorically.

Within a few years of the treaty coming into effect, the India side started to allege that some Nepali companies were circumventing its provisions by exporting products such as hydrogenated vegetable oil, copper wire, zinc oxide and acrylic yarns duty-free, when these items were outside the range of finished products envisaged by the treaty. Notwithstanding the fact that these products constituted only a negligible proportion of the industrial GDP of Nepal, the Indian side wanted to review the treaty. Some state governments in India actively argued that the treaty should be repealed. Neither the Government of Nepal nor the private sector could raise their voice against them.

In the wake of India's wavering stance on the treaty, some industrial entrepreneurs in Nepal held a meeting at Everest Hotel in Kathmandu to discuss the matter. They were particularly disgruntled with the FNCCI for failing to champion the cause of Nepali industries. All the participating entrepreneurs stressed the need for a 'think tank' to address the concerns of the Nepali private sector.

It was this gathering that decided to create the CNI.

The FNCCI took strong exception to the formation of the CNI. They charged us with setting up a parallel institution to avenge my electoral defeat. We were accused of 'fracturing the unity of entrepreneurs' by forming the CNI, despite the fact that Padma Jyoti, Suraj Baidya and Jagadish Agrawal had already planned to form a parallel organization after Mulmi won the election at the FNCCI. They had already drafted the statute for that organization. We prepared the CNI's statute by effecting minor changes to that draft.

The federation officials then took competition to an unhealthy extreme by trying to block the registration of the CNI. Even Prime Minister Sher Bahadur Deuba supported them. Due to relentless pressure from the FNCCI and from the government itself, we were unable to register the CNI for almost a year. Finally, we came up with an idea. While all attention was focused on the district administration office of Kathmandu to block our move, we quietly got the CNI registered by the district administration office of the neighbouring district of Lalitpur. Once an organization is registered, even the government cannot scrap it without solid reasons.

The FNCCI president, Ravi Bhakta Shrestha, and the office, bearers even published a public notice in the media to oppose the institution of the CNI. Ravi Bhakta is a close friend of mine now. We are partners in United Insurance Company. He acknowledges that the FNCCI tried to block the formation of the CNI during his tenure as president.

Despite the obstacles in its early days, the CNI, over the span of a decade, grew to the level of the FNCCI as a private sector umbrella body. Media organizations strongly supported us in this cause. The reputation I had earned as president of the FNCCI, the goodwill towards me among high-ranking government officials, and the support from many national and international quarters, also proved helpful.

We have always thought and acted with the nation's interests at heart. Whether it was the Economic Summit aimed at raising the monthly salary of every Nepali citizen to at least Rs 12,000, or the Partnership Summit inviting the former Malaysian prime minister Mahathir Mohamad to chalk out an economic strategy for Nepal, we have always given the topmost priority to economic agendas. The CNI has played an important role in drafting legislations pertaining to SEZs, the investment board and new industrial policies. Today, the CNI has its own modern secretariat. It earns more than it spends and is rapidly expanding its base.

It is not that we have never collaborated with the FNCCI, but we will always stand up for our rights.

The Maoist trouble

Industrialist Shashikant Agrawal loved getting together with friends. Some of us would meet at the Saino Restaurant at Durbar Marg in downtown Kathmandu three to four times a week at his invitation. Also invited were diplomats, high-ranking government officials and even prominent media personalities. These gatherings were distinctive for our frank discussions on current affairs.

During one of these gatherings in March 2007, the FNCCI president of the time, Chandi Dhakal, broke the news that trade unionists affiliated with the Maoists had physically attacked the owner of Woodland Hotel in Durbar Marg.

I was shocked to hear this. Shashikant Agrawal, Bhusan Dahal of Kantipur Television, Prakash Shrestha, chairperson of the Hotel Association of Nepal, and a few other friends were also present. We all knew the owner of Woodland Hotel personally, and were also aware that workers affiliated with the Maoist party had been harassing him for some time.

Though the Maoist party had joined peaceful, mainstream politics, many of their cadres were yet to mend their ways. A strike at the hotel had turned violent, with the owner brutally attacked.

'This is a serious offence. Hari Shresthajee is critically injured,' Chandi said. 'He's been admitted to the emergency ward of Bir Hospital.'

We rushed to the hospital.

Shrestha was writhing in pain. His body was badly bruised, his face bloodied and bloated. He could hardly see or talk. His clothes were torn. His loved ones, who were attending him, were indescribably distressed.

I brooded for a while, and then my blood started to boil. What was this? I thought. Why was a hard-working man who employed hundreds of people bashed so mercilessly by his own employees? Did they see physical violence as the only way to protest their grievances? Was no one safe from such attacks? If this could happen to a man like Hari Shrestha, how safe would the general public feel in the wake of this attack? And why would any entrepreneur want to invest here?

The image of Hari Shrestha lying bloodied and bruised in the chaotic environment of Bir Hospital seemed to symbolize not just the status of entrepreneurs and professionals but also that of the ordinary people of Nepal in those days of political transition. We were fooling ourselves with false assurances and sympathy for the emerging power. Weary of the drawn-out conflict in the country, we accepted any agent of change as an agent of good. We did not want to see the slyness and insincerity of those who were claiming to transform the country.

The sly do not understand the language of tears. The only emotion they understand is fury.

Chandi and I issued a strongly worded condemnation of the attack from the hospital itself. The next day, we decided to stage a protest by gathering most of the entrepreneurs and professionals available in the capital. Our plan was to hand over a letter of protest to the government demanding security and to caution the state against any recurrence of such an incident.

The next morning, we all gathered at Hari Shrestha's residence at Durbar Marg to console his family and express our solidarity with them. Many friends from the FNCCI and the CNI turned up.

Suddenly, someone broke the news that a mob of Maoists was heading towards Shrestha's house to attack us.

We immediately called up the home minister and some senior police for help, but they refused to take us seriously. This left us with only two choices: to run for cover or to stand our ground and face them. We chose the latter.

In a while, we heard the news that the Maoist cadres who were planning to attack us had decided to turn back.

This averted danger for the time being. Nonetheless, it was important to let the Maoists know we had not been intimidated. Garment entrepreneur Prashanta Pokharel took my arm and urged me to sit down in the middle of the road. I did as bid. Chandi followed suit. One by one, all the attendees from the FNCCI and the CNI sat down too.

Vehicular traffic ground to a halt as we blocked the road. A large crowd started to gather, joining us, encouraging us to continue our protest. We then decided to march to the official residence of the prime minister at Baluwatar. Girija Prasad Koirala was the prime minister. We marched to Baluwatar, chanting slogans against the Maoists' atrocities. News of the protest led by the two umbrella bodies of the private sector spread like wildfire across the country. Entrepreneurs, professionals and ordinary people alike rushed to join our march from all over the city. An unprecedented crowd gathered outside Gate Number 3 of the prime minister's residence.

We sought an appointment with the prime minister to discuss our concerns, but he refused to meet us. We were told he was occupied with some urgent work. This left us even more outraged. We decided to hold a press conference right there in front of Gate Number 3. I do not know who arranged for the chairs and microphones in such a brief span of time. Some two dozen journalists also instantly appeared for the press conference.

We organized a mass assembly of industrial entrepreneurs and professional organizations at Basantapur Durbar Square in downtown Kathmandu the next day to protest the growing anarchy and lawlessness in the country. The government, realizing how angry and determined we were, finally woke up. We were invited for talks.

The two top Maoist leaders, chairperson Pushpa 'Prachanda' Kamal Dahal and his deputy, Dr Baburam Bhattarai, were at Mahendranagar at the time. Prachandajee telephoned us from there. 'Don't step up your agitation. We'll discuss the matter once we return to Kathmandu,' he told us.

We were sick and tired of their false assurances and false amiability. The attack on Hari Shrestha was the trigger that ignited our pent-up anger and resentment against the Maoists who had been attacking the private sector for a long time.

'Fine. We're ready for dialogue but not for closed-door negotiations,' we told him. 'The talks must be held in public.' They cut short their stay in Mahendranagar and returned to Kathmandu the next day. We met at Radisson Hotel. Many news channels streamed the meeting live. The top Maoist leaders attended, and some leaders of the UML too. All of them committed to stopping the attacks on the private sector.

The ruling seven-party alliance and the Maoists then went on to issue a written commitment to industrial security. The Maoists also moved out of Surya Carpet Industry, which they had captured some time earlier.

Certificate of Origin row

A festering battle between the CNI and the FNCCI over the issue of Certificate of Origin (COO) eventually took a political form.

A COO is a document used in international trade attesting that a product is wholly produced in a particular country using local raw materials. The ministry of commerce had authorized the FNCCI to issue these certificates, but had not enacted the decision. Previously, only the Nepal Chamber of Commerce used to issue COOs.

When we, the officials of the CNI, first approached the government in 2002 to authorize us to issue COOs, Mahesh Lal Pradhan, then minister for industry and commerce, would not lend us an ear. Later, the ministry tried to address the matter by facilitating talks between us and the FNCCI, which only meant procrastination. Many years later, after Chandi Dhakal became president of the FNCCI, we reached a kind of understanding. They agreed to share the revenue collected through the issuance of COOs. The FNCCI levies Rs 12 per Rs 100 of exportable products as a service charge, which works out to Rs 6 crore annually. But, as they did not honour the agreement, we decided the CNI would issue COOs on its own. The customs office, however, would not accept our certificates.

I then approached the ministry of finance. 'Show me the law that bars the CNI from issuing COOs and I will stop issuing them immediately,' I told them. They could not cite any law. Customs started to accept the documents we issued.

Once, an export consignment was stuck in Kolkata because the Indian authorities declined to recognize the COO issued by us. Kolkata is the largest port of foreign trade for landlocked Nepal. I urged the commerce secretary to telephone our consulate general in Kolkata. The matter was settled once he discussed the matter with the Indian authorities. We were now an agency authorized to issue the COO.

The FNCCI did not like this at all. It lobbied the ministry against us. But the commerce minister, Rajendra Mahato, supported us. 'I'm not going to take away the CNI's rights,' he told them. However, under growing pressure from the FNCCI, the government, through a Cabinet meeting, came up with what it saw as a compromise. It directed the FNCCI to give Rs 1.3 for every COO issued by it to the CNI. This amounted to Rs 50 lakh to 60 lakh a year. In exchange, we would stop issuing COOs. We kept our part of the bargain, but instead of sharing the revenue as the Cabinet had suggested, the FNCCI sent us a letter stating it would provide only 25 percent of the Rs 1.3 per COO.

I was outraged. I convened a press conference at the ministry of commerce itself. Minister Mahato was also present.

'The FNCCI has disobeyed an order from the government,' I said.

'We told them what our decision was,' Mahato replied. 'Why don't you take it up with the FNCCI?'

I raised my voice.

'An order from the government has been blatantly disregarded,' I said. 'But instead of doing something about that, you're asking us to settle the matter directly with the FNCCI? Is that federation greater than the state?'

This was back in April 2010. Following this high-voltage drama, the commerce ministry reviewed its previous decision on 21 May 2010 authorizing the CNI, the Chamber of Commerce and Trade and the Export Promotion Centre, besides the FNCCI, to issue COOs.

This was a big victory in the CNI's fight for its rights against the FNCCI.

Part iii: Rebirth

10

The Turning Point

The first turning point in my professional life was my contact with Kiran Sherchan while I was studying for the Intermediate Certificate of Commerce at Saraswoti Campus in Kathmandu.

1973
Kiran had just returned after completing a hotel management course in Japan. He was running Laligurans Hotel at Lazimpat, a diplomatic enclave in Kathmandu. I was quite impressed with the way he talked and carried himself. He was slightly older than I. Being a St Xavier's alumnus, he had a wide range of friends and a broad way of thinking. On the other hand, I was raised in a traditional Marwari family and had gone to a general school. I thought Kiran was the person who would help me broaden my horizons. He was the one who could pick me up from a blind alley in Khichapokhari and lead me into the new era that Kathmandu was entering.

I started to adopt his ideas and mingle with his friends. I was able to make the acquaintance of Neer Shah, S.K. Singh, Ram Bhattarai, Rajendra Rijal, Divya Mani Rajbhandari, Rasendra Bhattarai and many others from the social elite of those days. They were close to the seat of power in one way or other. Rajendra's father, Nagendra Prasad Rijal, had been prime minister a number of times. Neer Shah was very close to Prince Dhirendra. Neer and Kumar Khadga, King Birendra's brother-in-law, were siblings. S.K. Singh was also a close relative of the royal family.

In the beginning, I felt they did not want to mix with me. They were members of the establishment and came from elite families, while I was a boy who had just graduated from a school and who was trying to start a business. Moreover, they looked askance at anyone who was from the Marwari community. However, the distance between us gradually narrowed. Two things brought us together: style and adventure.

I had long hair and wore bell-bottoms that were in vogue then. To top it all, I wore stylish leather boots, and was also often seen slinging my guitar over my shoulders and singing with Kiran and his friends. I would also roam New Road and King's Way, trying to impress the girls. I would attend parties thrown by the social elite of Kathmandu and spend hours at the upscale Indira Café on New Road. I also had my hobbies of motorbike riding and later, of driving fast cars. The Austin Healey two-seater, which I had got after staging the hunger strike at home, was our favourite toy. Kiran and I drove to Darjeeling many times in that car. We would also go on jaunts to Nagarkot and Kakani. We were fond of movies, travelling as far as Raxaul, Muzaffarpur and even Patna in India to watch new Bollywood releases.

Someone, probably one of our friends from Birgunj, brought the news one day: 'A new film has been released in Patna.'

'*Zanjeer*,' Kiran said. 'Amitabh Bachchan is the hero.'

We took out the car. We hit the brakes, so to speak, only after reaching Birgunj, having had our foot on the accelerator all the way down from Kathmandu. The friend who had tipped us off about the movie joined us there. There was no space for a third passenger in the Austin Healey, but we could not ditch him. So we left the car in Birgunj and went into Raxaul in a mule-driven cart. At Raxaul, we took a rickety public bus and reached Patna late in the evening. We had travelled some 600 kilometres to another country to watch a movie. Nepalis do not require a passport or a visa to enter India, but we were so crazy about movies that we would not have baulked at the journey even if a visa had been mandatory!

When I returned home on the third day, I felt like a criminal confronted by the police. Father's earlobes were vibrating. He blasted me. I felt so weighed down with remorse that I could not utter a word.

Two days later, Kiran and I again whizzed away to Kakani.

I had learned a lot about fashion and style through hobnobbing with Kiran. We would order new designer clothes from boutiques in Hong Kong and Bangkok. Sometimes we travelled to those places just to buy clothes. It was cashing in on that exposure that I opened Arun Boutique in Kathmandu, the first fashion outlet in Nepal.

Back in those days, advertising to promote a business was almost unknown. I, however, wanted to advertise the Saree Sansar and Ghar Sansar outlets within Arun Emporium. Kiran was related to the writer Bhupi Sherchan. I went to Bhupi's house with Kiran and asked him to write a poem for me. He instantly wrote four lines, right in front of us:

> *Nari sundar phool ho bhane*
> *saree usko bahar ho,*
> *usko sundartalai chamkaune*
> *yo nai anupam upahar ho.*
> (If a woman is an exotic bloom
> then her saree is her spring,
> it is the priceless gift that enhances
> her beauty.)

This poem by Bhupi featured in the advertisements for both Saree Sansar and Ghar Sansar.

'Okay, let's do business together,' I said.

'What business?' Kiran asked, surprised.

'Something special, something creative.'

We were sitting by a window at Indira Café.

Dusk was falling rapidly.

It had been raining and the leaves of the sacred fig outside the restaurant were thoroughly sodden. Through the window, we could clearly see drops of water dripping from the drenched leaves. The water gushing from the projected roof of the restaurant drummed in our ears, probably battering the corrugated steel sheets of the roof of one of the houses below. The chatter of the people inside the restaurant had been muffled by the downpour. Now that it had stopped raining, soft voices could be heard. The couples in there, who were waiting over tea or coffee for the rain to stop, were suddenly restless to leave. The tables became empty, one after the other.

Kiran and I were in no hurry. It was our daily ritual to pass our time at Indira Café in the evening before heading to a disco where we would party until late.

Kiran was brooding over something, his eyes fixed on the rain-washed road.

'Sir, you don't get new ideas by wracking your brain,' I said. 'Wait until an idea just spontaneously pops up in your mind.'

We paid the bill and left.

The loud western music at the disco drowned out our voices. Even our shrieks sounded like whispers. On the dance floor, couples were boogieing with their hands on each other's waists. The exposed backs of the women clad in backless evening wear changed colour like chameleons in the disco lights. And when their male partners' hands roamed over those backs, we who only stood around watching the action, would ache with desire. Some of the men would take to the dance floor after emptying their glasses at the bar. After exhausting themselves on the floor, they would again hit the bar.

That was a popular discotheque in Kathmandu.

Leny (Lendup Dorjee), who was displaced from Bhutan, had opened a casino at the Soaltee in 1968. The discotheque was located inside the casino, where the Shahs, Ranas and other aristocrats and members of the social elite gathered in the evening. Most of the parties there were informal or private. The unmarried came with their partners. The married, too, came with their boyfriends or girlfriends. It was rare to see married couples there together. Many young hippies, both Nepalis and foreigners, with their dreadlocks and baggy pyjamas, also frequented the discotheque.

Thanks to my association with Kiran, I got a chance to witness the flourishing nightlife of the early 1970s in Kathmandu, which the hippies oddly called Cat-Man-Do.

I had never seen the discotheque empty, right from the time I started going there. While the rest of Kathmandu was sleeping soundly, this place, with its flashy, coloured lights, kept going all night. The movers and shakers came to this discotheque. They drank there. And they also danced. This was the same class that went on shopping sprees to Hong Kong and Bangkok because they did not find enough to spend their money on in Kathmandu. They would spend their nights at discotheques and parties, tipping the waiters after every drink. During their leisure time, this lot would also make jaunts to Nagarkot, Kakani and Pokhara.

They were very limited in number but they were loyal customers who spent the day waiting for nightfall. They were addicted to nightlife the way some people are to drugs. I could also see that the number of foreigners visiting the discotheque had been increasing because of the large numbers of hippies flocking to Kathmandu. All of them were eager to spend their money on a good night out.

An idea spontaneously popped into my mind, something special and creative.

We too would start a discotheque. We named it Copper Floor because the dance floor was made of copper. The discotheque, which I launched in partnership with Kiran at Laligurans Hotel at Lazimpat, was my first independent undertaking. There were other discotheques in Kathmandu—Peter's Place and Foot Tappers on King's Way—by the time we opened ours. To stand out from the competition, we imported a sound system from Singapore and disco lights and other accessories from Hong Kong. Kiran and I went there to select the equipment.

We set up a 'members' club', charging Rs 2500 for annual membership. There were around 300 regular members. Most of them were either blue bloods or diplomats. Prince Dhirendra and Prabhakar Rana, the great grandson of Juddha Shumsher, also frequented our discotheque. Sudhir Rai, a senior captain with Royal Nepal Airlines, was the voluntary disc jockey. Women, too, thronged our place. Around half a dozen female flight attendants from Royal Nepal would visit regularly. All the men were interested in them. Our discotheque was also the meeting place for film stars from the Nepali movies. Many famous personalities of today would come to the discotheque accompanied by girls whom they would introduce as their girlfriends from Darjeeling or Kalimpong. I too was attracted to some of the girls, and some of them were attracted to me.

Copper Floor became a successful business venture.

Father was not very pleased with my decision to start a discotheque, though he did not actively oppose it. He wanted me to look after Arun Emporium, but I was not interested in the retail business. I wanted to do something novel and creative like Copper Floor. I think the fact that his son was at least involved in a business gave him some consolation.

I would always return home between 2 a.m. and 3 a.m. I would take off my shoes and try to climb the stairs stealthily, like a cat, so as not to disturb my parents. It was a wooden staircase, however, and it would creak on even the lightest step. Father would wake up. Sometimes he would be waiting for me. I would sneak into my room and close the door lightly, only to find father there. It would scare the hell out of me.

Still, my father did not scold the son who came home like a thief in the wee hours of the day.

'Oh, you've come,' he would say. 'Have you eaten?'

'Yes,' I would reply timidly.

'In that case, you'd better go to bed.' He would close the door as he left the room.

Father had unusual confidence on me. He was confident that any son of his must have intrinsic business sense and would never let him down. That was why he never interfered in my work. And I never let him down either. Even when I was hanging around with friends, I never smoked or drank alcohol, though I do smoke and drink now.

Many people were under the impression that we had opened the discotheque just for fun. They thought it was all about drinking to excess and dirty dancing, and held the place in contempt. But it was purely business for us. Though afternoons were leisure time for us, Kiran and I were totally disciplined and thoroughly professional, I would say, when it came to our job.

The broader society, of course, could not comprehend this. Chaudhary's son comes home at midnight! I became the talk of the town. Some people even started to defame my father indirectly: 'His son is spoilt rotten', or 'His son has fallen into bad company'. Some even tried to poison my father's mind against me. However, malicious gossip could never affect the relationship between my father and me. I wanted to give a fitting response to my detractors, but before I could do so I became even more notorious, under circumstances I would never have wished for.

Tinku was my cousin, son of my mother's sister. Because my aunt had financial difficulties, my mother had taken care of Tinku as a member of our own immediate family from the time he was four or five years old. Mother would say, 'I have four sons, Arun is the third and Tinku is the youngest.'

Then, one day, Tinku suddenly disappeared.

There was absolute panic at home. We put notices in all the newspapers. We informed the police. But the boy was nowhere to be found until five days later, when the body of a child was found in a blind alley in Tebahal, close to our neighbourhood.

We were horror-struck. It was gut-wrenching. My mother broke down.

Father and I went to identify the body. As we reached the alley leading to the Nepal Airlines building, a foul smell turned our stomachs. Many policemen were there. I was too afraid to face what might lie there but father went ahead. It was Tinku. He had been murdered.

'Judging by the state of the body,' a policeman said, 'he must have died four or five days ago.'

The police started to take statements from us, day in and day out. Sometimes they summoned father and mother, and sometimes just me and my brothers. I became the prime suspect! I was suspected of killing my cousin to prevent him from getting a share of our inheritance. The police appeared to have made that assumption solely on the basis of my profession as a discotheque operator and what was to them my flamboyant lifestyle. They went to Laligurans Hotel and to Copper Floor to conduct investigations. I noticed that people I had thought were friends now started to turn their backs on me. At the hotel, I felt unwelcome. One day, Kiran openly told me, 'The police obviously see you as a suspect. This might lead to big trouble for all of us.'

I was speechless.

Had some other friend said that to me, I could have endured it. However, my closest friend, the very one I turned to for sympathy and support, was, it appeared, trying to get rid of me in my moment of crisis. Nothing embitters the heart so much as betrayal by an intimate friend.

On the way back home, my head was spinning. Everything in front of my eyes looked shaky and blurred. I walked straight into my room, locked the door, covered my face with a towel, and cried my heart out for a long time.

The police would have sucked us dry had Indra Bhakta Shrestha not come to our rescue.

Indra Bhaktajee (prominent industrialist Ravi Bhakta Shrestha's father) was a family friend. His father treated my father as his son. Both grew up together in the same neighbourhood. Ravi Bhakta and I became good friends too. At a time when the entire neighbourhood had stopped supporting us, Indra Bhaktajee came to our rescue. His son-in-law, Narayan Prasad Shrestha, was head of administration at the royal palace. 'No one in Lunkaran Das's family would be capable of an act like that,' Indra Bhaktajee told his son-in-law. 'I can personally guarantee that.'

Narayan Prasadjee immediately directed the zonal administrator of Kathmandu, Surya Prasad Shrestha, to 'conduct the investigation properly and impartially and stop harassing the family'.

At the height of the Panchayat era, such a directive from an officer at the royal palace made the entire police administration stop and take notice. The officers who used to summon us to the police station for interrogation became nervous. I must assume they had been planning to extort money from my father, a wealthy Marwari businessman, as they saw him, by framing me or possibly one of my brothers for murder. After Indra Bhaktajee's intervention, the case took a new turn and fresh investigations began in earnest. It took less than two days for the police to find the real culprits.

A couple of carpenters who had worked in our house had abducted Tinku. They had noticed how my mother pampered him, and came up with the idea of kidnapping him for ransom—just a few thousand rupees, ironically. They waited for an opportunity and grabbed him. Tinku, however, started to cry at the lodge where he had been held captive. They gagged him by stuffing rags in his mouth and the child choked to death. In panic, the kidnappers stuffed his body into a bag and dumped it in the alley in Tebahal. Both the kidnappers pleaded guilty.

This horrible event did not destroy the close relationship we had with my aunt's family. My mother took good care of her sister throughout her life, and we still support her family today.

I, however, become disenchanted with my friends. This is how the world treats you, I thought. You have to fight your own battles! You need to stand up, and give a hand to yourself. The people I had thought of as firm friends had turned away from me when I was in trouble. Once the trouble had passed, perhaps they would have liked our friendship to go back to the way it was, but I now turned away from them.

I quit Copper Floor.

I decided to become a chartered accountant.
I had to go to New Delhi to appear for the entrance examination for chartered accountancy. I did not have good contacts in Delhi back then, in 1975.

In those days, I had a close friend, Sudhir Rai. He was employed at the reception of Hotel De L' Annapurna on Kingsway. He had a red Toyota Corolla. In the evening, after office hours, he had a second job, hiring out his car as a taxi with himself as the driver. I have done rounds of the city in his taxi. We would drive, and I would pay him for his time.

Sudhir was born and brought up in Dehradun. He had keen interest in music. He was for many years a drummer in a band with his friend Malcolm Edwards in New Delhi before he settled in Kathmandu. Sometimes he pitched in as the DJ at Copper Floor.

After completing the formalities for the CA entrance examinations, I said to Sudhir, 'I have to go to Delhi to appear for these exams. How do I go about it?'

He agreed to accompany me. We went to Delhi.

Malcolm Edwards had a two-room apartment there. He took me to his flat. We stayed there for around fifteen days while I wrote the exams. There were also other guests at Malcolm's place. There was a large cushion in the living room. I would sit on it to study during the day, and sleep on it at night.

Sudhir always wanted to fly. He had taken lessons at a flying club while he lived in Delhi. One day, he took me to the club. The aircraft parked there looked like toys to me. He asked me to sit in one and then got in to sit beside me. I thought he was kidding, but he suddenly turned on the ignition and started the plane. The toy-like plane jolted along like an empty kerosene can on a bumpy road. I did not know whether he could actually fly the aircraft though he had said he had trained to fly. The ear-piercing sound was enough to scare the wits out of me. I was completely shaken with fear; I felt I was suddenly being hurled out of a Ferris wheel.

I then realized the plane had taken off.

'Look around! Just look around!' Sudhir was yelling. I felt nauseated whenever I opened my eyes. How could I look around?

Once the turbulence subsided, I started to feel a bit less frightened. Slowly, I opened my eyes. The plane was flying over Delhi. Seeing how petrified I was, Sudhir burst into laughter. I was still very afraid. I looked out at the body of the aircraft. It looked so fragile. How could it resist the strong wind blowing against it? I turned towards the pilot, thinking here was a rookie in the cockpit. Could he actually fly the plane?

'Don't be afraid! Don't be afraid!' he said, trying to cheer me up as we circled over Delhi.

I was petrified again when we descended. He would have to try hard to land the plane, but the strong wind would lift it up and crash it down, I thought.

Sudhir later went to Canada to learn flying. He no longer flies those toy planes. He flies Boeings with Nepal Airlines Corporation.

As for me, I did not pass the CA entrance exams.

Early at the helm

Big business houses dominated the Federation of Nepalese Chambers of Commerce and Industry (FNCCI). These included the Golchha Group, the Dugar Group and the Madanlal Chiranjeelal (MC) Group. They had almost monopolized the quota for export of jute and other industrial products. Small and honest businessmen like my father had to struggle for a small share of the quotas. For the big houses,

the FNCCI was just a tool to dominate trade by staying close
to the helm of power. To sharpen that tool, they fielded and
elected their own candidates. By keeping the FNCCI under
their control, they could leverage benefits in the controlled
business environment of the time.

Indra Bhaktajee decided to stand for election to the
FNCCI in 1978. He sought my father's support. Father was
indebted to him. He was not just a childhood friend but had
also helped free me from the false charge of Tinku's murder.

On the other hand, the big business families had
announced their candidate—Juddha Bahadur Shrestha. This
was the same Shrestha out of whose premises we ran Arun
Emporium. This put my father in a spot. As the election
fever rose, the Marwari community issued an order that its
members should support Judhha Bahadur.

Without mincing words, my father told Juddha Bahadur,
'I have a family bond to Indra Bhaktajee and I have already
pledged my support to him. Please don't put me in a difficult
position.'

Juddha Bahadurjee was not angry or disappointed with
my father.

'I understand your predicament,' he replied. 'I know you
have a familial relationship with him. You should stand by
him and I will accept that.'

Both the candidates secured equal number of votes in
that election. Indra Bhaktajee won the election through a
lucky draw. Father, however, did not join his team of office-
bearers. Rather, he brought in Hulas Chand Golchha from the
competing panel as a vice president of the FNCCI.

I told my father, 'They've used you again.'

The leaders of the Marwari community were infuriated
with my father after that election. They could not digest the

fact that a man from their own community had gone against them, and branded him 'anti-Marwari'; father fell ill within a few days of the election.

One day, when I returned home at sunset, I saw father lying in his bed, with mother sitting beside him. I headed straight to my room upstairs. I heard my mother call out just as I was about to open my door, and ran down the stairs.

Father's face looked pale. He was breathing with difficulty. His forehead and nose where bathed in sweat. Mother was fanning him, and from time to time would wipe away the sweat from his face with her hands.

I was dumbstruck. I just stood and stared at him.

'Call the doctor immediately,' mother said.

There was no phone in that room. I dashed to the room where the phone was and called our family doctor Sachche Kumar Pahadi.

'Call the ambulance immediately,' he said. 'I'm on my way.'

Father's body was drenched in sweat by the time Dr Pahadi arrived. He checked my father's pulse and placed a stethoscope on his chest. The doctor's eyes said it all. When the ambulance arrived, Dr Pahadi would not even let my father get out of bed. He brought father downstairs, lifting the bed itself. Mother could not stop weeping.

The ambulance raced. I clasped father's hands but there was no response. His hands were cold and sweaty. I looked at father and at Dr Pahadi. The doctor was checking my father's heart with his stethoscope.

'He's had a heart attack,' he said softly.

I froze with terror.

Suddenly, my life had taken an unexpected turn. Father was on life support in the ICU. My brothers were not fully grown up. I had just graduated from Shankar Dev Campus in Kathmandu and, at twenty-three, apart from the discotheque venture from which I had now disassociated myself, had had no real responsibilities. And here was Dr Pahadi telling me, 'Your father cannot continue to work now. Make sure he gets complete rest.'

I felt as if a storm had swept away my world, as if I was a bird that had been flying free and was now trapped in a cage.

Our family business was at a critical juncture at the time. Father had just launched Pashupati Biscuits. We had only just received a licence for Maha Laxmi Maida (White Flour) Mills. Our stainless steel, synthetic yarn and hosiery factories had closed down. India had started to impose restrictions on the import quota for goods coming from Nepal on the grounds that the system was being abused. There were disputes with the Kedias and the Jatias who were managing our factories. Only Arun Emporium was doing well.

Then came another shock.

I would frequently accompany my father to Bombay and to Vellore, a small town in the Indian state of Tamil Nadu where he was undergoing treatment at a large Christian missionary hospital. Father had employed one of his distant cousins, whom we called Uncle Rajkumar, to look after Arun Emporium and Arun Impex while we were away. We thought Uncle Rajkumar was loyal to my father. However, when we had just returned from one of our trips to Vellore, he came to see father. He inquired about his health and initially seemed concerned, but when he was about to leave, he handed a letter to my father. Father asked me to read it aloud. It said:

'I have served you faithfully for many years. I had a lot of other opportunities which I never pursued just for your sake, even though I wanted to start my own business. Now it's time for me to think about my own welfare. I want a 25 per cent partnership in your business. Please don't misunderstand me. I believe a 25 per cent share is my right after having served you for so long.'

We were shaken to the core by Uncle Rajkumar's demand. It appeared that the people we trusted to look after our business interests were betraying us. We had had a bitter experience with Binay Agrawal in the flooring and furnishing trade, and now Uncle Rajkumar was following suit. His demand was absolutely unjustified, especially in the light of my father's failing health and the situation we were in. Father had never promised to make him a partner in the business. Outside of business, we treated Uncle Rajkumar like a member of the family, but within the business he was a paid employee like any other. We had not seen the greed lurking behind his concern for his 'brother'. He had raised the issue of partnership at a time when my father was unable to work and fighting for his life and—Uncle Rajkumar must have presumed—in no position to refuse him.

It seemed Uncle Rajkumar had been planning this move for a long time. He had already opened a shop, run by his brother, in Birgunj, and was hoping my father's ill-health would indirectly benefit his own business. However, his crude demand for a 25 per cent share in our business exposed the true extent of his greed. I decided to give him a fitting reply. This was a crucial and decisive move I made on the chessboard of my business world. Had I conceded to his demand, it would have given me more freedom in some ways. With him running the business, I would have had less responsibility and more free time, and could even have gone back to spending my evenings at Copper Floor. But that would have delayed my entry into the battlefield of business by many years.

I moved my first piece on the chessboard.

Father asked Uncle Rajkumar to meet him in his room a few days after receiving the letter. I was also present.

'I understand your feelings,' father told him very calmly. 'You're right. You have been taking care of my business for a long time and you shall continue to do so.'

Uncle Rajkumar's face brightened with joy.

Father continued, 'Binod has nothing to do. Take him with you and teach him the trade. He'll be able to assist you while I'm out of the picture.'

Uncle Rajkumar could not disagree. Perhaps he thought there was no threat from a boy who tried to avoid work even when his father was around. Perhaps he thought he could make me dance to his tune.

My first move was successful.

It was time for the second.

I would stay at the shop for a while and then return to my old ways. Uncle Rajkumar was content. Once I came up with a proposal, 'Uncle, let's go on a trip to Japan.'

'Why would we go to Japan?' he asked.

'Let's go on a buying trip. We can meet the wholesalers personally and bring stuff back with us if we find anything good,' I replied innocently.

He was probably surprised and annoyed that I seemed to be taking an interest in the business, so I quickly dispelled that impression. 'If you go to Japan, it gives me an excuse to go with you,' I said. 'We can mix business with pleasure.'

His expression changed.

My second move too was a successful one.

While Uncle Rajkumar went out to meet business contacts in Osaka, I would pretend to hang around in the markets. One evening, I coaxed him into going to a discotheque with me. Our relationship became less formal after we started visiting the discotheque together. He began to open up. I would ask questions about the business in a seemingly light-hearted way and he would give me information quite freely. I was like the camel in the fable that wanted to get its nose into the tent. Uncle Rajkumar also became more generous with his time. Earlier, when he called on business contacts, he used to leave me behind in the hotel, but now he started to take me with him, introducing me as his nephew. Establishing personal relations with these contacts and having them recognize me as a legitimate representative of the family business was exactly what I wanted. I wanted to become the camel that displaced the owner of the tent.

We would visit the production and sales centres to select clothes and other items. By day, we would inquire about prices and seek quotations, and by evening hit the discotheques.

Uncle had decided to befriend me, and I continued to pick his brains at every opportunity. By the end of that month-long visit to Japan, I understood every aspect of our business dealings there: our contacts, our sources, prices, how the goods were shipped to Nepal, how customs clearances were obtained, and who our clearing agents were.

My third move had been successful. I now contemplated my fourth.

I started to stay longer at office and began looking into the accounts. At times, I would check the accounts myself. Even at that point, I think, Uncle Rajkumar did not see me as a serious threat.

One day I said to him, 'It must be really tough for you. You have a lot to look after, on top of the accounts.'

'Yes, indeed,' he replied.

'I'm not of much help. Why don't you hire someone who knows a bit about the job?' I suggested.

'Whom shall we hire?'

Seizing the opportunity, I made my move. 'There's someone I know who's good at keeping accounts.'

Uncle Rajkumar did not reply.

The very next day, I handed over the entire account-keeping job to Indu Badani, someone I trusted completely. Uncle got quite a shock and went to my father to complain. 'Let Binod do whatever he wants,' father said, to sidestep the issue. 'I can't handle it any more.'

When he heard my father's response, it dawned on Rajkumar that we were planning to ease him out of the business. Naturally, he decided not to cooperate. He tried to keep some details of the accounts to himself and refused to answer any questions, which led to tension in the office. Meanwhile, I had already established direct contact with the Japanese producers and distributors. I started contacting distributors in Korea and Thailand as well. I started to place orders myself, and also to clear the goods, contacting the customs clearing agents myself. Through Indu Badani, I already had control of the accounts. Uncle Rajkumar no longer had a real role in the business.

I made my fifth and last move. I handed him a letter. He read it out in front of me:

'You have helped us a lot in running Arun Emporium and Arun Impex, and I am grateful to you for that. However, since I have now started to run the entire business myself, there is no longer a role for you. Hence, after you collect your severance pay, I bid you farewell.'

Uncle Rajkumar was dumbstruck.

I had given him a fitting reply, exactly six months after he had handed his letter to my father.

I had won the game in just five moves. Uncle was defeated at his own game.

I now wanted to bring the Pashupati Biscuit factory in Biratnagar fully under my control. Two brothers, Bajrang and Radheshyam, were managing the factory. I suspected they had ideas similar to Uncle Rajkumar's. Father had given a 10 per cent share in the project to each of them as his working partners. After father fell ill, they were running the show.

I had to manoeuvre my pieces on the chessboard, just to gain control of my own family's enterprises. I went to Biratnagar and, during a meeting with the brothers, told them, 'The competition is getting tough. If we don't become more professional, we're not going to survive.'

They asked what they could do.

'Let's hire chartered accountants. Let's bring in market researchers to study the market. Let's identify where we are lagging behind and explore the possibility of exporting,' I said, setting out my plans.

They did not agree with my plan to hire experts. They would rather have taken care of everything themselves. Perhaps they guessed I had an ulterior motive. But I took a firm stand and appointed two chartered accountants, M.R. Maheshwori and J.R. Bhandari. Then my supposed partners' real intentions became crystal clear. They refused to cooperate with the chartered accountants. The chartered accountants told me they were refusing to provide them essential documents, which made it impossible for them to do their job. I pleaded with them to hang in there.

The brothers were so brazen that they started being deliberately obstructionist in their dealings with me. If they knew I had arrived in Biratnagar, they would simply leave the place. Faced with such a degree of non-cooperation, I opened an office for myself in Biratnagar and continued to move my pieces from there. In the meantime, I launched Maha Laxmi Maida Mills. Father had agreed to give shares of 10 per cent each to the working partners there too. I kept up the pressure on the partners in Pashupati Biscuits pushing them more and more until they gave up and left the business.

We managed to set up a kind of independent industrial structure in Biratnagar.

I had won the second game of chess.

I spent a lot of my time in Biratnagar in those days. After putting a system in place for Arun Emporium and its subsidiary firm, I entrusted Indu Badani to look after that business in Kathmandu. I then focused on expanding the biscuit venture, including production of the raw materials for it. Establishing Maha Laxmi Maida Mills was part of that plan. We also started to produce the packaging for the biscuits. We developed new brands and began researching the market in the eastern hills of Nepal and in India. I travelled to the towns in the eastern hills—such as Dharan, Dhankuta, Ilam and Panchthar—and from there to the north-eastern Indian states of Sikkim, Assam and Meghalaya, with model packets and promotional materials for Pashupati Biscuits.

Within a year of launch of the promotional campaign, Pashupati Biscuits was well established in the markets of

Nepal and was becoming increasingly popular in north-east India. After jute during my father's time, Pashupati Biscuits became the second product we exported. By 1980–81, it had found a good market in India.

The building in which our corporate office is located—at Sanepa in Kathmandu valley—is known by many as 'Chaudhary's radio office'.

Around sixty years ago, father had loaned money to Surendra Shumsher Rana, a member of the Rana oligarchy. Twenty years later, Rana summoned my father to tell him that he could not pay back the money but would instead give him a plot of land at Sanepa as compensation. In those days, the area was nothing but farmland. The plot was close to the Surendra Bhawan maternity hospital where I was born. There were no other buildings in the vicinity. Rather than risk receiving no repayment at all, father accepted the deal, but the plot of land remained idle for a long time.

After the expansion of Pashupati Biscuits and Maha Laxmi Maida, I was looking for a new area of investment. Through family sources, I came to know that the deputy inspector general of police, Narayan Singh Shah, had a good relationship with the management of the Japanese company National Panasonic. Through Shah, I made contact with National Panasonic and, after protracted negotiations, got the contract to assemble parts for National Panasonic Radio in Nepal.

This was my first collaboration with a multinational company.

Around thirty years ago, I built a single-storeyed building on that plot of land at Sanepa and started producing radios. I also set up a small office there. People called it 'Chaudhary's radio office'. After the business expanded, I added another storey to the building and decided to relocate my office there from Khichapokhari. Another reason I decided to relocate my office was that friends would frequently call in at Khichapokhari. They would drop by in the evening and I would have to devote considerable time to socializing when I should have been working. I was sick and tired of it.

When I was setting up the corporate office at Sanepa, I had one important thing in mind. Now that I was collaborating with a multinational company, I knew I had to project a different image of myself. If you want to be successful, then you have to project an image of success. I hired an interior decorator for an ultramodern design for the flooring and furnishings. Father's experience in the field was a great help. We had some difficulty choosing the right colour for the curtains. People came up with so many different options. The window of my office on the top floor of the Sanepa building overlooks the entire city of Kathmandu. Why would I want to block out a sight like that? I decided not to put up curtains at all. The flooring and furnishings have changed many times over the years. The colour of the walls has changed too. But the window still does not have any curtains. My desk faces the window, and I still have a sweeping view of Kathmandu. There is also a balcony with a small but nice garden outside my office.

The collaboration with National Panasonic took my confidence to an all-time high. I was filled with enthusiasm and started to look far and wide for new opportunities through my professional contacts, friends and relatives.

I soon found myself collaborating with Suzuki Motors of Japan. I had met a high-ranking manager of Suzuki Motors during one of my visits to Japan. They were looking for an authorized agent in Nepal. I immediately forwarded a proposal to them. Two other Nepali companies were also interested. Suzuki gave conditional, temporary agent status to all three of us; whoever sold the most vehicles in a six-month period would get the authorized dealership. This was an innovative way of doing business, pitting the parties seeking dealership against each other. A true businessman never works harder than when he fears losing a lucrative business opportunity. Suzuki's proposition also ensured that our business dealings with Japan ran smoothly even during the trial period.

I put all my energy into the project. My contacts helped me a lot. Within six months, I got the Suzuki Motors dealership, defeating my two competitors. It was a quantum leap from radios to automobiles, not just in terms of cost and size of business but in relation to the company's market expansion and organizational growth. Later, Maruti of India also entered into a collaboration with Suzuki Motors and our dealership was changed to Maruti Suzuki's. My youngest brother Arun still looks after that side of the business.

I was growing, and so were my business and my office.

The scattered energies were synergizing. I had formed a big hub from a number of comparatively small and disparate businesses. I was collaborating with multinational companies such as National Panasonic and Suzuki Motors. The foundation for a big and robust company with its own corporate headquarters was being laid. I had taken the leap from traditional business management into the corporate world. Sitting in a tall building, my horizons grew wider.

My dreams began to grow new wings. I was ready to explore greater heights.

The banner of Bhuramal Lunkaran Das Chaudhary was already displaying a new avatar: the Chaudhary Group.

11

Salaam Bombay

'What will you do now?' my father had asked me after I passed the School Leaving Certificate (SLC) examination with flying colours. I was ranked among the top five in the exams, which is still dubbed 'the iron gate of life'.

I glanced at my mother. Her eyes danced playfully. I understood her signal. Only a little earlier, I had told her what I wished to do, and she had told me that father had to approve it.

I never had the guts to ask my father for anything directly. But now that I had done so well in the exams, I somehow mustered up the courage to make my request.

'I want to see Bombay. Please let me go.'

Father looked at mother. Mother looked at me. I lowered my gaze to the floor.

Father walked out of the room. Mother too lowered her gaze, hinting that she was not happy. I sprang to my feet and grabbed a pair of pants from a hanger.

'Where are you going?' mother asked.

'Out,' I snapped.

As I was about to wear my pants, my father reappeared. He was accompanied by Shyam Sunder Sureka, an employee at Arun Emporium. Father had brought him from Muzaffarpur in India to keep our accounts. He was always well groomed, and used fragrant hair oil and a dash of perfume. As soon as he entered, his perfume permeated the entire room.

Pointing towards me, father told Shyam Sundar in Hindi, 'He wants to see Bombay. Take him around there for fifteen to twenty days.'

I wanted to hug him and say that he was the best father in the world, but I could not. Rather, I was overcome with shyness. Mother was smiling at me. I replaced the pants on the hanger and quietly left the room.

Besides being an Indian national, Shyam Sundar had already been to Bombay. The fact that they were sending their child away for the first time could have been disturbing for my parents, but they felt my safety was assured with an experienced man like Shyam Sundar accompanying me. As for me, I was doubly excited about the trip because Shyam Sundar was taking me.

Mother started to weep when she applied the auspicious vermilion powder to my forehead while seeing me off, as if I were going on a worldwide expedition, and not to a city in a neighbouring country. To me, it was actually as exciting as setting off on a world tour. It was the first long journey of my life.

Father gave me ten Rs 1000 notes, adding that he had also given some money to Shyam Sunder.

I grabbed my bag and followed Shyam. We took a bus to Birgunj and then headed to Muzaffarpur. There we caught a train to Bombay. That was my first rail journey.

Father had also handed over a letter addressed to a cloth merchant by the name of Gulraj Babulal in Bombay, whose firm our family had been dealing with since my grandfather's days. Babulal lived near the Kalba Devi temple in Bombay.

After stepping out from the Victoria Terminus of the Indian Railways in Bombay, we caught a three-wheeler to the temple area. We did not have any problem finding Babulal's residence. Everybody there knew Gulraj Babulal because of his old and established business.

I handed over the letter father had sent him. He read it intently and then said excitedly, 'So you are Lukarandas's son! And you want to see Bombay, right?'

I nodded.

Gulraj Babulal was a fun-loving person who also encouraged me to have fun. 'Eat, drink and be merry! You don't need to worry about a thing,' he told me.

Shyam Sunder and I had a ball in Bombay. We ate, drank and pampered ourselves in so many ways!

It has been a long time since I last visited the Kalba Devi area, though I visit Mumbai, as the city is called now, frequently. As a result, I do not know how the area is faring these days, but back then, it was a very interesting place to hang around.

It was a big mundi for cloth merchants. They would sit on thick cushions and trade cloth all day long; at night, they would dust the same cushions and lie down on them. Babulal laid cushions out for us too. We would roam the city throughout the day and return to his place at night to dream of the city.

We would be jolted out of our dreams when it came to answering nature's call in the morning, when we had to wait in a queue for our turn to use the communal toilet shared by the entire neighbourhood. It was operated on a first-come-first-served basis, so those who woke up late had the most agonizing wait. Luckily, this ordeal I faced in Bombay was not that extreme.

I was pretty shy about taking off my clothes and having a bath in the presence of another person. I never had to experience anything like that in Kathmandu. The two-week long stay in Bombay, however, forced me to get over my self-consciousness. There was not a single proper bathroom in the neighbourhood. All they had was a public tap where women would queue up from the wee hours of the day to fetch water for their homes. Someone would always try to push into the line and the other women would shout and curse that person. To bathe, you had to somehow manage to get a bucket of water from that tap and take it to an almost open bathing area for men nearby. There was another bathing area strictly for women on the other side of the tap. People would be busy applying soap to their body and socializing while bathing.

Initially, I would hurriedly apply soap, pour water over myself and run out of the bathing area as quickly as possible. I did not even rinse the lather off properly, and my body would itch through the day. To add to that, the humid climate of Bombay made me perspire heavily. Soon, I started to bathe properly, regardless of who might have been looking at me.

The mundi would open between seven and eight in the morning. We would wake up at six, pack up our cushions and freshen up. We would have breakfast and dinner at Babulal's place and, in between, would eat out while exploring the city.

I really relished the famous *pav bhaji* of Bombay, which is ubiquitous on all the sidewalks of the city. Despite its other shortcomings, the mundi served food that was great and filling. The merchants would keep their own cooks, who were popularly known as 'maharaj'. They offered a thali, a plate of assorted vegetables, fritters, yoghurt, milk, poppadum, salads, and several other items, besides rice and rotis.

Shyam Sunder would say, 'The way they feed themselves and others is simply exemplary.' I would say, 'Agreed. But you don't feel like eating anything when you think about the toilet.'

I wanted to tour Bombay on those three-wheelers, but we did not have enough money for that. Father had given us only a limited amount to spend. Though he had told us we could call him up if we needed more, we did not want to bother him. We travelled around the city by public bus and train.

I was crazy about movies. How could I possibly visit Bombay and not see the homes of famous movie stars? I would take Shyam Sunder around and show him the houses of superstars like Dev Anand, Amitabh Bachchan and Rekha. God knows whether they were indeed the houses of these stars, but my heart would start to race like a local train as soon as we approached those sprawling bungalows. I would think to myself: What if I run into Amitabh Bachchan or Dev Anand? What would I say? What would I do? Would Dev Anand still remember me, the boy who ran from pillar to post in Kathmandu searching for black Jaguar socks for him? Would he recognize me if I reintroduced myself to him? He was yet to pay for the socks!

I was jolted out of these reveries by Shyam Sunder who would suddenly grab my hands and pull me towards him.

'Stop daydreaming, would you?' he snapped at me once.

But then, he too was mesmerized by the city.

'Guess what? Every evening Amitabh steps on to his balcony to wave at his fans gathered outside,' he said, waving his hands Amitabh-style. That got me even more excited. When would the evening come when Amitabh would appear at his balcony so that I could wave at him in such a way that he would notice me? We spent around four evenings in front of his house but he never did come out to his balcony.

Shyam Sunder was embarrassed. 'He must be away on a shoot,' he said, putting on a brave face.

We visited the Gateway of India.

Travel writers label the entire city as the Gateway of India. The historical monument is a twenty-six-metre-high basalt arch, erected in 1924 to commemorate the visit of the British monarch George V back in 1911.

Another important historical landmark stands nearby—the Taj hotel. The first monument symbolizes British colonial rule while the second epitomizes the defiance of it. Legend has it that towards the end of the nineteenth century, Mumbai industrialist Jamsetji Nusserwanji Tata was barred from entering a local hotel where only Europeans were allowed. Remembering that insult, Tata vowed to build a hotel in the city that would not only allow unhindered access to Indians, but would also stand among the best hotels in the world.

His dream became a reality in 1903. There were only seventeen visitors when the Taj hotel was inaugurated that year. Today, it is considered among India's proudest monuments. Its international clientele has included celebrities ranging from prominent political leaders to rock stars—Louis Armstrong, Mick Jagger, Madonna, Brad Pitt, Bill Clinton, Jacqueline Kennedy Onassis, Margaret Thatcher, George Bernard Shaw, Prince Charles, and many more. The wealthy are happy to call it their temporary home. The middle class aspire to stay there one day. As for the poor, it represents just a wonderful dream.

Even today, one can see at any time people simply standing outside the hotel, watching the movement of vehicles in and out. I was part of that crowd during that first visit.

I came to know about the significance of the Taj hotel much later in life. On my first visit to Bombay, I was dazzled by the royal caravan of vehicles that entered the hotel premises while I hung around the Gateway of India. I even sat down on the pavement in front of the hotel to keenly monitor the activities inside the hotel. A tall and sturdy Maratha gatekeeper would open the door of each car that drew up to the hotel and salute the guests. The guests would then proudly walk into the hotel. Some of them were friendly and offered a tip to the gatekeeper, probably Rs 50 or maybe even Rs 100. This would lead to the gatekeeper saluting them again.

I could hardly restrain my excitement on seeing all this.

'What's this all about?' I asked Shyam.

Shyam was waiting for an opportunity to air his general knowledge. He launched into a lecture: 'This is the greatest hotel in India. They call it the Taj hotel. The biggest of the film stars, industrialists, leaders and foreigners, all of them stay here, eat here.'

'Let's go inside and see for ourselves,' I suggested.

He stared at me.

'Do you see that guard over there?' he said, pointing to the Maratha gatekeeper. 'He would grab you by your neck and drag you out of the hotel.'

I felt intimidated. As we left, I kept turning back to look at the hotel.

To me, the guests who had entered the hotel amid salutes from the gatekeeper appeared the most wonderful people in the world. Who could they be? And what kind of facilities must that hotel be providing? Could I ever in my life enter the hotel, receive a salute and enjoy all the facilities it offered?

I lay awake for most of that night on Babulal's cushion.

Today, as part of Taj Asia, we are in partnership with that same Taj hotel. We own and operate luxury hotels and resorts in many cities in Sri Lanka, the Maldives and Malaysia, and are planning to expand further. I visit Mumbai frequently in connection with these ventures. And whenever I visit, there is only one place I stay—the grand old Taj hotel.

Most of the suites in the hotel cost between Rs 50,000 and Rs 1 lakh per night. All of them face the Gateway of India. Every time I stay there, I make it a point to look out of the window and drift back to the past. The Gateway of India, the Taj hotel, the road leading to the hotel, the pavement . . . all remain the same; even the gatekeeper resembles the Maratha gatekeeper from my memories. The royal caravan of vehicles enters the hotel in the same way it did decades ago, and the gatekeeper salutes the proud guests just as his predecessor had in the past.

Nothing seems to have changed.

I too am the same person, even though my status has changed.

Back in those days, I would squat on the pavement looking at the hotel with wide eyes. Today, I look out on the road from the costliest suite in the hotel, owing to my partnership with its owner.

My eyes would sparkle with wonder back then and they still sparkle today. I am the same boy who once squatted on the pavement to behold the splendour of the hotel, the son of an ordinary businessman, who dreamt about the hotel and went on to live that dream. Yes, I am the same boy, now retracing his footsteps from that pavement to this suite.

Somehow, I believe that destiny and not just my own hard work, has brought me to here. I often try to show these footsteps to my sons, Nirvana, Rahul and Varun. My life journey has taken me from that point to this point, I tell them; you guys are starting from here, and now I am going to see where your journey takes you.

12

Birth of an MNC

The Government of India had organized an investment conference to which Nepal was an invitee. The government decided to include some of us entrepreneurs in the official delegation. A meeting was convened at the ministry of industry to discuss this.

'Do you know why India is organizing this conference?' I asked the government officials during the meeting. There was no answer.

'The Indian government is organizing the conference to attract foreign investment,' I said. 'Why do you want to send us to the conference when you know very well that our law doesn't allow a Nepali to invest abroad?'

The government officials were speechless.

'Are we supposed to go there as mute spectators? Are we supposed to back away, citing the law of the land if someone comes up with a good investment proposal?'

They could not utter a word.

'We will take part in the conference if you can give us a concrete guarantee that we will be allowed to invest in India if a good proposal comes up,' I added. 'Otherwise, we don't want to go there to embarrass ourselves.'

The central bank and the ministry of industry then discussed the matter at length.

They concluded that they could not provide us a concrete guarantee on the matter, as the law prohibited investment in other countries. But they were quick to suggest that we could initiate reforms and that they would offer us moral support to any good investment proposal in India. The government, however, is yet to complete these reforms.

As for me, I have already expanded my business around the world, paving my own path.

This section is about that chapter of my professional life in which I took up the challenge to transform the Chaudhary Group into Nepal's first multinational corporation. That challenge—or rather, fight, I would say—is still going on.

When I lost the election for the post of the FNCCI president in 1996, I was so disturbed by the defeat that I left Kathmandu immediately afterwards and headed for a retreat in Bharatpur with Lily. I felt embittered by my defeat which had taken place despite all my efforts to raise Nepal's private sector up to international standards. But this dejection later gave way to a sense of moral freedom. I now had the opportunity to explore the boundless possibilities that had been dormant in my mind for quite some time. I clearly saw two paths ahead of me: one leading to expansion of my own business to an international level, and the other taking me into the arena of active politics. After carefully weighing both options, I decided that the time had not yet come for my active involvement in politics.

My choice was made: I vowed to take the plunge into the international market, a new world for me.

Sometimes a defeat opens the door to more success in life. Had I not lost that election, I might have still been stuck in the world of FNCCI politics, and my business interests might have been limited to the country of Nepal. I want to give credit to that defeat for pushing me in new directions, to new heights. If one believes in fate, only destiny could have written that subplot of my life. I was disenchanted with my friends and colleagues, and with everything else that held me emotionally attached to Nepal. This was the time for change.

Today I feel no disenchantment with anybody or anything. On the contrary, I am filled with gratitude towards all the visible and invisible powers that contributed to my defeat. My happiness today is born out of the sadness I experienced then; I am successful today because I was unsuccessful then.

That was the time of globalization. Huge business empires were competing to invest beyond the national boundaries. In South Asia, Indian business groups such as Reliance, Infosys and the Tatas, which had been operating under the socialist model promoted by Jawaharlal Nehru ever since the country's Independence back in 1947, were also internationalizing their businesses. They were compelled to quickly adapt to the wave of globalization. Those were the days when home-grown vehicles such as the Ambassador and the Padmini were dominating the Indian market. Telecom was the monopoly of a state-run giant. Suddenly, the country switched to economic liberalization and these companies faced tough competition from international players. Indian industrialists then sought a 'level playing field', arguing that if foreign companies were going to be allowed to enter the Indian market, then they should also be allowed to invest abroad.

My campaign to establish a multinational company is based on the same notion—that if foreign companies are allowed to invest in Nepal, we must also be allowed to invest abroad. If Maggi can be allowed into Nepal and compete with our Wai Wai, why cannot Wai Wai take on Maggi in India? Today no nation can stop the wave of globalization. The government must allow its citizens to take their enterprises across the world. It is only a matter of time before the state wakes up and faces this reality.

South Korean President Park Chung-hee had invited all the leading industrialists of his country to a meeting to tell them it was high time that Korean companies followed in the footsteps of the Japanese. All the leading companies in Japan are in private hands. The state supported them in their global expansion, and they have all become multinational companies today. Emulating Japan's model, Park Chung-hee helped Korean companies to grow internationally. To achieve this goal, he handed over specific sectors, such as automobile, power and construction, to each of the leading industrialists. Owing to the direct backing of the state, each of these companies rose to distinction. They grew significantly in size and competence, and were able to take on the world.

Park Chung-hee's message to the Korean industrialists was loud and clear: stop competing among yourselves and start competing with the world. This is the story behind the success of companies such as Hyundai, Samsung and LG.

The Nepali leadership may not have the vision and determination of a Park Chung-hee, but I was convinced that they would not block my way if I sought to grow internationally. Moreover, I was not ready to extinguish my dream just because of a dearth of laws to regulate such a move. I had also heard that the information technology and software industries had flourished in India under similar circumstances. India did not have a law to regulate the software industry when it switched to economic liberalization. Had Azim Premji of Wipro and Ratan Tata of the Tata Group waited for the state to enact the law, India could never have made the strides it has in the field of IT. At times, an entrepreneur must have the guts to brush aside incomplete or impeding legislation for the right reasons.

The fledgling that I was in the world of international business, I attempted my flight, nevertheless.

Singapore

I have been familiar with this place since the days we brought foreign goods for Arun Emporium from here.

In those days, Nepal had close relations with Singapore, which was a trading hub of South East Asia. Most of the goods from third countries were brought to Nepal through Singapore. Not all the goods shipped from Singapore were manufactured on the island, but most of the global companies had their authorized dealerships there. Obviously, Singapore was a popular market for traders like us.

I made many friends, both personal and professional, during my trips to Singapore. Some of my close friends even ended up settling there.

When I started to think about expanding my business beyond Nepal, Singapore was naturally the first destination of choice. I thought I would open a modest office there to begin with. I filed an application with Nepal Rastra Bank, seeking permission to open a branch office of the Chaudhary Group in Singapore. The central bank did not respond. I am talking about the year 1995. Finally, the bank did approve my application—but almost fourteen years after it was filed! Even the Supreme Court had not taken more than five years to rule in my favour in the Nabil Bank case.

I do not actually want to hold the regulators responsible for the red tape in Nepal. The crux of the problem lies in the law of the land. The existing Foreign Investment Control Act bars Nepali citizens from investing abroad. We have to show our source of income to open even a bank account in foreign currency. If the law were to be stringently followed, a Nepali national would not have been able to open a bank account in India, even for the education of his children. The biggest challenge for me was to minutely explore the loopholes in the law so that I could circumvent it and be immune from legal challenge.

I found a loophole in a provision pertaining to Non-resident Nepalis (NRN) in the Income Tax Act. A Nepali who lived outside the country for more than 183 days a year was an NRN in the eyes of the law. He was free to invest abroad. To take advantage of this provision, I decided to become a temporary citizen of my homeland by staying abroad for 183 days a year. Today, my sons Rahul and Varun look after my business interests outside Nepal as NRNs. I coordinate with them from Nepal, in the role of guardian and consultant. It would be no exaggeration to say that this is part of my broader strategy to expand my business internationally, and that this strategy is entirely within the law.

I laid the foundation for a multinational company in Singapore in collaboration with established foreign entrepreneurs such as Mahbubur Rahman, Abdul Awal

Mintoo, Jal Shroff, Yusuf Mohamad and Kamal Kishore Sharma. As the strategy partner, I took the lead when it came to preparing the business model, exploring areas for investment and expanding the business network. They, as working partners, allotted me equal shares. Even though the Act relating to foreign investment barred us from making investments abroad, the Foreign Exchange Act did not bar us from getting shares in a foreign company if we received them free of charge. All we had to do was to notify the central bank about it. Many Nepalis own shares in foreign companies through this procedure.

The start-up company followed a kind of venture capital model, one very popular in international trade. Big business houses across the world have set up venture capital outfits. When they come across a new business idea, they can mobilize the venture capital instead of directly investing in the project. It was this kind of venture capital that I accessed to fund my business expansion worldwide. Rahman, Mintoo and a few other friends came on board.

I have already mentioned Rahman and Mintoo in the context of the purchase of shares in Nabil Bank. Both of them are promoters of NB International, which holds the majority of shares in Nabil Bank.

Jal Shroff is a prominent industrialist based in Hong Kong. He is the chairperson of the international company Fossil Inc., which is listed on Nasdaq. Fossil has branches in more than ninety countries around the world. I had met Shroff at a World Economic Forum meeting.

Yusuf Mohamad is the chairperson of a leading Japanese business firm, Mieyo Boyeki Shokai. Its trade has spread from Japan to Korea, Hong Kong, Singapore, Pakistan and the Middle East. It mainly trades in cloth, synthetic yarn and weaving machines. Actually, Yusuf is a friend of father and I got to know him during the days when father used to import clothes from Japan.

Kamal Kishore Sharma is a family friend. He is related to my wife. Based in Singapore, Kamal is the founder managing director of Global Trade Well Private Limited. He has been in the polyester yarn trade for more than twenty years and has invested considerably in the markets in both the Far East and South Asia. The main reason for my choice of Singapore for international trade was my close ties with Kamal Kishore.

I explained my model and plans for the international expansion of our business to these 'strategic investor' friends. What returns would they get if they deposited their capital in a bank instead? Five to 10 per cent. And if they invested the money in stocks? Ten to 12 per cent. I proposed a plan that projected an annual return of 20 per cent on their investment. They were convinced.

After agreeing on the fundamentals, we did a bit of brainstorming for naming the company. I wanted the name to be representative of the Chaudhary Group, either directly or indirectly.

One day, Nirvana entered my office with a file. He placed it on my desk and walked out of the room. I opened it. There was an A4-sized paper with a word printed on it in a big font: Cinnovation.

I did not understand the meaning of the word. There was another computer printout beneath the top sheet. On this paper the word was broken up like this: C+ Innovation, and the term was explained: Chaudhary's Innovation.

Now that I understood the meaning of the word, I felt it was exactly what I wanted. It was linked to the Chaudhary Group and at the same time it was something that could be of international appeal. I telephoned Nirvana immediately. He was, in fact, waiting for my call. As soon as I said hello, he asked, 'Papa, did you like it?'

'Brilliant!' I replied.

I wrote an email to all my partners telling them that the company's name—Cinnovation—had been decided upon.

By evening, their replies were already in my inbox.

'Beautiful.'

13

The Multinational Journey: Partnership with Taj

The Tatas are a distinguished Indian business house. Indian Hotels Company Limited (IHCL), the hospitality arm of the Tatas, runs world-class hotels, resorts and palaces in many countries under the brand name of Taj and other sub-brands. The Taj hotel in Mumbai is one of them.

A friend of mine, Rajiv Gujral, was a senior executive with the Taj Group. He was vice-president of the international arm of the group. We were both members of the Young Presidents' Organization (YPO) and became good friends from meeting at YPO conferences. After establishing Cinnovation, I made a proposal to Rajiv: 'We want to open a hotel in Nepal in collaboration with your group.' The Taj Group had invested in the Annapurna hotel, but the amount involved was not significant. I also knew that they had some disputes with their Nepali partner, Helen Shah.

'I will put your proposal to the board,' Rajiv replied.

Taj's board of directors was favourably inclined towards my proposal, but they were not willing to make further investments in Nepal until their dispute regarding the Annapurna hotel was settled. 'We are, however, willing to work with you on a project in Sri Lanka,' Rajiv said.

The Taj Group had opened a hotel called Taj Samudra in Sri Lanka around twenty years ago. The hotel was close to defaulting on its loans. The promoters were now in a quandary—should they file for bankruptcy or not? Filing for it could affect Taj's reputation. They could not make additional investments in the hotel either, as the company's internal policy discouraged investment in any conflict-torn country. To overcome this situation, they were looking for a reliable partner.

I travelled to Sri Lanka with Rajiv Gujral to see the hotel.

This gave me an opportunity to get first-hand information about Taj Samudra and other Taj subsidiaries. Even the Sri Lankan partners of the Taj Group were reluctant to invest any more in Taj Samudra. The Liberation Tigers of Tamil Elam (LTTE) had just blown up seven aircraft in a single attack. Investors were panicky. They were more than happy to leave Sri Lanka even if they could only recover half the amount they had invested there. The bankers were of a similar mindset.

Despite all this, I still felt confident about the project. I felt that I could get a good deal if I negotiated well with the banks at a time when investor confidence was at an all-time low. Moreover, the banks that had lent money to the hotel were planning to invoke the guarantee, etc. A project that everyone is trying to get rid of is the easiest to negotiate for.

'I am ready to rescue the Sri Lankan project,' I said in my proposal to the Taj Group, sent through Rajiv. 'But for that you have to agree on a 50 per cent partnership.'

Though I had floated a proposal to 'rescue' this project in Sri Lanka, my real goal was different.

After inspecting the Taj Samudra in Sri Lanka, Rajiv and I had visited the Maldives. There we had stayed at the Taj Lagoon. It was a very modest hotel, which charged around US$80 a night. Against the backdrop of the high-end tourism market of the island nation, this hotel was nothing more than a lodge. Taj had another hotel in the Maldives, Taj Coral Reef, which was just constructed and yet to open.

In just two days of the Maldives sojourn, I came to realize that both these hotels were dogged by internal financial problems. I saw the Maldives as a silver lining against the dark cloud of Sri Lanka.

Negotiations with the Taj Group began. My team of negotiators included R.C. Bhargava, who was then chief executive of Maruti Suzuki, and currently chairman. His presence alone made our side dependable and strong. The ILFC's venture investment banking CEO, Shahzaad Dalal, and Nabil Bank's CEO, D.C. Khanna, provided additional support.

I told the Taj Group's CEO, R.K. Krishna Kumar, 'Taj is a big company and highly respected throughout the world. That's why I am here. But let me tell you that nobody knows that your hotel group is a global brand.'

'Leave alone the world, you don't have much of a presence in Asia (except India) itself,' I continued. 'The Oberoi is much better known.'

Krishna Kumar was impressed by my candid approach.

'This is the reality that we all know,' he said. 'What do you have in your mind, young man?'

I floated the idea that in current times, all world expansion is based on joint ventures. If you can find investors with a strong network in a particular region, that would not only help to raise capital but would also expand the company and the Taj brand rapidly. Krishna Kumar understood and appreciated the network we had built in the ASEAN countries over the last forty years in the course of our other businesses; he took my proposal as an opportunity to grow the Taj brand, apart from also refinancing the existing projects that were suffering as a result of over-leveraging.

'Though created back in 1903, the Taj Group is limited to a handful of countries besides India. If you want your company to become a global brand, then you have to strike separate partnership deals in Asia, the Middle East, Africa, Europe and America so that local partners can help you establish the brand quickly.

'We have old ties with many countries in Asia. But Taj has no presence in ASEAN. We can play a pivotal role in expanding Taj across Asia by using our network,' I said. 'This is possible only if we become a strategic partner involved in its growth and not just one of the investors. Our partnership is meaningful only if we have a role at your policy-making level and in the process of rejuvenating your brand.'

They eventually agreed to my proposition.

I then disclosed to them my biggest desire, the one that had brought me to the negotiating table, but in a very relaxed manner.

'I have been to the Maldives, and I could see that both the Taj hotels there are in bad shape. The Lagoon has tarnished your image. It is not fit to be branded a Taj,' I said.

They agreed.

'Why don't you upgrade them?' I was slowly coming to the crux of the matter.

'Financing is an issue,' was the frank reply.

This was the best possible opportunity for me.

'If you agree, then I am ready to rescue the projects in the Maldives too,' I said. 'Let's agree on a package.'

They did not think twice before accepting my proposal.

Taj not only agreed to my proposal but also offered to create a very special mechanism to support the growth of our joint venture in terms of cash-flow generation. The management agreements were signed for our joint venture—thus, Taj Asia was born. We had created an equal partnership with one of the world's premier groups and owners of the Taj brand. A provision for rotating chairmanship of the board was a huge feather in my cap. For our family, this was the giant step marking the beginning of our creation of a multinational venture.

The Taj venture was my first international expansion.

Many in Kathmandu were surprised when they heard about our partnership with the Taj Group.

How could a person like me, who had no knowledge of the hospitality industry, land such a deal with Taj?

Nobody can make a quantum leap in any field without good planning. And I had timed mine very well. The reshuffle in the Taj management and the restructuring of various debt-ridden projects just before our agreement with them played a crucial role in my landing the deal on my terms. I had, at the right juncture, floated my proposal for a partnership with Taj, through Rajiv Gujral.

After the inception of Taj Asia, I went to Sri Lanka and the Maldives for strategic planning. We held serious negotiations with the banks that had financed the Sri Lankan hotel for restructuring of the loan.

'If we cannot keep this hotel afloat, you can never recover your money,' I told the bankers. 'I'm ready for the refinancing of the project. You have to exempt the interest and a part of the principal.'

My partners and I did not have to try too hard to convince the banks. This marked my first successful step towards fulfilling the promises I had made to the Taj Group. Krishna Kumar was very impressed.

I then started to discuss ways to restructure the hotels in the Maldives. I proposed a plan to transform both the hotels into landmarks on the island nation. 'Let's reconstruct the hotels in such a way that a room that now fetches only $80 a night could fetch $500,' I said. 'This could be a prelude to the Taj Exotica brand you are planning there.'

Though all the leading global hospitality chains, including Four Seasons and Intercontinental, were present in the Maldives at the time, only one hotel matched our concept of Exotica—the Soneva Fushi, operated by a company called Six Senses. Sonu Shivdasani, a businessman from London, and his wife Eva, had leased an island in the Maldives for their personal use. Later, they decided to develop a high-end resort on it. The resort was an instant hit! It became so popular that it became the costliest resort in the country, overshadowing all its competitors.

'If we want to run a hotel in the Maldives, we should stop competing with the Hilton and Sheraton. Soneva Fushi, Four Seasons, Aman, and the Intercontinental should be the benchmarks for our brand,' I told Krishna Kumar.

A man with a keen understanding of the concept of brand, Krishna Kumar could instantly relate to my idea. He accepted it.

He at once telephoned an interior decoration company from California, which was working on renovating the Taj in Mumbai, and asked them to propose a master plan for conversion of the Taj Lagoon into a high-end resort.

Today, Taj Exotica Resort and Spa (the erstwhile Lagoon) is among the three best hotels in the Maldives. A suite in the hotel, which once cost only $90 a night, can now fetch up to $900. After its revamp, the Taj Coral Reef—operated under Taj's Vivanta brand—fetches around $500 a night.

This is my first success story at the international level. After setting its Maldives properties on the rails, Taj Asia turned to Malaysia and Thailand.

We entered into a management contract with a resort called Rebak Island, a 390-acre property, and built the Taj Rebak Marina Resort on it. It is one of the ninety-nine small islands off Malaysia called Langkawi, a fifteen-minute ride by ferry from the Langkawi port.

Once the hotels promoted and managed by Taj Asia became popular, we received many proposals from around the world for management of hotels. Krishna Kumar would forward the proposals to me as soon as he received them. I would conduct a field study to determine the financial feasibility of the project. He would trust me to such an extent that my judgement on any new proposal would be the final judgement of the entire group. A proposal submitted by the Carlyle Hotel of New York was rejected solely on my discretion.

Once Krishna Kumar offered a very good deal to me. I still rue my failure to grab it.

He told me, 'We're buying the Land's End hotel in Bandra, Mumbai. You should join us as an equal partner.' ICICI Bank had extended a huge loan for that property, and now wanted the Taj to take it over without touching the loan. The Taj was about to take over the hotel at a negligible price. But I could not see that. I insisted on a 50 per cent partnership in the management, which they refused.

Sometimes you become penny wise and pound foolish if you do not properly calculate the benefits to be made in the future from a project. Taj wanted to include me in the Land's End hotel project, overlooking its own policy not to forge partnerships with any party in India. However, I was obsessed with the petty issue of partnership in the management. At that time, the hotel cost less than Rs 50 crore (in Indian currency). Today it is valued at around Rs 1500 crore.

I badly regret having lost two projects in my life—the Butwal Power Company and Land's End hotel.

The Taj Group was expanding rapidly. It was also coming up with new strategies to establish itself as a world-class hotel management company. As part of that goal, it brought in Raymond Bickson, a towering personality in the international hotel sector, as its managing director. It was from his time at the helm that Taj started to categorize its hotels according to the quality of the properties and their location.

I am talking about the year 2003.

In the changed context, the Taj Group's priority was no longer limited to Taj Asia. They started to focus on worldwide growth and expansion. I began to feel that Taj Asia would not grow significantly, and felt that my aim of expanding Taj Asia across the globe was not going to be accomplished.

This occurred to me for the first time when we were negotiating a deal in Mauritius.

We were planning to develop new properties in Mauritius as part of our aim to establish the Exotica brand across the world. Rajiv Gujral and I travelled to Mauritius to conduct a feasibility study and chose a site for the proposed project. The son of the deputy prime minister of the country somehow got to know about the land deal. He approached his father-in-law with a proposition: 'Taj Asia has chosen a plot of land at a particular place to set up a hotel. You should approach them and, if they are ready for a partnership, then I can assure you that that plot of land will be leased for the project at a very low price.'

Mauritius has adopted a very good business model to woo investors. You do not have to buy land in that country, you simply lease it from the state. Now that his son's in-laws were interested in the deal, the deputy prime minister was more than happy to offer a good deal to Taj.

The father-in-law came to India and proposed to Taj that he would take care of the land deal and even invest in the hotel; at the same time, he would let Taj manage it. Taj had to neither invest in the hotel, nor share the management fees.

The Taj Group was more than happy with the deal. But I was embittered. We had travelled such a long distance together and seen so many dreams come true, but now they were dumping me just because they got a more lucrative deal from somebody else.

I felt that the new management of the Taj Group was not very interested in including us in their upcoming deals either. Things started to slow down. A project would take months for implementation. I would work day in and day out on a hotel, but Taj was in no hurry. They could not—or did not—want to keep pace with me.

Taj must have had its reasons for treating us the way it did. By the end of the 1990s, it had set up a huge network of hotels in India. This network was not under our partnership. Even when Taj sealed the joint-venture deal with us, it was already running thirty-five hotels in India. Today they run over 110 in the country. Moreover, we were not the only partner Taj had. It had dozens of joint ventures with companies like ours. It would be wrong to expect the Taj Group to focus only on our partnership. If you look at it from Taj's perspective, you can see that what it did with us was quite natural. But that does not change the fact that I felt sidelined. It was not a deliberate move on their part. We were just a small partner for them, considering the size of their operations. But this hardly went any way towards satisfying my hunger for success. This truth disappointed me the most.

I thought it was now high time that I devised a new strategy rather than just cling to hotels and resorts affiliated to Taj. I needed to expand in a new direction on my own.

This led to the next chapter of my drive to expand globally.

14

CG Hotels & Resorts

200 hotels by 2020

'When we think about high-end tourists in the hospitality industry, we should imagine those who lead a regal life. They live in a palace that costs millions of dollars and ride in cars that cost hundreds of thousands. And when they travel, they look for hotels that cost thousands of dollars per night.'

Steve Fitzgerald, chief executive of Conservation Corporation of Africa (CCA), a leading ecotourism safari company, once said: 'They have never roughed it out in their lives. We make them rough it out, and sell them experience. Tourism is all about selling experiences.'

'What kind of experiences?' I asked him when we met.

'Trekking, mountaineering and rafting are popular in Nepal. These are components of a great experience,' he said. 'But that's not enough to ensure sustainable business. You have to learn to keep it exciting for the tourists.'

He pointed to a far-off hill from where some boulders would fall down from time to time. 'We see numerous sights like that when we go on a trek,' he added. 'We can keep the tourists excited with the help of sights like that.'

'How?' I was asking him, as though I were a curious child.

'Make that sight like a scene in a movie. Look excited. Pretend you're a bit nervous. Point to the site of the landslide and say, "Oh, look at that falling boulder!" Tourists who are trudging uphill will stop for a moment to look in that direction. Then you start telling stories about landslides, how many landslides occur in Nepal each year, the damage they cause, the number of people killed. If someone was killed at that site, then don't forget to tell that tale. Encourage them to take photographs of the place.

'After you move on from there, stop at another point and, pointing to the ground, exclaim, "See! A cow has just left its sign here!" They'll be at a loss for a moment. They'll be thinking, "What crap is this idiot showing us?" Then you tell them about the importance of the cow in rural life. You tell them, "We revere the cow as a sacred being." Many will be surprised and intrigued when you tell them that killing a cow carries a life sentence in Nepal, just like murder.'

I was starting to get his point.

'You can make each trip a learning experience. Draw their attention to the river that meanders on your left or right. Ask them to listen attentively to the songs of the birds. Tell them a story about a small village you pass on the way. Dance to the tune of local folk music. This is how you win the tourists' hearts.'

He gave me an example from CCA.

'Our lodge is among the most expensive in Africa. But we don't even have electricity. Early in the morning, we gather our guests at a spot in the lodge and tell them. "Now we will teach you how to make toast in a place where there is no electricity or a proper stove." We take them inside the kitchen, hand them loaves of bread and teach them to make toast on a coal-fired oven. Those millionaires and billionaires are excited to be making their own toast like that, and they don't mind paying ten to twelve times more at our lodge than they would at other hotels with better facilities.

'It's not that we can't bring electricity to our lodge. And our staff certainly know how to make toast. But our guests find the way we do things more exciting. They feel that they are really in the middle of the jungle. This is what I call selling experience with excitement.'

I was highly impressed with Fitzgerald's mantra.

There is tough competition among the big hospitality companies to woo top-notch tourists. These tourists make at least one overseas trip a year. They usually fly in their own private planes. Most important, they are not afraid to spend big money. At first, this kind of tourist would only visit a handful of countries in the Americas and Europe. Companies like CCA have drawn them to Africa.

As I was exploring options to expand my business internationally, I proposed to Steve that we jointly start an inbound travel company in the Asian market.

An inbound travel company brings tourists from across the world into selected countries and then hands them over to local hotels. I wanted to make the best use of CCA's global network. If we could draw their high-class tourists to the Asian market, we would benefit a lot. We already had the expertise to manage hotels and implement travel packages.

Steve was interested.

Cinnovation and CCA signed an understanding to explore the possibility of a joint venture. We started to look at possible wildlife destinations in Asia.

I wanted to first explore that possibility in Nepal, so I brought Steve and other senior officials of CCA to tour the conservation areas. My detractors spread rumours that I was planning to take over all the conservation areas in the country! Even experts in the field opposed me without bothering to know the truth. They could not see how tourism would benefit if CCA made Nepal one of its destinations.

CCA decided not to come to Nepal. They thought it was too hard to put the required infrastructure in place. The government was uncooperative too.

We then looked at India. CCA liked some of the forest areas in the state of Madhya Pradesh. I put forward a proposal for wildlife tourism in the state to the chief minister Shree Digvijay Singh. He not only welcomed the proposal but also asked his tourism minister to take us around the state's national parks in a government chopper. However, we had a tough time convincing the state administration about our plans. The rules were so stringent that it was next to impossible to develop wildlife tourism if we were to follow them. We took some officials from the forest ministry on four trips to South Africa at our expense to show them how wildlife tourism operates. We took them on jungle safaris and showed them how the lodges operated. The African model finally convinced them that our plans could work.

1 November 2006. Bandhavgarh National Park.

The first lodge we opened in partnership with CCA and Taj was Mahua Kothi in Bandhavgarh National Park. As per the terms of our deal, CCA brought the tourists in using its global network. This was our first experience in operating and managing a jungle lodge. The Taj India Safaris package became popular.

After the success of Mahua Kothi, we started Baghvan lodge in Pench National Park. Though not as famous as the other national parks, Pench was a great destination for jungle safaris. At the time of writing this book, we are planning to include air travel in the jungle safari package. India Safari and Tours, in association with Federal Air, are planning to manage the tourist flow to our wildlife resorts.

I proposed to the CCA that we expand our partnership to other Asian countries too, though not in the wildlife sector. It is very difficult to run a wildlife tourism business in most Asian countries as the conservation areas are owned by the state. As an alternative, I wanted to sell Asia as a cultural destination. I saw tremendous potential for eco-cultural tourism in China, Myanmar, Laos, Cambodia and Vietnam.

The promoter of the CCA, Mark Getty, rejected my proposal outright.

'Asia is not our baby,' he said. 'Non-wildlife is not our baby.'

Around that time, an old friend of mine, Mark Edleson, was planning to launch hotels under a new brand called Alila. He has more than thirty years of experience in the fields of finance, real estate and tourism in South East Asia. He is associated with many successful hotels and tourism enterprises. He was the founder of the Nusa Pacific Group that operates high-end hotels in Indonesia, and also a founding partner of GHM Indonesia, which runs many boutique hotels. He is also a founder partner of Mandara Spa, one of the world's leading spa brands, besides being a partner in the Aman Group.

He was about to use three or four properties he had bought from Aman to launch his new brand in Indonesia when a series of bomb blasts rocked Bali. These dealt a serious blow to the tourism industry in Indonesia and to Edleson's fledgling brand, Alila.

I discussed the changing priorities of the Taj Group, CCA and Cinnovation with Mark.

'You're trying to promote your Alila brand, but a brand can't grow only with management. You must be in a position to invest in it if needed. There are many promoters whose businesses are floundering for lack of investment, but with adequate funding, those hotels could pick up. You should include me as a strategic partner,' I told Mark. 'Let's develop new areas in the hospitality business and take your brand and our company to new heights.'

I had long-standing ties with the other partners of the Alila Group. They accepted my proposal. For the first time, Cinnovation inked a partnership for a hotel chain brand. We acquired a 30 per cent stake in the Alila brand.

We wanted to collaborate with Alila in four sectors: high-end boutique hotels, eco and cultural tourism, wellness resorts and business hotels. I could see a good market for medium and higher-medium business (budget) hotels in the emerging markets of the Indian subcontinent, Africa, the Middle East, ASEAN and China. The number of tourists across the world was rising, but the money they spent on hotels was steadily declining. Most of them were on the lookout for cheaper hotels that offered good facilities. It was my belief that boutique or luxury hotels would not expand as quickly as budget hotels, and I convinced Mark about this. We set up a separate company called Amitra Hospitality. Though we had sought an equal partnership in the company, Alila gave us only a near-equal stake of 49 per cent in it.

They were also not very excited about opening business hotels. One day Mark told me bluntly, 'This will distract us from our main purpose. Boutique hotels and wellness resorts are our speciality and we shouldn't be going into areas beyond our expertise.'

But my dream was not limited to these hotel categories alone.

15

Zinc: Our Own First Global Hotel Brand

Edleson, my partner in Alila, had deputed a manager to assist me in developing my own business hotel brand. His name was Tim Halett.

I sent Halett to Dubai to explore the markets in the Middle East. The hospitality industry was growing at an astounding pace in the Middle East at the time. We had also invested in the real estate sector there. My youngest son, Varun, was stationed in Dubai to look after our real estate enterprises. We had plans for the launch of our business hotel brand in the UAE, considering its geographical location, its rapid economic growth and expanding market.

But our plans had to be jettisoned. Soon after I sent Tim to Dubai, the global economic crisis hit, dragging down the whole of the Middle East too with it. Dubai's economy and its market crashed like a house of cards.

Mark introduced me to another seasoned hospitality manager, Eric Levy. I entrusted him with the responsibility of developing the new business hotel brand and to mobilize capital for it from international financiers. He worked out of our Singapore office. We had already set up Cigen Corporation (Zinc Holdings now) under Cinnovation (now CG Corp Global) to look after our hospitality wing. My second son, Rahul, had started to take care of this operation from Singapore.

Our business hotel brand was conceived in Singapore, with Eric, Rahul and another person, Jason Dean, playing a big role. There was a fourth person too—David Keen—without whom our brand could not have been established effectively. David, an established brand guru in international hospitality, had operated a brand consultancy company in Bangkok called Keen Media. Now he has founded a global company, Quo, in London.

'I want to create a company whose business will spread across the world,' I told David during our first meeting.

'It's not up to the company to spread its business across the world. It is up to the person who runs the company,' he replied.

Then, pointing his index finger at me, he asked, 'Do you have that capability?'

'I have the confidence,' I replied.

'Confidence can't run a company,' he snapped at me. 'It takes money and it takes time.'

'I don't have either,' I said.

He was speechless with surprise.

'I'm a small entrepreneur from a poor country,' I said. "And I'm already fifty-four years old.'

He grinned at me and shook his head.

'So it's like building a castle in the sky?' he said, challenging my ambition.

I was not going to give up. I said, 'I come from a Himalayan country. I can come close to the sky by climbing a mountain.'

'It demands a lot of hard work and perseverance.'

'I'm not scared of hard work and I'm pretty determined.'

He smiled.

'So, what do you expect from me?'

'I want to open a hospitality company that will be known all over the world.'

'That is up to you. How can I possibly help you there?'

'I will create the company and you will introduce it to the world. Branding establishes a hospitality company. I want the best brand from you.'

As soon as I said this, he sprang to his feet and extended his hand to shake mine.

'I think working with you is going to be exciting,' he said.

'I feel the same.' I shook his hand firmly.

David and I discussed the core aspects of the company. I told him about my experiences with Taj, CCA and Alila. I told him how passionate I was about creating a global brand. 'The partnership with Taj gave me exposure and association with a famous brand, but it did not give our company its own identity. Only the name Taj appeared everywhere. They called it Taj Asia under the Taj Group. Now I want to establish a company with its own distinct identity to be the international face of Cinnovation.'

I also told him about my long-term plans for the brand.

'Once our brand is established in one sector, it should be possible for it to extend to other sectors as well. I have come across a lot of brands that suit hospitality but are not appropriate for other sectors,' I told him. 'I need a brand that can be used for other products such as alcohol, jeans, real estate, airlines or any other area for that matter, besides hospitality.'

He listened intently.

After months of discussion, David called me up from Bangkok. I was in Kathmandu.

'I want to show you your dream company,' he said, without beating around the bush.

I was so eager to see what he had created that I caught the first flight to Bangkok the next day. That evening, David organized a small gathering for his presentation. Around half a dozen guests from the hospitality and other sectors were present, as well as some of his colleagues and the four of us— Eric, Rahul, Jason and I.

The lights in the room were switched off.

The slides he had prepared were projected on a white wall.

We were holding our breath; David's was the only voice to be heard.

The presentation ended in ten minutes. The lights were turned on.

I went straight to David and hugged him tight.

He had indeed come up with a unique, unparalleled and richly loaded word for our company. The Oxford dictionary defines it as 'the chemical element with the atomic number 30, a silvery-white metal which is a constituent of brass and is used for coating (galvanizing) iron and steel to protect against corrosion.'

It is also a natural nutrient found in food, which helped fight diseases, heal wounds and assist in the growth of the foetus.

Our new brand would be Zinc.

A person becomes most restless as he nears his destination. I was like someone who had just sat through an important exam and expected the results to be known in just a few days' time.

This was January 2010.

Having finalized the brand, our Singapore office was working towards making the new company a reality. We had already finalized some projects in Nepal, India, China and Dubai. We bought a building that was under construction in Greater Noida near New Delhi to open our Zinc City hotel. We had also identified land in the Indian cities of Surat and Kochi, and initiated three projects in Nepal. I wanted to open a hotel with a huge mall and other facilities at the place where the Food Corporation's godown was located at Thapathali in Kathmandu. We were trying to finalize a deal to lease the land while working on the design of the hotel. We were also designing hotels and resorts in Chitwan, and had already identified projects in China and Dubai.

The Zinc brand was about to take off.

We designed a website for the company, incorporating information about all the proposed projects. I had Zinc business cards printed, and told all my friends about the new company.

Unfortunately, destiny had something else in store for us!

Zinc was forced to make an emergency landing as soon as it took off.

Eric Levy, whom I had entrusted with building the company, was offered the position of head of global development at the Pan Pacific Group, one of the world's leading hospitality companies. He could not reject the offer. He moved on, wishing me the best of luck with our new company.

Without Eric, I felt that one of the pillars of our company had suddenly collapsed. Had the company already been up and running by the time he left, it would not have been so tough. But ours was a fledgling company. As if this was not enough, Jason could not keep pace with me. 'Establishing a new brand is a huge risk,' he told me. 'We can't afford to take that risk at this point. Instead, we should be forging a partnership with one of the existing global brands.'

I could not agree with him. We already had partnerships with Taj, CCA and Alila, and if we were to simply enter into new partnerships, there was no point whatsoever in building our own brand.

Jason and I parted ways.

Suddenly, I felt my dreams for my own multinational hotel company was coming to nothing. I felt an entire year of hard work had gone to waste. I felt like a king robbed of his kingdom. I had the brand and the projects, but no organization. I had a dream but nobody to help me realize it.

Zinc had stalled.

A person feels most dejected when, after a long journey, he falls flat on his face only a few steps short of his destination. I was like a student who could not pass an exam despite studying for an entire year.

Zinc-InVision
One day David called me from Bangkok. 'I'm coming to Kathmandu to see you.'

He arrived the next day.

Zinc was David's brainchild. 'It should never have been stalled this way,' he said.

I knew that of course, but I was helpless about it. How could we run such a huge company?

'Don't focus on organization,' David suggested. 'We have projects, we have a brand, and we have the capacity to mobilize capital, but we lack an organizational structure. There must be someone with a good, existing organization who lacks the other things we have.'

David wanted us to look for a joint venture with an internationally established company. I had not liked the idea when Jason suggested it, but now I had no choice.

As David was a hospitality expert, he knew many people in the field and many entrepreneurs in Asia. He introduced me to Michael Thomas, who operated three hotels in Thailand, all making good profits. We held four or five rounds of negotiations, but could not work out a deal.

I held talks with half a dozen other companies but with no success. Some of them had good organizational structures but could not accept our conditions. Others accepted our conditions but did not have a good enough organizational structure. Eventually I met Chris Stafford, a man who visits Nepal once a year to play elephant polo. He told me, 'I had a boss, Kevin Beauvais. He has more than thirty years' experience in the hotel industry. He headed Marriott's Asian operations for twenty-five years. Then he became the chief executive and director of Minor International PLC. He was the one who established the Four Seasons resort and Anantara brands in Thailand.

'He has now established his own company called InVision after a dispute with Minor International. He's operating six hotels. He's a well-respected and established figure in the hospitality industry.'

I was intrigued. I began to make inquiries about Kevin Beauvais.

'If I'm not mistaken, Kevin is struggling to operate his hotels,' Chris went on. 'But he does have a good and strong organization.'

'Should I call him up?' I asked. Chris gave me Kevin's telephone number.

I told all this to David. As soon as he heard Kevin's name, he was overjoyed.

'I have an excellent relationship with him,' he said. 'He's perfect for you!'

I was surprised. If Kevin was so perfect for me, why had David not suggested his name earlier?

'I just don't know,' he said. 'Somehow it slipped my mind.'

Sometimes you run from pillar to post searching for something, oblivious of the fact that it is actually lying at your feet. David immediately talked to Kevin. The next day, I received a message: Kevin Beauvais wanted to meet me. He was coming to Nepal.

It was late July 2010. I was planning a pilgrimage to Mansarovar, one of the sacred Hindu lakes located in Tibet. Kevin came to Kathmandu. We held talks at our Sanepa corporate office for two hours. I told him clearly, 'I will be the majority shareholder in the company. Cinnovation will have 51 per cent and InVision 49 per cent.'

Kevin agreed to those conditions.

I also said to him, 'I'm aiming to establish my own brand. To facilitate our merger, we will start by renaming our company Zinc-InVision. Eventually, however, all the properties will be only branded Zinc.'

I wanted to bring the hotels currently operated by Kevin under the Zinc brand. In other words, I wanted InVision to be merged into Zinc. Kevin accepted this as well. His only condition was that his sub-brand GLOW should continue to exist under the Zinc brand. Today these properties are branded 'GLOW by Zinc'.

I accepted his proposal because I saw no point in suddenly destroying an established brand.

But I had yet another condition: I had to be the senior partner in the company. In return, Kevin would hold the position of chief executive. Even Rahul's portfolio would be below his.

'We can work out a deal only if you agree to this structure,' I told Kevin. 'I'll give you the status and respect you deserve, and I assure you that the interests of your group will not be compromised. Even my son will report to you. But you have to report to me.'

In two hours of talks, we chalked out a framework for Zinc-InVision.

The most important aspect of our partnership is our reciprocal relationship. We do not create properties where Kevin already has his, and vice versa. InVision has a strong organization with thirty-five managers, something we do not have, while we have the experience of working with leading brands such as Taj, CCA and Alila. And, while international financiers are eager to fund Cinnovation, InVision does not have that kind of clout.

Kevin and I share a common dream. We are equally ambitious and work well together.

This is how you establish a big company. What is the use of burdening yourself with more of the same things you already have? It is better to aim for something that can significantly expand not only the size of your organization but its capabilities too. In the context of Zinc and InVision, complementary capacities have come together to form a company that is ten times bigger than either individual outfit. This company is headquartered in Bangkok.

Insofar as Zinc Holdings is concerned, it is a new avatar of Cigen Corporation under the Zinc brand. This company takes care of the equity we have invested in the many hospitality companies/ventures with Taj, Alila, Jetwing, CCA, Amaya, The Farm and IST. The market value of these companies is more than US$500 million today.

Naturally, all the partners and investors were happy that Zinc Holdings could achieve such a lot within only a few years. They started to urge us to achieve even more, assuring us that they were ready to pump in the necessary capital. This led to the formation of Z-I Capital Partners. This group helps us mobilize capital to establish hotels. It is a mutual fund of both the partners in Zinc-InVision and other financiers, and is headquartered in Singapore.

Today we are giving the final touches to our projects in many countries in the China–ASEAN subregion, the Indian subcontinent, the Middle East and Africa. We are also searching for another established company—again, one without a strong brand identity, but with a strong organization—to enter the hospitality sector in the Chinese market. Our strategy is to expand our business worldwide.

However, later, with our acquisition of a majority stake in Concept Hospitality, we decided to have Concept as our brand's global management company instead of InVision Hospitality.

Before anything else, we are entrepreneurs. An entrepreneur creates opportunities. He adds a new dimension to a product at the right time and sets a new price for it. And he goes on to woo other investors on the basis of the newly established price. Had we not devised this strategy, we would not have been able to create such a big company. My sons have also been actively engaged in doing this for the last ten years.

We hear every now and then that global business firms such as the Tatas, Birlas, Reliance or the Mittals have bought projects worth billions of dollars. Actually, others invest for them. They do not invest in these projects themselves. What an entrepreneur does is create confidence in the investor that he can turn something small into something very big. Once he gains that trust, the investor is won over. There are many individuals and organizations in the world that hold huge capital and are always waiting for the right entrepreneur and opportunity to invest. Every bank, every private equity company, every venture capitalist, wants to invest money to earn more. Huge pension funds and insurance companies are sitting on billions of dollars in the international market. All of them want to invest their money to earn more. These capitalists are on the lookout to bet on the strongest horses in the field. The biggest challenge facing an entrepreneur is to establish himself as the strongest horse. If you can convince investors that you are the ace stallion on which they should place their bet, you can go on to fulfil all your dreams.

Once you start achieving in the field of business, you will see things differently. Instead of one and one adding up to two, you will see the potential for one and one to equal eleven.

Zinc Holdings is the story of an innovative idea, and the support that idea got from those who believed in it. It has reinforced the universal business truth that if an entrepreneur has a dream, and the resolve and the managerial skill to realize that dream, then capital will never be an impediment.

Doubletree by Hilton Hotel, New York

New York's lively atmosphere and impressive buildings have always inspired me. When I took the first step to expand my business to the United States in 2005, I turned to the Big Apple. In April that year, I had visited New York for an executive programme at the Wharton School of Business. The institution invites senior executives and promoters of companies across the world to attend these month-long executive programmes. Rahul was in the US too, in the fourth year of his studies, and wanted to start his career there. His area of interest was hospitality. I believed that hotels would be the best option for me if I were to start a business in the US.

Having finished my course at Wharton, I was staying at Taj's The Pierre in New York. I wanted to travel around the country and explore business opportunities. Though I had been discussing my intentions with Rahul for a long time, we had not yet found an opening. This time around, an interesting development took place.

Having heard that I was in New York, Sushi Mohinani, son of my friend in Sri Lanka, invited me to lunch at his apartment. Nirvana and I had attended his wedding reception in Bali only a few months ago. Sushil was in the garment business in the

US, but in the course of our conversation he told me what he would really like to do. 'If I got the chance, I'd invest in the hotel industry here,' he said.

'What do you mean "if I got the chance"?' I asked.

'I couldn't possibly run a hotel in a country like the US by myself,' he said. 'I'd need a good partner and a good deal as well.'

'In that case, let's work together,' Rahul suggested, and both turned to me for my response.

What could have been a better proposition than jointly launching a hotel in New York with the Mohinanis? They had the experience of working with a leading global brand such as Aman. They were already operating two hotels in Sri Lanka and one in the Indian state of Rajasthan. I had been looking for an experienced and competent partner like Mohinani; to add to that, he was my son's friend too. All this made the idea very tempting.

'If you want to work together, I have no problem with it,' I said.

The brief discussion with Mohinani at that apartment on 55th Street, Second Avenue, Manhattan, New York, prepared the road map for my American journey. Rahul and Sushil scouted possible locations in New York, Washington, San Francisco and some other places in the US. We mobilized the brokers in all those cities. They would keep me updated, and I would give them my feedback.

Still, we had to wait for almost one and a half years to identify a project we really liked. That was a Radisson Hotel close to JFK Airport in New York.

22 December 2006

I could not sleep that night. I was so restless that had I been a bird, I would have flown instantly to New York.

We were about to sign an agreement to open our first hotel in the US. But I was in the Maldives, entrusting Rahul to follow up on the deal. I had no idea they would be ready to finalize the deal so fast. Rahul and Sushil had been negotiating with the Radisson management for a month in room number 1724 at the Hilton in Manhattan. That night there was a sudden breakthrough in the negotiations.

I would call Rahul every now and then to inquire about the latest position and conditions being offered. I would feel reassured as soon as I spoke to him; however, no sooner would we hang up than I would become restless again and call him back.

'Now get some rest, Papa. Don't worry about the deal. I'll take care of it.' When Rahul said those words to me, it was 4 a.m. in the Maldives but 9 p.m. in New York. They were at the tail end of the negotiations. According to Rahul, only a few legal clauses remained to be settled. They were in a mood to strike a deal that night.

I lay down in bed but could not sleep. As soon as I closed my eyes, I would become overwhelmed with anxiety, as though Rahul were desperately trying to contact me but my mobile phone was somehow switched off.

I would get up and look at my phone.

At one point I dozed off, only to be jolted awake by the phone ringing. I leaped like a deer to get it but before I could even say 'Hello' Rahul shouted at the top of his voice, 'We made the deal!'

My eyes, dulled by lack of sleep, suddenly dilated.

'Finally, we have taken our first step into America,' Rahul said.

Doubletree is a brand of the Hilton chain. A hotel can seek Doubletree franchise if it meets all the standards set by Hilton. After buying the Radisson, we upgraded it to a full Doubletree.

Many other opportunities in the US have come my way, but for the time being this is the only business we have there. More than anything else, this hotel has given us the satisfaction of showing that a family from a small country like Nepal can successfully expand its business the most powerful country in the world, that too in New York, one of the world's most expensive cities.

16

Iconic Properties

An important thing I have learnt in life is that you do not necessarily need to create something big. If you want to make a mark globally, you should create something that the world loves. It can be a product, property, or anything else. Working on this realization has helped me establish myself in the hospitality business in a very short time. Today, through our joint ventures, we are associated with some of the world's most iconic properties.

Taj Exotica and Taj Vivanta

As I mentioned earlier, when we wanted to start our hospitality business, destiny took us to the Maldives. We could have always retained Taj Lagoon as a mediocre property that charged US$80 per night. But I was part of the effort that transformed Taj Lagoon into Taj Exotica, run by an equal partnership between the Taj Group and us. Today it is known all over the world and is considered one of the three best hotels in the Maldives.

It was not an easy task to carve out this niche for oneself in a country with a culture of raising the bar when it comes to the quality of hospitality. While those in the hospitality business all over the world compete to offer cost-effective products and services, the Maldives is a place where everyone resorts to one-upmanship in another way. If your property can charge US$1100 per day, your neighbour will strive to create a similar property that can charge as little as US$500 per day.

To carry forward that legacy, we transformed a property called Coral Reef into Taj Vivanta. That was our second resort in the Maldives. We feel proud to be associated with these properties, which continue to earn international awards.

Taj Samudra

Taj Samudra, which hardly charged US$20 dollars a day during the period Sri Lanka was mired in conflict, has been transformed through huge investments into the best hotel in the country. Everybody talks about it. The presidential suite is of 6000 square feet, probably the biggest in the whole of South Asia. These days, if Sri Lankan officials have to conduct meetings with very important guests, this suite is their venue. Our hotel has added to Sri Lanka's distinction and reputation. It has become an iconic property, something in which the whole nation takes pride.

The Farm at San Benito

The wellness industry has become a big business today. Everyone wants to feel and look good. There are some big properties in the West that movers and shakers from all walks of life, including Hollywood stars, patronize for wellness treatments. We decided to bring that luxury to Asia, taking over an average property called The Farm at San Benito in the Philippines and upgrading it. The whole world now knows about it. It has become a symbol for wellness and has earned a reputation for the organic food we grow inside the property. No alcohol or meat is served at The Farm, and yet the whole world wants to go there.

Taj Safaris

Unlike Nepal or Africa, India was not particularly well known for its wildlife except, perhaps, for the Bengal tiger. We brought in CCA, a respected wildlife tour operator in Africa, and created a circuit in Bandhavgarh, Pench, Panna and Kanha, dotted with lodges in those parts of Madhya Pradesh that were not even accessible previously. Nobody had gone there before because it was so difficult to reach the inner recesses of the dense forests inhabited by a host of wildlife. But we knew that trekkers and wildlife enthusiasts are not put off by physical hardship. They are the sort of people who are excited rather than deterred by such challenges. If someone yearns to see a tiger in its natural habitat, he or she deserves a chance to fulfil that wish, especially if he or she is prepared to pay handsomely for the experience. At the same time, however, we also need to provide a degree of comfort and luxury to those who go on safaris. With that in mind, we created Taj Safari Lodges.

Jetwing Vil Uyana and Jetwing Sea

I am personally very passionate about one of our investments in Sri Lanka under our joint venture with Jetwing. It is Vil Uyana in Sigriya, the golden triangle of Sri Lanka. Vil Uyana, over the years, has won many accolades, distinction and recognition as Sri Lanka's best and unique eco-friendly resort. It not only commands the highest tariffs in Sri Lanka, but its design, service standard and the overall ambience are considered to be unparalleled in the country. It is situated on agricultural land, with walking routes along paddy fields surrounded by man-made water bodies. We have created a destination that has been highly rated by travel magazines and blogs.

Zinc Hospitality

It is not that we are only interested in iconic properties. We also operate many other kinds of properties in many different parts of the world, as I have mentioned in the previous chapters. We are promoting Zinc in Africa and Nepal. However, I have always wanted to be associated with dream properties, the sort of places where people might go only once but remember the experience for the rest of their lives. I am thankful to God that I have had the opportunity to create some of these iconic properties. I am so proud of them.

Our plans of growing Zinc in India under Zinc management did not gain much ground. In retrospect, I have to admit that the decisions we made—of partnering in the Greater Noida project, of opening a GLOW, and of acquisition of the site in Kochi—were too far ahead of their time. Our efforts to build a vibrant organization in India at a huge investment proved to be ineffective, and the plans had to be shelved. We had already got these projects designed by a Singapore-based firm with high-quality Singaporean designers, and had done everything possible to get them going. But I concluded that greenfield ventures are not the wisest projects to undertake in India. This is not only our experience, but that of many of the world's other hotels. The cumbersome approval processes related to land and the many other requirements simply make such projects unviable. We quickly decided to divert our focus to other markets and kept these projects on hold. We shifted our energies to Sri Lanka and Africa, where a lot has happened, which I will discuss in the following pages.

Concept Hospitality

A few years ago, the opportunity to acquire a controlling interest in Concept Hospitality, a company that had thirty-five flags under well-known brands like The Fern, Fern Residency and Beacon, had come to the table. Our friend Homi, who is also a very well-known hotel consultant, had brought the deal, but soon we learnt that it had gone in favour of the Singapore-based Silver Needle, a company promoted by Nadathur, in partnership with Narayana Murthy, of Infosys. Perhaps Rahul had heard somewhere that the deal with Silver Needle had run into problems. I had written off this deal in my mind, but Rahul kept pursuing it. Two years later, Rahul called me up one day, hugely excited, 'Concept is back on the table.' I was surprised. I called up Homi who said, 'Yes. You have to give full credit to your son, Rahul, who had been pushing me for the last two years even though I was not very optimistic. It was his sheer persistence that has brought the deal back to the table.' It took us six months of negotiations to strike a deal with the private equity firm Busi from New York for Concept.

Param Kannampilly, founder of the company, has an immaculate reputation in the hotel fraternity in India. His son, Suhail, is equally dynamic and runs the operations seamlessly. In the Silver Needle deal, so far as I know, Param's and Suhail's role would have been negligible. But in our case, we were looking to not only acquire a company but also people with a proven track record, whom we could trust 100 per cent and who could drive CG Hotels & Resorts to greater success. The

Concept acquisition was a perfect fit in this respect. An ideal partnership had been sealed.

We stitched together our global and regional presence, integrating all our regional management companies in Africa, the Middle East, Sri Lanka, Nepal, Thailand and China. Concept brought in a strong management platform with a strong team of professionals—not to mention its own three brands—to consolidate and drive these scattered regional entities. The deal was formally announced during HICSA 2015. Our new corporate holding company, CG Hotels & Resorts, replaced the erstwhile Zinc Hospitality. CG Hotels & Resorts not only has Zinc under it but also encompasses Fern and GLOW. Today, eight global offices operating eighty-eight hotels under eight different brands in eleven countries come under CG Hotels & Resorts. We are in the process of creating the necessary infrastructure in terms of global sales and marketing and a strong technical service team to support our global expansion. A new, strategic growth plan is being crafted to bring 200 hotels under the eight brands into the CG fold by 2020. All the required organizational changes are in place, rebranding has been done, and our new website is in the process of being launched. It was also a logical move, therefore, to house the headquarters of CG Hotels & Resorts in Mumbai, where Concept is located. We are looking to soon open a much bigger office in our own premises, to perhaps create a company that will one day operate the largest number of hotels with a much bigger geographical footprint.

17

Destination Dubai

Around nine years ago, I had taken part in a retreat in Egypt organized by the Young Presidents' Organization. My wife and our youngest son, Varun, were with me. When we were returning, Rajiv Gujral of the Taj Group joined us.

Before leaving Egypt, he proposed that I visit Dubai with him for two or three days. 'I have some work there,' he said. 'You should take the opportunity to have a look at Dubai.'

I was not very interested in Dubai. I had been there several times while negotiating for Nabil Bank with Emirates Bank International. It was largely a desert. A decrepit market by the sea, I thought. Dubai was also largely perceived as a haven for gold trade in the region.

This image of Dubai was so strongly engraved on my psyche that I had never returned there after the Nabil Bank negotiations. Even when I travelled to Europe or America, I did not transit through Dubai.

'No! Dubai has been transformed,' Rajiv told me. 'Just go there once. You won't believe your eyes.' He managed to persuade me to go with him.

By the time we reached our hotel in Dubai from the airport, I was already repenting having lost touch with Dubai for so many years. Looking this way and that out of the car, I saw that the roads were much wider and more inviting. Huge buildings and flashy malls had sprung up. Construction work was taking place at an astounding pace. I was staring at Dubai as though it were a child I had last seen years ago that had grown up into a handsome youth.

'You're right,' I told Rajiv. 'This place is on the move.'

That stopover in Dubai was enough for me to get to know the city inside out. Sheikh Mohammed, the ruler of Dubai, had devised a plan to transform the city into the most sought-after destination in the world. And how was he going about it? By creating everything to attract tourists: ponds, lakes, islands, mountains, even snow . . . everything nature had held away from Dubai.

He envisioned a man-made city with all the beauties of nature.

Today Dubai is like Indraprastha, the abode of the Pandavas in the Mahabharata. It has the biggest shopping malls, the tallest towers, the best designed buildings, leading financial centres, the best hotels in the world, Formula 1 race tracks and World Islands, a copy of the map of the world. And the list is still being added to.

I was looking for an international destination for my real estate business, and here it was in front of me—Dubai.

I told Rajiv: 'I'm going to stay a few more days. I want to explore business opportunities here.' He felt quite proud because he was the one who had talked me into coming to Dubai.

I started to explore projects that I could invest in. I sounded out real estate brokers. One of them took me to the Jebel Ali zone to show me a project under construction. Two hundred buildings were under construction in that busy hub of the city.

'This is the biggest housing project in Dubai,' he said. 'If you buy here today, you can sell it at a 20 per cent profit within three months.'

You could purchase a house by depositing 10 per cent of the total price in the first three months—in other words, make a 20 per cent profit for 10 percent investment in the property, making for a 200 per cent return on investment. But what about the risks? What if the houses could not be sold? The realty market in Dubai was going viral. While sellers were queuing up in other places to dispose of their properties, buyers were lining up to purchase properties in Dubai. Multinational companies from across the world were thronging there.

I liked the scheme. But I had one reservation. The real estate company demanded a three percent commission for the sale, and that was a huge sum. I asked for a few days' time and went to meet the hospitality manager of the project developer, a company called Nakheel. As soon as I introduced myself as a partner in Taj Asia, he was impressed. 'Taj has only one hotel in Dubai. You ought to open more,' he told me.

'We won't directly be involved in hotels in Dubai. The Taj Group itself handles that,' I told him. 'But I'll definitely convey your message to them.'

We opened up to each other easily during that first, brief meeting. He took me to meet his chief executive.

Nakheel is a leading state-run construction company. To meet its head was a huge opportunity for me. If I could make a good impression on him, then we could possibly work together on projects in Dubai, and not just the one at Jebel Ali. But how would I impress him at our first meeting?

Shaking hands, exchanging business cards and complaining about the three per cent commission on the sale price of a house were not going to help. I came up with another strategy. I told him, 'We are a worldwide company. We believe in fair business practices. We have partnerships with many multinational companies, including Taj, Suzuki and National Panasonic. We are bankers ourselves. We are the ones who look after Nepal Arab Bank, which was once operated by Emirates Bank. I have come here to invest, as I was impressed with Sheikh Mohammed's vision of the future.'

'Why do you say that?' He was palpably nervous.

His nervousness only boosted my confidence. I told him bluntly, 'People within your company, through the brokers outside, are demanding a three per cent commission from me on the purchase of a property at Jebel Ali. I was not expecting this in the realm of Sheikh Mohammed. If the property is actually underpriced, I am ready to pay more. But what is the meaning of underhand dealings involving commissions? If I get to meet Sheikh Mohammed someday, I'll definitely tell him that such practices are undermining the realization of his dream. I'll say that those who want to invest in Dubai should be encouraged, and not discouraged by dubious activities.'

As soon as I said this, I could see he had become so nervous that his lips were parched. I saw two possibilities: either I would get a good deal, or I would be chased out of Dubai.

I had hit the bull's eye. He started to defend himself.

'What you have heard is absolutely false,' he said. 'We don't have any policy of seeking a three per cent commission on sale of property.'

He rose from his seat and pointed to a map of the Jebel Ali project. 'Tell me, which building do you want?'

The properties were not yet officially in the market, and this man was asking me to choose the property I wanted! That was the first real estate project of Cinnovation.

Here, I would like to mention that eventually this project proved all my concerns right—such as no appreciation, no sales, and delays—but it also proved my intuition and gut feeling correct as it became one of the very successful projects, giving us identity in market and decent returns on our investment.

And all this happened during my brief, unplanned stay in Dubai.

The first impression is the last impression. This adage, which I have been hearing since childhood, applies perfectly to business.

My meeting with the head of Nakheel illustrated this. That meeting helped establish my stature in Dubai's realty market. My meeting with the head of Dubai Properties, Hashim al-Dabal, was equally fruitful.

The meeting was set up with al-Dabal as part of my plan to expand my business in Dubai. He was the CEO of Dubai Properties which was the master property development arm of Dubai holdings. They had all the strategic land banks and plots in the so-called New Dubai vision. Ahead of the meeting, I discussed what I had in mind with my colleagues, asking them to prepare a presentation that clearly mapped out our plans and goals.

On the day of the meeting, as we stepped into a lift in Dubai Properties Tower to get to al-Dabal's office on the twentieth floor, I asked my colleagues, 'Are you guys ready for the presentation?'

They looked at each other and both turned red with embarrassment.

'What's up?' I was surprised.

'I haven't prepared the presentation,' one of them said and, pointing to the other, added, 'I thought he was going to do it.'

I turned to the other. He was pointing to the first one. Nobody had prepared the presentation! I was exasperated. I am already in the lift, the meeting is due to start in ten minutes and I have nothing to show! It had taken a great deal of effort to secure even the short meeting we had been granted. If we did not go ahead with it, we might as well say goodbye to Dubai's realty market. It was a now-or-never situation for me.

The lift was gradually ascending. Nobody spoke a word. My colleagues were completely embarrassed while I was trying to focus and decide in just a few minutes how to conduct myself during the meeting. By the time the lift reached the twentieth floor, I had readied myself physically as well as mentally. When I recall that moment, it gives me an insight into what has helped me achieve success. When the two were struggling for an excuse for their blunder, I was thinking and planning to avail this opportunity in our favour even without having the desired ammunition and with a team of lost soldiers.

As we sat in front of Hashim al-Dabal, my colleagues were at their wits' end. They did not know how I would handle the meeting. As for me, I felt calm and composed.

'Sir, I know you are a very busy person. Each and every minute is precious to you. That's why I don't want to take up your time with a formal presentation. It's not possible to explain my business plans and models to you in a meeting so brief as this. We can meet some other day for that. Today I want to only explain my business idea to you since a business idea *is* everything. Other frameworks, work plans and presentations are trivial things in comparison. I can email them to you to read at your leisure. I feel that when you get to know of my idea about a partnership between us, you'll be interested in learning more.' As an entrepreneur, I take my business decisions on the basis of idea and conviction. Number crunching by an accountant or impressive presentation from management graduates is only required to support the decisions taken. That's why I would like to avail every minute of our meeting to share my conviction in the business idea and commitment towards our partnership.'

I spoke for exactly fifteen minutes. In those fifteen minutes, I told al-Dabal everything—about the establishment of the Chaudhary Group to the leap we have taken into the field of hospitality and our dreams for Dubai real estate.

'I am quite impressed with you, Mr Chaudhary, and would like to thank you for utilizing this time in meaningful discussion rather than colourful presentation. I come across that every second meeting,' al-Dabal said, taking a long breath.

At the end of the meeting, I signed an MoU with Dubai Properties. A presentation was never required after that.

That is what I meant by saying that the first impression is the last impression.

Following the Jebel Ali property deal with Nakheel and the MoU with Dubai Properties, we were ready to take Dubai's realty sector by storm. We formed a new company to look after this venture—Sunstar Developers, an autonomous company under Cinnovation.

We did not make the profits we hoped to from Nakheel's property. The project got delayed. The buyers who had promised to purchase the property changed their mind. There was cut-throat competition in the market, with real estate projects mushrooming everywhere. Some of the projects started after ours were completed before ours! We could not sell our property for a premium price even after waiting for six months. As millions of dollars were locked up in the first project, we did not dare opt for a second one.

A good thing about the realty market is that even if one cannot sell one's property in time, it does not entail a complete loss. You can always recover a portion of your investment by selling the property at a lower price. If you want to recover all your money, you have to wait for the market itself to fully recover. You have to be financially very strong for that. Those who can keep themselves afloat eventually come out of crises.

It was not easy for us to wait for very long with an investment worth Rs 200 crore at stake. We waited for a few months. Eventually, we decided to dispose it of by breaking it up into smaller units. We learnt a good lesson from that first project in Dubai.

I believe that the Dubai market was a perfect match for my working and decision-making style. I made better returns on those investments where I took decisions on the basis of my intuitions rather than on market study or expert's advice—

be it investment in Taj, Wai Wai, hotels in Sri Lanka or CBD Projects in Dubai. I remember that we purchased ten villa plots in Dubai Land, which we sold with profit in due course unlike others who panicked and sold either at the cost price or less than that. We saved 2 per cent transfer charges by not getting it transferred in our name and letting it remain in the name of the previous owner. The seller requested my colleague for an appointment with me. 'How can he keep such a huge investment in my name, without knowing or meeting me even once?' he wondered. It was one of my decisions based on intuition.

We then made acquaintance with the HDS Group of Dubai. We decided to build our own properties instead of buying structures built by others. Constructing a building on a plot of land owned by others would raise the cost of production, and you could not sell the property at a competitive price. This was one of the problems with the Jebel Ali property. Here again, when we were signing the deal, my team suggested that we were paying higher than the market rate. I replied that this was not our cost but our investment in the project and relationship. Over time, both the project and relationship have proved to be one of the strongest and most satisfying.

Sunstar Developers started to work with the HDS Group on two projects in Dubai—HDS Sunstar Tower 1 and HDS Sunstar Tower 2. Before starting construction, we publicized the concept, layout and overall design so that interested buyers could get a fair idea of the project they were putting their money into. This idea worked.

Huge presales in both the towers were enough to make us forget the pain of our initial loss. Location was the strongest point in the two projects' favour. Both the towers are located in the business district of International City, which is considered the centre of Dubai. The location also easily connects to Sheikh Zayed Road, the main arterial road in Dubai. People have now started to stay in the towers.

Sunstar is now known as CG Realty. Meanwhile, Zinc Middle East is collaborating with Sunstar to set up hotels under the brands of Zinc and GLOW by Zinc, and also hotels in partnership with the Taj Group. The first hotel is coming up at Jumeirah Lake Towers in Dubai. We have a couple of local partners, Rajiv Shroff and Jayant Ganwani. We are planning to open Taj Vivanta by the beginning of 2016 as the premier hotel in that area.

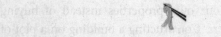

World Islands
World Islands is a unique human creation.

It is a network of small man-made islands in the Arabian Sea and is a microcosm of the world. The islands represent every country, including Nepal.

Nakheel, with whose housing property we entered the real estate business in Dubai, is the creator of World Islands. Cinnovation, along with some partners, bought an isle called Nova Island and started construction work on it around seven years back. Our plan is to build a private villa on the isle on the crystal blue sea, and to sell it off at a premium price. We think its total cost will be in the order of US$200 million.

Actually, the World Island I really wanted to buy was 'Nepal'. Sadly, it was already sold, along with 'India'. My wish to own a 'Nepal' in a world within the world could not be fulfilled.

However, the entire World Islands project started to fall by the wayside in the wake of the global recession of 2008. Other mammoth projects such as Pam Jebel Ali and Water Front were also impacted by the crisis. Now there are more serious issues, such as erosion of the islands and problems related to compaction and connectivity.

Taj Vivanta at JLT, Dubai

Once I was invited by the ruler Sheikh Mohammed in Dubai to attend an international event. There I met a lovely gentleman named Raju Shroff, son of one of the top textile traders in Dubai who was also engaged in real estate. In the course of our conversation, we developed immense mutual fondness. We spent some quality time together. I kept in touch with Raju and introduced him to my boys. During my subsequent visits, Raju was kind enough to invite me to his house for dinner, during which he proposed to me his site at JLT districts. My mind was all the time in search of possibilities for a hotel in Dubai, but many of our earlier plans to establish Zinc there had fallen through for one reason or other. Dubai is not an easy or predictable market. My experience was that the local partner plays a key role, and that his reliability is paramount. I immediately asked Raju to show me the site. What I saw was unbelievable. The site's location and positioning, with three sides open—one facing the golf course, the other the Burj Khalifa, and the third the Burj Al Arab—and surrounded by Marina View, Emirate Hills and Sheikh Zayed Road, was unique. I immediately deputed Rahul to meet up with Raju and formalize the commercial terms, which he did.

Over the years, Taj had reached a point where decision-making had become complicated; there were too many opposing forces within the system trying to pull each other down instead of working together as a team. It hurt to see a great company like Taj, under the great banner of the Tata Group, suffering a destiny it did not deserve. Many decisions had seriously dented the company's bottom line. For two consecutive years, Taj had to write off hundreds of millions of dollars annually. At a time when hotel companies were marking unprecedented price-to-earning ratios, Taj's market shares were tumbling. Coincidentally, it was at the same time that a new leadership emerged at the Tata Group, with Cyrus Mistry taking over the reins from Ratan Tata. I had heard that Mistry brings with him a very down-to-earth and practical approach in doing business, and likes to work with the group partners. Shapoorji Pallonji, the family that Cyrus hails from, is the largest shareholder of the Tata Group. It was for the first time that a non-Tata person had been chosen to lead the globally renowned conglomerate.

Nirvana had socially known Shapoor, Cyrus's older brother, and had encouraged me to meet Shapoor many times. Somehow, that did not happen. Once the change became official, I asked Nirvana to arrange a meeting with Shapoor Mistry. Shapoor was unbelievably polite when I called on his office and, to my surprise, he knew exactly everything that was happening at the Taj Group. I did not realize that he was also on its board. He knew how joint-venture partners like us were being treated, and that many opportunities had been neglected. He gave me a completely new sense of confidence in rebuilding my relationship with Taj. He advised that

I should meet with his brother Cyrus and work towards correcting the past; 'correcting the past' in the sense that we had done nothing new over a period of fifteen years, and remained where we had started—the Maldives and Sri Lanka. Although an investment in Phuket had been made, there was no headway there. On the contrary, there was a desire on Taj's part to sell the land and exit. Despite sitting on a gold mine like Samudra with ten acres of land, opportunities had been wasted. Taj Asia, as the name itself signifies, was opened to create hotels in Japan, Korea, Hong Kong, Singapore, Indonesia and Thailand. But for years, it remained almost dormant. My frustration at seeing opportunities ripe for the picking but not being taken forward was eating away at my insides. That had pushed me to create our own brands and to do what we did. Still, my heart was always with Taj because that brand had given me my unique global identity as a hotelier and had also been my business school when it came to the hotel industry.

I eventually met with Cyrus, a very unassuming man and a very patient listener, and yet very confident of himself. It did not take me long to understand that he had already done his homework. Not only did he know about us, but he was also aware of our background and history. He candidly asked me to wait for the new MD to take over and then work towards rebuilding our relationship with Taj. He went on to express his great respect for our partnership as one of the most profitable joint ventures of Taj and acknowledged the role we had played in keeping it that way. He not only offered to introduce the new MD of IHCL, Rakesh Sarna, to us, whom I am now working closely with, but also introduced us to the heads of many other verticals like Tata Power, Tata Communications and Tata Motors. Cyrus wanted them to grow with us in many sectors in Nepal. The letters he had written to all these functionaries illustrate Cyrus's respect for our partnership.

Subsequently, I received an invitation to an event for the formal induction of Rakesh Sarna as the new MD of the Taj Group and a farewell to Raymond Bickson. I decided to attend. It was a short but very impactful meeting with Rakesh. He immediately said we must meet and spend some quality time together without delay, giving me the feeling that he too knew the background pretty well. I had heard that during his thirty years of association in senior positions with the Hyatt Group worldwide, he was known for his quick decision-making, his commercial astuteness and his friendliness towards the hotel's partners. It is no wonder that Hyatt thrives in partner relationships and maintains a huge respect for the role that the partners play in the growth of the organization.

I met Rakesh soon over lunch, and had a very long, candid conversation with him, giving him the full background of the reasons why we decided to move on and create other joint ventures as well as our own brand, which he completely appreciated. But he was quick to state that what had happened was history and that we now had to work together, not only to strengthen our existing business and exploit existing opportunities, but also to re-execute the vision behind the creation of Taj Asia. We formed a task force and created a new road map to establish twenty new Taj's in ASEAN, the Middle East, China and Africa (territories where we have already made significant headway). My request for an independent and dynamic CEO to drive Taj Asia was immediately addressed, and we are pretty much on track to move rapidly to once again make this company a very vibrant one.

Today I get a great sense of pleasure in working with Rakesh. We speak almost the same language and think along the same lines. This has also reshaped the destiny of Taj Safari and, as a consequence, we have brought in our very high-end resort in Meghauli at the Chitwan National Park—which we wanted to open as a Zinc—under the Taj Safari fold. This will also help turn around Taj Safari as a company.

To me, Taj as a hotel brand is no different from my own brand Zinc. I have now started viewing opportunities objectively. Wherever we feel that the Taj brand fits in better, we bring Taj in. That was exactly what led to turning the Jumeirah Lake Towers (JLT) into a Taj Vivanta. I was amazed to witness the personal attention to detail Rakesh brought to the table. At a Mumbai meeting with the Taj Vivanta designers, Rakesh literally redesigned the JLT hotel right in front of my eyes. Later, I learnt he had also led the technical services department of the Hyatt Group and had built several hotels. We are both very keen to grow this relationship and hope to extend this to our new joint venture called Summit. Our vision is to make Summit the most iconic hotel in Nepal, and we are moving towards that goal.

18

The Globalization of Wai Wai

Aim: A billion-dollar company

I was waiting for my baggage at Dubai airport. A large number of Nepali passengers got off a Qatar Airways plane that had just landed. Most of them were young.

I asked one group that had deplaned, 'Where do you work, brothers?'

I have forgotten the name of the company that had employed them but they had come to work in its security department.

'And what has brought you to Dubai, brother?' I was asked.

'I am Binod Chaudhary. I have some business here.'

'Oh,' some of them responded, apparently not much interested in me.

I then quietly waited for my baggage to arrive.

The baggage belt started to move. Suitcases started to surface on the belt. As soon as the young men spotted their suitcases, they would run to grab them. In a while, I saw four or five cartons of Wai Wai noodles on the belt, and some of the young men rushed to grab those too.

Placing my suitcase on a trolley, I moved towards them.

'What do you have in these Wai Wai cartons?' I asked.

'Wai Wai noodles, of course,' one replied.

I was surprised.

'Why did you bring so many of them?'

'Yah,' one of them said, 'you don't find them here.'

I was so delighted I wanted to jump up and down. I wanted to hug them and tell them, 'Brothers, Wai Wai is my product.'

But I could not do that. They were not interested in me at all. Also, a part of me felt I could not claim Wai Wai as my product alone as it has been owned by so many people.

I decided at that very moment that I would ensure Wai Wai became available across the world, or at least in those parts of the world where Nepalis lived so that they would never have to take cartons of Wai Wai with them or ration their supplies of it when they left the country.

If export can be treated as international expansion of one's business, we had expanded a long time ago, because we have been exporting Wai Wai to India for more than two decades. If it is the establishment of the first factory abroad that marks the internationalization of a product, then Wai Wai was internationalized more or less simultaneously with our realty business.

The north-eastern region of India has been a major market for Nepali products for many decades. This region comprises Darjeeling, Sikkim, Assam, Meghalaya, Nagaland, Arunachal

Pradesh, Mizoram and Tripura. Even Bhutan is considered a part of this region these days. People of Nepali origin have a strong presence in the region. We had set up a basic distribution system in the region while we were exporting Pashupati Biscuits three decades ago.

We enhanced the distribution system for Wai Wai. We devised a new strategy for market promotion by appointing Nepali students going to India for studies as our brand ambassadors. They were not supposed to sell Wai Wai in their colleges, but only introduce their friends to the brand. This idea was a hit. Wai Wai became explosively popular, not only among Indian students of Nepali origin, but also among Indians and Tibetans.

After successfully establishing our product in that regional market, I thought it was high time we set up Wai Wai plants at the international level.

We established CG Food India Private Limited under Cinnovation. This fast-moving consumer commodity business was duly registered with the authorities concerned at Guwahati in Assam in 2002. The first Wai Wai plant outside Nepal came up in Assam, though we would have preferred Sikkim, a better site for us in many ways. It is a mere four-hour journey from Kathmandu to Gangtok. You can fly from Kathmandu to Bhadrapur in about forty-five minutes, from where Gangtok is just a few hours' drive away. Also, the people of Sikkim share the lifestyle, culture, food and habits of Nepalis. An Indian from Delhi would feel an alien in Sikkim, while a person from Kathmandu would feel right at home.

However, we faced a major problem in Sikkim—foreigners were not allowed to buy land there, and you had to give 51 per cent shares in the enterprise to the local residents who provided land for the factory. This was unacceptable to me.

Assam was our alternative.

At that time, the United Liberation Front of Assam (ULFA), an armed guerrilla group, was stepping up its activities across the state. The security situation was critical. The state was lagging behind in development, and poverty was widespread. On the other hand, India's Central government was pumping billions of rupees into the state. It also introduced an industrial promotion package, which included provision for a plot of land in any part of the state to be leased at a nominal charge for ten years. Electricity was heavily subsidized, and there was a ten-year exemption from income tax too. The state government gave a transport subsidy for importing raw materials and exporting finished products. Additionally, for every Rs 1 crore invested in a project, the state government would provide a grant of Rs 30 lakh. Lured by these facilities, we decided to make Assam the first site for CG Food India.

Meanwhile, another interesting development took place.

I was in Delhi on business, and the senior cardiovascular surgeon at Escorts Hospital Dr Naresh Trehan took me to the site of a proposed project.

Dr Trehan is a renowned doctor in India. He initially practised in New York, and later shifted to India to establish Escorts Hospital at the request of former prime minister Rajiv Gandhi. He has received some of the highest civilian awards, such as the Padma Shri and the Padma Bhushan. I had set up Norvic Health Care Centre in Nepal with his assistance. Now, he was bringing the Medicity project to India to provide global medical facilities under one roof, and was proposing that I open a hotel there.

I have deep respect for Naresh and Madhu. They have always been good guardians to Nirvana, right from the time he joined Doon School. Naresh has stood by my side since the time my father took ill. Despite being incredibly busy with not only his medical practice but also his diverse interests in many spheres of life, he has always had the time to help, guide and assist me, whether as a friend or as a businessman. There have been many times when we have run into serious problems that Naresh solved.

Naresh too has a high degree of confidence in me. When he was parting with Escorts and starting Medanta, he asked me to partner him. I had a few rounds of discussion with his partner Sunil Sachdev. Unfortunately, Sunil could not fulfil the required formalities suggested by our lawyers. It was a big investment for us at the time, and that too for a minority position. I told Naresh I would like to opt out of the project but would assist him as a friend if he wanted to use our investments to bridge over any problems on the way. In hindsight, I have no hesitation in admitting that I made a wrong decision. Instead of listening to the lawyers and thinking about the technicalities, I should have thought of the project as an initiative of a visionary like Naresh, and known what he was capable of creating. My involvement in Medanta in whatever small role as a partner would have taken our presence in India, our honour and our respect, to new heights. I still tease Naresh, telling him: 'You still owe me the promised shares which you've not given me.' Naresh, notwithstanding all this, remains a great friend and guide to my family.

We were now speeding towards the site, when he suddenly swerved the car around.

'Oh, my God!'

I was bewildered.

'I'm going to be finished,' he said. 'I have to go back to the hospital for five minutes.'

'What's the matter, brother?' I asked.

'I had given an appointment to the Sikkim chief minister, Pawan Chamling. It slipped my mind,' he explained. 'I'll see him and come with you.'

We returned to the hospital.

Chief Minister Chamling was waiting for the doctor when we reached the hospital. He was with his wife and an aide. After finishing his brief check-up, Dr Trehan introduced me to Chamling

The very next day, Chamling and I were chatting at Sikkim House in New Delhi—not in Hindi, but in Nepali.

I told him how I had wanted to set up a Wai Wai factory in Sikkim but was forced to go elsewhere. 'You won't sell land to foreigners in Sikkim,' I said. 'How can you expect foreign investment?'

He responded immediately: 'That's not on. We are so close to each other. Nepal is hardly three hours' drive from Sikkim. How could you possibly go to Assam to invest? You have to come to Sikkim. I'll make all the necessary arrangements.'

He told me: 'Please visit Sikkim and see for yourself how popular your Wai Wai is among us.'

'But I can't give 51 per cent partnership to others for leasing their land,' I said.

'Forget about that. Just think that you have already found a plot of land in Sikkim.'

He put me in a spot.

I had made all the arrangements to set up the plant in Assam, and the state government there was pledging huge subsidies. On the other hand, the chief minister of Sikkim was insisting I had to open a factory in his state.

'I'm interested,' I said. 'But can you provide us with the same subsidies provided by the Assam government?'

'Just wait three months. I'll give you even more facilities,' he replied. 'The legislation has already been tabled in the House. It should be ratified within three months.'

After such a strong commitment from the chief minister himself, what more could I have asked for?

So it was that a conversation that began about establishing a hospital in Sikkim ended up about setting up a Wai Wai factory.

'A hospital is a very sensitive matter,' I told him. 'We'll discuss it later. But I promise you that I won't turn down your request to set up a Wai Wai factory.'

'That's a deal.' He rose from his seat in excitement and shook my hand firmly. 'You are welcome anytime. Just let me know which site you like and I'll arrange it for you.'

We immediately withdrew our plans for Assam and started to work on the Sikkim project.

At Rangpo, by the banks of the Teesta River where our Wai Wai plant is now located, we received seven acres of land from the state government on a long-term lease at a negligible rent. The market price of the land itself must be around Rs 15 crore in Indian currency. As Chamling had pledged, the bill was endorsed by the House within three months. We got the licence to open a plant in Sikkim, with better subsidies and facilities than offered by Assam.

This is what I call an investment-friendly climate!

Now it was my turn to fulfil my promises to Sikkim. I opened the factory in a record time of seven months.

CG Foods India's first factory came into operation in April 2006. The plant has a capacity of 11,000 tonnes of finished noodles, or 120 million packets a year, and is operating at full capacity. We are producing, in addition to Wai Wai, Kwiks cheeseballs, *bhujia* and other snacks at the factory.

While issuing the licence for the factory, Chamling told me, 'The state government does not expect a penny from you. We're giving everything to you. I also don't want any personal favours from you. I would, however, ask you for one thing: the people of Sikkim must be employed in your factory.'

I gave him my word: 'Chief Minister, I will be the largest employer in Sikkim within two years. This is my promise to you.'

I fulfilled that promise, employing around 500 Sikkimese people in the factory within two years. That year, we added another plant of even higher capacity in Sikkim, our second phase of expansion in that state. More than one thousand local residents were now working for us.

The establishment of the Wai Wai plant in Sikkim created great astonishment across Nepal.

This was probably the first instance of a huge investment by a Nepali entrepreneur outside the country. Not only that, investing in India was itself a controversial matter. How could the Chaudhary Group invest in India in a blatant breach of the Act that prohibits a Nepali citizen from investing outside the country? However, I had not flouted any law. The factory in Sikkim was registered in the name of CG Foods India and not the Chaudhary Group. And CG Foods is a company owned by Cinnovation, a Singapore-based company.

I am eternally grateful to *Kantipur*, the leading national daily of Nepal, for its firm support to me. At a time when a heated debate was going on in the country for and against our decision, *Kantipur* gave us support. The message was clear: if foreign companies could have unhindered access to invest in Nepal's market, a Nepali company must also be allowed to invest abroad. My Wai Wai factory in Sikkim was a wake-up call to the policymakers and politicians in Nepal.

Shortly afterwards, the finance minister and the governor of the central bank publicly stated that the government had initiated the process to bring restaurants and other companies run by Nepalis outside the country within the ambit of the law. 'Many Nepalis are using back-door means to invest abroad. We shall let them invest using the front door by bringing those investments within the realm of law,' Finance Minister Dr Ram Sharan Mahat said.

Even at the time of writing this, we are yet to get permission to invest abroad through the 'front door', as envisioned by Dr Mahat, but the Act that forced us to use the back door has been amended. And all the stakeholders seem unanimously in favour of reform.

'Please do come and invest here. After all, Sikkim is yours.'

This is what Pawan Chamling had told me during our first meeting.

He has always kept his word to me. It is not that I did not face any administrative hurdles in Sikkim, but I do not remember anything that seriously impeded the project. If I approached Chamling with a problem, he would summon the ministers and secretaries concerned and settle the matter immediately.

One problem we faced related to the land we had leased at Rangpo. It belonged to the state-run Mining Corporation. From the time we began construction there, the managing director of the corporation started to harass us under one pretext or other. Many times, he switched off electricity and water supply to our site. We also had to use the corporation's gate to reach our site, as we did not have a separate entrance. One day, the MD padlocked the gate, so our employees could not enter the site, and their vehicles were lined up outside the gate.

When the employees told me about this incident, I immediately telephoned Chamling. He instantly transferred the managing director out, purely on the basis of what I had told him He later requisitioned the land and moved the Mining Corporation elsewhere.

The last time I met him was on 11 September 2008.

He had given me an appointment at 7 p.m. that day at his official residence in Gangtok. I arrived there with Lily and Nirvana. He was busy in another meeting, but after twenty minutes or so, he turned up, apologizing for making us wait.

'Oh, I made you wait for so long!'

We had brought *khada*s in his honour. He offered the same khadas to us, saying, 'You are the guests, not I!'

I thanked him for the support extended by the Government of Sikkim to help us establish the Wai Wai factory at Rangpo. He would only smile.

'Sir, do you remember how we accidentally met at Dr Naresh Trehan's place in Delhi?' I said, taking him down memory lane. 'Our Sikkim journey started from that point.'

'How could I forget that!' he said, folding his hands. 'You are our masters. Is there anything else I can do for you?'

I thought it was a good opportunity to ask of him a favour. 'A lot of the land of the Mining Corporation is still vacant. If you let me utilize that land, I'll set up an industrial park there.'

I pushed my sofa a bit forward and leaned towards him to explain my plan. 'We can bring investors from abroad. We can build roads and other infrastructure to develop an industrial centre.'

He nodded.

'Well, we're operating hotels and resorts in Sri Lanka, the Maldives and India. We would like to set up hotels in Sikkim too.'

'Please do that,' he said.

'Sir, we need land for that,' I said.

'We are constructing an airport at Pakyong,' he told me. 'We are planning to build big hotels, casinos and malls there. We have acquired 500 acres of land for the project so far and plan to acquire 500 acres more. We can lease some of that land to you. You come up with a master plan, I'll go through it.'

I could not have asked for anything better! I had merely wanted to propose a small industrial park, but he wanted to include me in his extensive plan for the airport!

'If you provide me around 100 acres, I promise to build a world-class hotel, park and mall there,' I told him.

'You just lodge a formal proposal for the airport project. I shall take it forward,' he told me as we were about to leave.

I thanked him profusely.

'You don't have to thank me,' he said, grabbing both my hands firmly. 'I am here for you. You are most welcome to invest here. After all, Sikkim is yours.'

Our vehicle of international expansion embarked on its journey from Sikkim. We were easily penetrating India's north-east. However, as Wai Wai was equally popular in north India, including Delhi, Dehradun, Punjab and Chandigarh, we had to install a plant in that region to supply those markets. It was not feasible to transport the product from Sikkim to north India. We would have had to increase the production capacity of our plants in Nepal if we were to export Wai Wai from Nepal to northern India. It was wise to build a plant somewhere in north India itself.

Rudrapur in the Indian state of Uttarakhand became our next destination.

The chief minister of Uttarakhand, Narayan Dutt Tiwari, had launched a special campaign aimed at industrialization and generation of employment in the state. As part of the campaign, he had acquired 2500 acres of land at Rudrapur to establish an industrial district. It is now known as the State Industrial Development Corporation of Uttarakhand, or SIDCUL. We were requested to take a plot of land there. We were looking for a site for a plant in north India, but we were not very sure that Rudrapur was a good choice.

We got three acres of land at Rudrapur just before the deadline for the land acquisition expired. Even after leasing the land, we did not immediately start work on the site. Our interest was finally roused only after the Tatas, Bajajs, Nestlé, Dabur, Haldiram, HP, Delta and other big brands started to throng Rudrapur. The Tatas operate on nearly half of the industrial estate, in around 1100 acres. Ashok Leyland has also established a huge plant at Rudrapur, but just outside the industrial district.

When these huge brands were coming to Rudrapur, why would we hesitate to go there?

In the first week of August 2006, we laid the foundation stone for the plant in Rudrapur. I thought the deadline for industrial production had been extended up to March 2010. I discussed the matter with the local officer of SIDCUL.

'The Central government has decided to extend the deadline. We're not concerned about that,' he said. 'However, if you fail to initiate construction work by 10 August, the entire plot of land will be revoked."

I was crestfallen. August 10 was less than a week away. I had to convince the SIDCUL officials within a few days that I had started the construction of the factory. We began gathering construction materials. Without even a basic design, we put up pillars at the four corners of the plot. Once they were up, we took photographs of the site and showed them to the SIDCUL officials, a day before the deadline expired.

The next day, they arrived at the site for inspection. Construction materials were piled everywhere, and the pillars were up. The officials were convinced that construction work had started, and left satisfied. But in fact, it was a trick. To avoid losing the land, we had orchestrated false construction work at the site. At times, a ruse like that is necessary to overcome administrative hurdles.

Once the administration was satisfied, we constructed the factory at our own pace. The deadline for commencement of production rolled near, but we were not ready, and it would have been foolish to pour money into production at that point, before ensuring that the entire north Indian market could be covered by the plant. SIDCUL, however, was in no mood to wait for us. They were struggling to cope with the growing demand for land, and were looking for an excuse to scrap their deal with any party that defaulted. Their officials started to pressure us to show proof that we had started production. Wai Wai's Hakka noodles was the result of that pressure.

Given the situation at Rudrapur, we needed a product that could be churned out by a small plant. We struck upon this idea of Hakka noodles, which required only a small production unit to prepare the dough and another machine to shred it. After that, we only needed to parboil the noodles before packaging them.

This product did not come anywhere close to the quality of Wai Wai. We have never produced noodles of this kind at any of our plants in Nepal and Sikkim.

Initially, the SIDCUL officials were reluctant to accept the Hakka noodles as our authentic product.

'This is not your Wai Wai, is it?' They had caught us red-handed. 'We are not going to accept this.'

'This is our new product,' I argued. 'How could you not accept it?'

Big or small, nobody could deny that the item was an industrial product. Moreover, how could they force us to produce the same product we did in Nepal and Sikkim? The SIDCUL officials were forced to accept my logic. We started production from that plant in May 2008. Meanwhile, the Hakka noodles became extremely popular.

Today, the plant at Rudrapur is as big as the one in Sikkim. It produces 120 million packets of noodles a year. We are planning to supply the entire north Indian market using that plant.

In the third phase, we expanded our production to Assam. We had switched from Assam to Sikkim at the eleventh hour, but we had no doubt about the market potential in Assam. Guwahati and many other places in Assam have close cultural ties to Nepal. It was also easy to reach the markets of Meghalaya, Mizoram and Nagaland from Guwahati. The subsidies provided by the Assam government were equally tempting.

We leased 7.5 acres of land at Chhaygaun, which is about sixty kilometres away from Guwahati. On 13 September 2008, I visited Guwahati for the first time to see the plot. The very next month, we began construction of the plant. Within a year, CG Foods India's third factory was commissioned. It is operating at its full capacity of 150 million packets a year. We have recently set up another plant of equal capacity in Assam.

My eldest son, Nirvana, looks after our FMCG ventures, both in Nepal and overseas.

I realized from my experience with CG Foods India that if you do a huge volume of trade in a big market you can achieve extraordinary vertical growth.

This had led to the suggestion from many stakeholders that we transform the company into a public holding and list it on the stock exchange in India. Many investors are also approaching us for a pre-listing placement of our company's shares. However, I do not think the time has come for us to convert it into a public company.

CG Foods India is now expanding at a fast pace. After our plants in Sikkim, Assam, Guwahati, Silchar (from where we can also easily cater to Nagaland and Mizoram) and Uttarakhand, we have further expanded to Chittoor in Andhra Pradesh, where our new plant has already started operations. Chittoor is fifty kilometres away from the famous Hindu shrine of Tirupati. The three major business hubs of south India—Hyderabad, Chennai and Bangalore—are equidistant from Chittoor. We are planning to carve a market of Rs 4 crore a month for Wai Wai in the region within two years. The Chittoor plant will not only cater to south India, but also address our export needs. From Chennai port, we can export our products to the Middle East and Africa. We are setting up another plant at Purnia in Bihar, which will begin operations from November 2014. Once our food park project at Ajmer in Rajasthan comes into operation, and we also start a plant at Indore, for which the Madhya Pradesh government has demonstrated strong support, we will be the only company in India with a pan-India presence of manufacturing facilities. We have plants across India with a strategy to have a plant in every three or four states, in such a way that the plants lie within a 600-kilometre radius across India. This gives us a huge advantage by way of faster penetration of the market across India. One must not forget a key rule of economics: supply creates demand.

Over the thirty-two years of Wai Wai's presence in Nepal, we have been able to start only five plants there, two of them small ones. Whereas, over a short period of six years, we already have eight plants in India. It is going to be nine soon. Our India production is twice Nepal's, and is growing at an average rate of 40 per cent. Wai Wai is a company that has grown without any ATL (above the line) publicity. Our greatest marketers and brand ambassadors are the three generations of Wai Wai lovers, the people of Nepal and northeast India, and the students from Dehradun and Darjeeling who flock to the many educational centres in India.

I had attended the Invest MP Summit along with Naresh Trehan and Ravi Jaipuria, and met with Minister Yashodhara Raje Scindiajee (sister of Vasundhara Raje Scindiajee). She is the minister of industry and in charge of promotion of new investments. We had a brief chat during the summit and promised to keep in touch. I was amazed to see that on my return after a few weeks, she reached out to me first. I see her as a minister who operates like a business CEO. She is available on BlackBerry messenger, on her mobile and on the Internet, and loves to engage with investors, much as a businessman does with his partners. She often says, in a lighter vein, that the job of promoting business does not belong to the babus alone.

Although we had bought a site in Gujarat to start a plant to cater to western and central India, comprising the states of Gujarat, Madhya Pradesh and Maharashtra, and although we had also been looking to cover these geographies with our Ajmer food park, we decided to explore the Indore option seriously. Many trips have been made to Madhya Pradesh, and our proposal is in the final stages. I hope the dynamic leadership of Madhya Pradesh and the persistently persuasive approach of Shree Yashodharajee sees us starting a plant there within the next year.

Even after setting up so many plants in India, we never had to advertise our product. That happens by word of mouth, as mentioned earlier, by the two or three generations who have grown up eating Wai Wai and who are our real ambassadors. They will not consider any other brand.

Having achieved for our company a pan-India presence, the time has now come for us to launch our brand in the Indian media. This will give another boost to Wai Wai in terms of its presence in the market, visibility, brand image and sales volumes. There will come a day when Wai Wai will give tough competition to Nestlé, or even take over as the top-selling brand of noodles in India.

We are expanding globally too. Construction of a Wai Wai plant has begun outside Dhaka in Bangladesh. We have finalized our deal with a very reputed group in Saudi Arabia to set up a plant there. We are actively engaged in expanding our business to Africa too.

Our experience so far shows that regional presence is crucial in the noodles market. Rather than one big plant in one place, I prefer to have smaller plants in many places within a country so that our product can be easily transported to any part of the country, thereby expanding the market for it.

Looking at the international noodles market in general, the biggest company in any country covers 55 per cent to 60 per cent of the market, followed by a distant second player with a coverage of 20 per cent to 25 per cent. The rest of the companies get a 5 per cent market share each approximately. Data from Japan, Malaysia, Thailand and many other countries show this pattern. In Nepal, we are undoubtedly the biggest player. In India, Maggi is ahead of the rest but we are a strong contender for the second position.

Utilizing the rights we have obtained from Thai Food, we have also begun exporting Wai Wai to Bhutan, China, Malaysia, Hong Kong, Singapore, Brunei and most of the countries in the Middle East. We also export to the United Kingdom, the US and Canada. We export to Bhutan from Sikkim. Once we gain a share in these markets through exports, we will set up plants in those countries. This is what we are doing in India.

I have summed up our general plan; however, I am contemplating something deeper.

To grow into a global company, we now need a two-pronged approach—organic and inorganic. Our growth so far has been organic; we have been adding one plant after another and enhancing the capacity of the earlier ones. Insofar as inorganic growth is concerned, an established company is acquired rather than creating a greenfield project. This approach expedites the rate of growth. We will now give equal priority to both organic and inorganic growth. We are looking for powerful FMCG companies across the world that we can take over for the diversification of our production and expansion of the market. These companies must have their own plants, products, brands and markets. For instance, we are yet to find a proper market in China. We can find one overnight if we acquire an established company in China instead of starting one from scratch. The same applies to ASEAN, Africa and the former Soviet Union. We are mobilizing investment bankers to facilitate our entry and growth in these potential markets.

Our organization has already reached a point where there is no alternative to growth and expansion. We have to consistently increase our investment in order to maintain the momentum of our organization. Our dream is to establish a global empire for Wai Wai in ten years from now. I am confident that we can achieve this goal.

According to the World Instant Noodles Association (WINA) data, around 100 billion packets of instant noodles are sold around the world each year. We are producing 1 billion packets out of Nepal and India. In other words, we account for 1 per cent of the total instant noodles produced in the world. If we can raise our share to 10 per cent in ten years, Wai Wai would become one of the five biggest instant noodles producers in the world. In that case, our company's capital, market, and trade should be around twenty times larger than they are now.

There are many stopovers and destinations in this journey. I, of course, do not know where this journey is going to end. Every time I reach a stopover, I vividly recall those young faces I saw in Dubai airport. They could not go without Wai Wai, even when they were compelled to go abroad in search of work. Think then about scores of our compatriots landing in airports all over the world with their cartons of Wai Wai. Many more must be urging their friends who are heading home for holidays to bring back some Wai Wai for them when they return. They must be using their own Wai Wai supply sparingly in case they run out of it.

I am not going to end this journey until I am able to at least take Wai Wai to all those places where the generations that grew up with Wai Wai are now located.

Given the current situation, what I can say confidently is that CG Foods (Global) will be listed on the New York Stock Exchange through the stock exchanges in India and Singapore.

This also means that I am going to realize my dream of building a billion-dollar company.

I received a proposal from Rabobank India: some companies were willing to invest in CG Foods, even as minority shareholders. I have been getting such requests for a long time now.

Ever since we expedited our expansion plans in India, many investment banks have been approaching us with proposals from many interested companies. They are even ready to pay an incredibly high price to become part of CG Foods.

I have a readymade answer to all those proposals: 'I am on a campaign to transform Wai Wai into a global company of a very high standard. This is the fire driving that campaign. And this fire is not going to be doused.

'Also, tell those who are sending proposals to buy us out that we are willing to buy their companies in India or other parts of the world, should they have any.'

Those who come up with such proposals mince their words. But I know very well that Nestlé India Limited is eyeing

Wai Wai. I also know that they are willing to forge a partnership with us for products such as Lactogen and Nescafé at the cost of CG Foods India. Hinting clearly at Nestlé themselves, I have told them, 'Let's keep the instant noodles aside for now. We are always ready if Nestlé wants to partner with us in Nepal.'

I take these proposals as a very positive sign reflecting our market value and stature.

On 11 January 2011, Wai Wai held its first formal press conference in India at the Taj hotel in New Delhi. Dozens of journalists from national newspapers and television channels had gathered for the conference. We were publicizing Wai Wai's latest sales figures.

The first question from the media was: Are you here to sell your company?

In those days, many entrepreneurs were setting up small companies so that they could sell them off to business houses once they had some presence in the market.

The question raised by the journalist reflected that trend.

'We are not here to sell our company,' I told them. 'We are here to buy more companies.'

19

The *Forbes* Story

One fine day, *Forbes* magazine invited me to attend its global conference in Singapore. I was very happy, though not very surprised; happy at the invitation from *Forbes* as I was not on its list of billionaires at that point, and not surprised as I was already an invitee to numerous functions of the World Economic Forum and similar global platforms. What really made me happy was *Forbes*'s recognition of my institution. It gave me a huge sense of satisfaction.

I attended that conference, which gave me an opportunity to meet the who's who of the corporate world and leading policy-makers from across the globe. There was also an interaction with Lee Kuan Yew, the legendary leader of Singapore. At the end of the conference, I felt the people I met there had many things in common. They were, basically, ordinary people like me who were either self-made or who had taken their modest businesses to the global level. I also had a lively talk with some of the regional editors of *Forbes* present there. Obviously, I felt elated about the event, but nobody gave me the faintest clue as to why I was invited.

I returned home and started going about my business. Soon afterwards, the *Forbes* guys started approaching us, inquiring about our activities. They even approached our bankers and legal advisers, seeking details of our global partnerships. It did not call for a lot of imagination to deduce they were probably doing some kind of background check on us. I think many businesses lose a *Forbes* listing because of an error of judgement at this point. They become apprehensive about giving out details about their businesses. I too was not completely without reservations; it did occur to me that the information they were seeking could be exploited by the wrong people, possibly by my competitors. But I thought it was a risk worth taking. What did I want to achieve through my business? Some entrepreneurs might want to retire after achieving the goal of just establishing their businesses. But my aim has been to establish the largest, most dynamic and most professional business group in Nepal in the first phase, and to take it to the regional level in South Asia and South East Asia, China, the Middle East and Africa in the next phase, to one day become a global player. So I assigned certain people from our organization to interact with the *Forbes* guys. I also started receiving feedback from our partners and bankers that somebody was inquiring about me. *Forbes* continued to invite my family to their events. This went on for more than two years.

Then, one day, Tim Ferguson, international editor of *Forbes*, telephoned me. I was already acquainted with him.

'Binod,' Tim told me. 'We want to do a story on you. I'm sending our Asia editor, Naazneen Karmali, to Nepal. She'll come from Mumbai and our photographer will come from Thailand.'

'Fine,' I said. 'Send them.'

Naazneen Karmali came to Kathmandu to interview me. She came across as very sharp, serious and thorough, yet frank and charming too at the same time.

'But this business is not just about me. It's about my family and my partners.'

'Yes, it will be a story about what you represent as the head of your family and what your group has achieved.'

Naazneen and I have become very good friends since then. What I found most impressive about her was her knowledge of the corporate world of the region, especially India's, like the palm of her hand.

Forbes went on to publish that story, which also mentions Nirvana and Rahul.

From the moment the magazine hit the stands, the deluge of response the story fetched overwhelmed me. Never in my life have I received that kind of response from all over the world for any of my achievements. There was a flood of congratulatory messages by email, on social networking sites and on the phone. It was like a volcanic eruption! To be brutally honest, a part of me was apprehensive that I might face attacks from certain quarters out of jealousy at the level of attention I was getting.

But I had nothing to worry about, and I am happy to say the article did not result in any kind of negative publicity. In fact, that was the first time I was convinced that people with positive energy outnumber the cynics and my critics in Nepal. The Nepali psyche is essentially a positive one, especially when it comes to anyone and anything that does the nation proud.

People, including those from the media, have often asked me how I feel about the recognition from *Forbes*.

I have said this repeatedly, and the media have also published it: there is no provision for a businessperson to get the Nobel prize. Recognition by *Forbes* is the highest honour a businessman can expect. I cannot ask for anything more.

Now, the *Forbes* listing is a petty numbers' game. Initially, we stood at number 1343 among the world's richest. In the latest listing, we have dropped to the 1400s. This setback was not due to any failing on our part but because of the fall of Nepal's currency against the US dollar. This numbers' game will continue year after year, but to be recognized by *Forbes* was a huge moment for me, one I treasure. I cherish it not so much because I am now a *Forbes* billionaire, but because I have been honoured by an internationally respected organization, which recognizes only those corporate entities that have been built in a transparent manner. *Forbes* stands for corporate governance and good business practices. Wealth is just one of its measures. If *Forbes* were to recognize wealth alone, then its list should have included far more businesspersons than it does.

Forbes has been publishing its billionaire list for the past twenty-seven years, and it is worthwhile to note what *Forbes* itself has to say about the process:

> Though we've been at it a long time, it is never an easy task. Our reporters dig deep and travel far. To compile net worth, we value individuals' assets—including stakes in public and private companies, real estate, yachts, art and cash—and account for debt. We attempt to vet these numbers with all billionaires. Some cooperate; others don't. We also consult an array of outside experts in various fields.
>
> The Forbes Billionaires ranks individuals rather than large, multi-generational families who share large fortunes. . . . In some cases we list siblings together if the ownership breakdown among them isn't clear, but here, too, they must be worth a minimum of $2 billion together, or equivalent to $1 billion apiece, to make the cut. We split up these fortunes when we get better information . . . Children are listed with their parents when one person is the founder and in control. Those fortunes are identified as "& family."

We do not include royal family members or dictators who derive their fortunes entirely as a result of their position of power, nor do we include royalty who, often with large families, control the riches in trust for their nation. Over the years Forbes has valued the fortunes of these wealthy despots, dictators and royals but have listed them separately as they do not truly reflect individual, entrepreneurial wealth that could be passed down to a younger generation or truly given away.

The best thing about *Forbes* is that it is a source of inspiration to all those who want to make it big in the corporate world by adhering to good corporate governance and not just by accumulating wealth by any means.

It has been rewarding in many wonderful ways to be featured in *Forbes*. It has given us a lot of visibility and added to our credibility. The moment people from the corporate world come to know that we have been recognized by *Forbes*, that becomes our biggest recommendation. Wherever we go, we get proposals for joint ventures from the top companies from that country or region, even though they may or may not know much about us. To be featured in *Forbes*, therefore, is the biggest recognition you can possibly get as a businessperson. It is also one that helps you grow, making you more responsible and more dedicated to good corporate governance. There have been many upsides to this *Forbes* journey.

An additional reward for a businessman like me who hails from a poor country like Nepal is that the *Forbes* coverage has added a new dimension to Nepal itself. Look, they say, Nepal has also arrived at the forefront in the global corporate arena, something nobody in this country could have imagined in their wildest dreams even a few years back.

Let me end this chapter with a beautiful story. One of my Sri Lankan friends recently hired a taxi in New York. He happened to take a cab driven by a Nepali. My friend started to chat with his cabbie as they drove along.

'Sir, do you know that we have a *Forbes* billionaire from Nepal?' the cabbie asked him proudly.

'He was pleasantly surprised when I told him you were a friend of mine,' this friend later told me.

So our recognition by *Forbes* has also inspired countless Nepalis, both in Nepal and overseas—which only adds to my happiness.

This recognition does come with its own challenges. Whenever I go abroad now, corporate and social leaders alike ask me why I do not do something for my country. Why can I not transform my country when I can create a global-level company? I feel a bit embarrassed. But then, they do not realize that it is very difficult to transform this country even if I wished to and had the resources to do so. Still, I feel pressured; I feel obliged to become a crucial component in the transformation of the country that was my platform from where I spread my wings globally. I have to justify the recognition I have been given. It is not a question of choice. Whether I can or cannot do this, only time will tell. However, it is not I but the next generation that is going to face the biggest challenges. If they cannot maintain the status we have achieved, it will not augur well for our group. I have already begun to limit my role in our organization. I do not run the business any more. I participate only in big policy-level decision-making, attend only important meetings, involve myself in hiring only the senior staff and focus largely on structural issues in the organization.

20

The Chaudhary Foundation

Engaging with the society has always been a way of life in the family traditionally. However, we formalized such activities under the banner of the Chaudhary Foundation in the 1990s, which continues to grow in many facets of philanthropic work related with the group both within and outside Nepal. In fact, post the devastating earthquake in Nepal of April 2015, this foundation has taken the centre stage in not only our personal lives, but also the life of the group.

The Chaudhary Foundation follows our group's belief in the power of relationships. It was set up to enhance our contributions to society by reorganizing our social initiatives towards a sustainable and focused model. This belief allows our foundation to prioritize initiatives in different sectors within its sphere of influence in a sustainable way. Through various partners, we are tackling some of the most critical issues in each of these areas. Our approach is to focus on a few critical issues through which we can adopt the best methodology and have the greatest impact. The Chaudhary Foundation continues to add to the portfolio of initiatives taken up by the Chaudhary Group over the past few decades. Focused and optimistic, the foundation is working with our partners to identify and implement innovative solutions that can help every person have the opportunity to live a healthy and productive life.

Post-disaster relief and rehabilitation work

On 25 April 2015, a devastating 7.8 magnitude earthquake struck Nepal with the epicentre in Lamjung district (north-west of the capital city, Kathmandu). The government reported that out of seventy-five districts, thirty-five were affected in the central and western regions of the country. Fourteen districts, namely Dhading, Gorkha, Rasuwa, Sindhupalchowk, Kavre, Nuwakot, Dolakha, Kathmandu, Lalitpur, Bhaktapur, Ramechhap, Solukhumbu, Okhaldhunga and Sindhuli were the most affected. According to government reports, the earthquake claimed nearly 9000 lives and destroyed around seven million houses. More than 25,000 people were injured.

Currently, the foundation is busy building 10,000 shelter homes for the people who were made homeless by the earthquake. It is also rebuilding 100 schools that were destroyed in the quake. Besides, it is also building twenty additional schools aiming to provide vocational livelihood training to the youth from the impoverished and disaster-hit communities.

Gyan Uday Scholarship

This was established in 2008 to give recognition to brilliant but financially disadvantaged students of public schools graduating from high school (SLC), to help them continue their studies. Until 2014, 708 scholarships have been distributed. Community schoolteachers contributing to help the students excel are also honoured as part of the scholarship.

CG Nepal Social Business

This is another core avenue of activity of the Chaudhary Foundation.

I have realized over the years that business houses become immortal not because of what they earn but because of what they give. However, giving is not an easy business. It is more difficult to give in a meaningful way than it is to earn. For instance, when we think of the Tatas, the Tata Memorial Cancer Hospital comes to mind first. Talking about Bill Gates, his social contributions have left a deeper impression on people's minds than his business activities. The same applies in the case of the Birlas and others. But I have also seen that many charities run by business families have fallen apart over time. Not all charities are sustainable, or have a sustainable impact on the lives of the people they aim to help. Our family has been running many different charitable campaigns over the years to engage with the people. One of them was a campaign called Sikchhit Nepali, Sambridha Nepal (Educated Nepali, Prosperous Nepal), which provided scholarships to children.

We are now building a research centre to study the ancient faiths and shrines scattered throughout Nepal. However, I have not been completely satisfied with these efforts. I have always wanted to do something more meaningful and of greater impact.

When I visited Bangladesh for Mintoo's son's wedding party, I had urged Mintoo to take me to Professor Muhammad Yunus. I wanted to explore the possibility of emulating the spectacular Bangladeshi model of microfinance in Nepal. Mintoo took me to the Nobel laureate. As we discussed microfinance, Professor Yunus began talking about social business.

'I have now realized that I can do only so much with microfinance institutions,' Professor Yunus told me. 'Microfinance alone cannot transform a country's economic destiny, though it can bring about social change. If you want to transform a country, it can happen through social business. The day business houses realize social business is the way to go, the country will transform.'

'What is this social business?' I asked.

'Social business is business done without any expectation of dividend,' he replied. 'But that business has to address social problems and it has to be sustainable.'

He then explained to me the seven principles of social business:

1. The business objective will be to overcome poverty, or to tackle one or more other problems (relating to education, health, technology access, or environment) that threaten people and society, not profit maximization.
2. Financial and economic sustainability.

3. Investors get back only their investment amount. No dividend is distributed.
4. After the invested amount is paid back, the profit stays with the company for expansion and improvement.
5. The business will be environmentally conscious.
6. The workforce gets market wages and better working conditions.
7. The business is done with joy.

I was very impressed with the idea.

The Government of Nepal once had the Yuva Sworojgar Yojana, or Youth Self-Employment Programme. But that was a rather politically motivated scheme to mobilize party cadres and to distribute subsidized loans to them. When it comes to genuine social business, merely distributing money is neither sufficient nor efficient. I think the most important components of social business include training and business incubation. What could young people with bright ideas do without the required capital to set up and run their own enterprises? Could they ever become another Binod Chaudhary? I had my small family business as my stepping stone, but what about them? This question had been haunting me for a long time. I felt I had finally found my answers now, thanks to Professor Yunus.

I started to work more closely with the professor. I invited him to Nepal in the context of an annual general meeting of the CNI.

'Let's start a social business in Nepal as a joint venture,' Professor Yunus proposed. 'We will give you the know-how and the system, and you build the organization.'

I was more than happy to embark on this, as by that time I was fully convinced that Nepal was the ideal place to run a social business. On the one hand, Nepal has not been able to tap its tremendous natural resources, while on the other, around 1500 young Nepalis fly abroad every day seeking jobs, as employment opportunities are scarce in the country.

At the venue of the AGM itself, we pledged US$1 million for the cause—not a small amount in the context of a small country like Nepal. This way, our organization would be sustainable, with or without me. Today the Nepal Social Business team has been working on a war footing to achieve its aims. It is getting support from other international organizations, including the Lions Clubs International.

Professor Yunus has been inviting me to many summits related to social business. I was a speaker at one of the summits in Dhaka. He also invited me to another function in Malaysia. In 2013, *Forbes* invited me to its 400 Philanthropy Summit in New York as a speaker. In attendance were the top philanthropists from across the world, including Warren Buffet, Bill Gates, Bono and Ted Turner. I was invited to the summit again in 2014. Nirvana attended that time around.

As I get more and more involved in social business and enter the bigger league of philanthropists, I am getting more and more confident that if we can properly position Nepal Social Business, we can raise millions of dollars for the cause. Let us face it, the US$1 million we pledged for CG Nepal Social Business is peanuts if we are talking about creating self-employment opportunities for our young people. The Chaudhary Group, on its own, cannot meet that challenge.

We are now working towards taking CG Nepal Social Business to the next level. We are trying to get the world's top philanthropists to join the project in Nepal. We tell them that if they engage with the people of Nepal through the social business programme, they will not have to spend a single penny on administrative expenses. The CG team takes care of the administration, free of charge. Today, there are about 5000 NGOs and INGOs in Nepal, and a whopping 30–40 per cent of the money pledged to them for social causes is spent on administration. This is a big irony. With CG, every penny spent in Nepal will be deployed for the core cause.

A major conference of the Lions Clubs International, with participation from around thirty countries, was held in Nepal some time back. The president of the Lions Clubs International, Barry J. Palmer, also attended the conference. I was invited as a guest speaker. There I talked about why I am deeply committed to social business. Palmer was so impressed by my speech that he suddenly rose from the dais and floated a proposal for a partnership with us. I was invited to their global conference in Toronto, where I was asked to make a presentation in front of some 18,000 Lions. Lions Clubs International signed a partnership agreement with us in Toronto itself.

For the first phase of our social business, we have identified five projects in the remote, hilly district of Jumla in Nepal where poverty is rampant. We have already trained young local entrepreneurs. We are ready to provide US$30,000 for each project. This is our pilot scheme. We will soon scale it up and cover ten more districts. Lions Clubs International has pledged US$2 million for the next phase, an amount sufficient to establish around seventy new businesses in Nepal run by young local entrepreneurs using local resources in such a way that they touch the life of the local residents. This is how we are planning to transform the economy of the country.

So far, young people in Nepal have had very little to look forward to. We are instilling hope in our youth. And the best part of it is that our solution is not charity. We will call for proposals, and our team will study them, and identify the projects for funding. The selected projects have to return the capital once they start making profits, after which the money will be reinvested in another project. As the entrepreneurs cannot get ownership of their projects until they pay back the capital, there is no possibility of misappropriation of funds. Further, each project we support will, in turn, have to support another social business. In this way, the young entrepreneurs also become the pioneer social business promoters in their region, creating a multiplier effect. There are other benefits too. One of the projects we are supporting in Jumla will manufacture malt-based nutritious food for children using local produce. Malnutrition is a major problem in Jumla, where life expectancy is as low as 47 against the national average of 65. Our project will address malnutrition, use locally produced raw materials, will create employment at the local level, and thus make for another viable enterprise in the country. Look at how many birds we are killing with one stone!

Mark my word, if Nepal Social Business functions as planned, someday the Chaudhary Group will be better known for social business than for Wai Wai or any other venture. I cannot tell you when that will happen, but I can tell you that we are moving in that direction.

Here, I would also like to add that I want to manage a programme designed on the lines of The Apprentice run by Donald Trump someday here in Nepal. I think it is a fantastic idea.

21

African Adventure

Africa is the story of a continent with unique, unparalleled natural resources and opportunities that are badly managed—a living example of the famous argument that if natural resources were the parameters determining the prosperity of a nation, Japan and Singapore would have been the poorest and perhaps Africa, Nepal and their like, the richest. Prosperity is all about quality of governance, leadership and the courage and vision to bring the economy to the centre stage. It is not politics-for-the-sake-of-politics that builds a country. It is politics for the sake of building a country that builds a country. Political decisions need to be directed in accordance with the country's inherent strengths to deliver a better quality of life to its people.

However, currently, one is beginning to see some of the African countries follow the very successful story of South Africa post the emergence of Nelson Mandela. It was Mandela's statesmanship that resulted in the end of Apartheid, bringing the whites and blacks together to build a resurgent nation. He had to persuade his people to forgive and forget. South

Africa wrote its Constitution in record time, moving on to become a cohesive nation, perhaps one of the most successful in the entire African continent. Some of the countries on the continent are trying to emulate South Africa, but many, still riven by Third World politics, are not. However, there is a growing desire among investors to go to Africa.

Ravi Jaipuria, who has started operations for Pepsi and KFC in east and west Africa, invited me to join him on one of his trips to the continent. Being a close friend and a sharp entrepreneur, he was the right person for me to travel with, to know what was really happening on the continent. I flew to Africa with him from Dubai in his private jet and spent a week touring Kenya, Tanzania, Mozambique and some other countries. I was very clear in my mind that Africa is no different from my own country, and if we could build a multinational from Nepal, then why not one out of Africa.

On my return, I identified an investment banker who brought a very attractive deal to the table—Britannia in Uganda and the House of Manjees, a household name for biscuits in Kenya going back a hundred years. Both were run by a local family who were partners in the companies; their majority ownership was with the Libyan government. A similar situation had resulted when Gaddafi's rule ended and a new political order emerged. There was a rush on the part of the new regime to sell the erstwhile investments of Gaddafi. We were successful in striking a deal after many months of protracted negotiations. We even posted our team in Africa to take over the ailing outfits and to turn them around. However, some elements in Libya as well as Africa did not allow that deal to happen as they did not want to let go of the hen that laid the golden eggs for their personal benefit. We decided to abandon those ventures.

Meanwhile, on one of my visits to Africa, I met a leading businessman, Alykhan Karmali. I had met him as a FMCG player, but as destiny would have it, we landed up in a joint venture for starting a series of Zinc hotels in the East African countries. Our first project was at Kigali in Rwanda—Zinc City which is going to be opened in December 2015. We subsequently acquired sites in Kampala, where a project is under design and development.

Our plans for a Wai Wai project in Africa, which had to be set aside when the Britannia deal was aborted, has also taken a new shape. The Kenyan government has invited us to set up a greenfield plant in Machakos, a new state under the new federal regime. We are now negotiating with another FMCG for an acquisition. Our partnership with a big Nigeria-based group for an FMCG company is also beginning to take shape.

In our renewed vision for Taj under Taj Asia, we intend to open a Taj in Nigeria too. Things are moving very fast on the global front. Our team in Dubai is working day and night. At this rate, we are certain to create a serious presence in both East and West Africa in the next five years.

PART IV: MY BUSINESS MANTRAS

22

The Mantras

Ever since I entered the world of industrial enterprise, I have had to assume responsibilities I was not prepared for. I was neither prepared nor had enough education or experience when I started off, but I took each development in my life very seriously. This helped me see clearly where I stood and where I had to reach. My one resolve was to not just take charge of the family business when I was compelled to do so by circumstances, but to take it to new heights.

Success is a relative concept. An ill-equipped club cannot produce a Maradona. That takes a good field and a government that understands football and is ready to promote the game. It also requires colleagues with sportsmanship and an audience that cheers, besides, of course, the skills and qualities of the player. Nobody can be the best by some fluke and retain that position by chance. I did not go to Harvard, MIT or Wharton. Banking on my own experience, I have, nevertheless, made decisions that even a Harvard professor would recoil from without several rounds of market surveys.

Drawing from my own experience, I would like to list some of the qualities and skills that an entrepreneur should possess. However, I would like to clarify that though I am elaborating on what I consider as my business mantras, they are not a sure-fire way to success.

High ambition

Our society has always accorded negative connotations to the word 'ambition'. This is the biggest obstacle in an entrepreneur's path. The stature I have achieved now is the product of my high ambition and strong will. Ambition whets your appetite for success, and that hunger propels you ahead. From the time I stepped into my father's shoes, I wanted to become bigger than the biggest business families in Nepal. All my plans and efforts were guided by the thought that there was no reason we could not compete with the big houses and ultimately overtake them.

Even today, there are many businessmen in Kathmandu, contemporaries of my father, who are content with their old grocery shops. Sometimes they envy us, cursing their own feeble willpower. If you do not want to expand your business, establish an industrial group or a multinational organization, you would do well not to opt for it at all. Rara noodles dominated Nepal's market when I launched Wai Wai in the country. Maggi from India also had a good hold in the market. Had the presence of these brands intimidated me, Wai Wai would have never happened, and the Chaudhary Group would never have achieved the heights it has today.

Organization building

Four decades back, the radius of our business extended to the corner of Arun Emporium at Khichapokhari, where our small office stood. We lived in the same building. We had a handful of employees. Even with these limitations, I decided to hire a chartered accountant, a professional secretary and employees who had good knowledge of the import and export business. No business firm would hire a CA in those days. Conduct of the business depended on whatever knowledge the family members had of it. Breaking away from that culture, I laid emphasis on organization-building. You cannot achieve huge goals single-handedly. You need an organization for that. You need a group of experts. That is how the sapling of Arun Emporium has grown into the huge tree of the Chaudhary Group.

Persistence

I have encountered many challenges and situations in my professional life that made me feel weak inwardly. I was often overcome with fear of losing the battle. Nevertheless, I never gave up. Though I was inexperienced when my father became bedridden, I left no stone unturned to grow Pashupati Biscuits and the flour mills. In the early 1980s, a powerful political camp tried to ruin me. I did not panic, but associated myself with an even more powerful group.

There are many more examples of my tenacity. I wanted to invest in energy and cement plants twenty-five years ago, but I was thwarted by man-made hurdles and unhealthy competition. From the Modi Khola project to Butwal Power Company, many of my plans for the sector came to naught. Despite all this, I remained determined to be a presence in the energy sector. Today we are planning joint investment with Coastal Energy, one of the leading power developers of India. As far as cement is concerned, we wanted to take over the state-run Himal Cement Factory many years ago, but got caught in the crossfire between two power centres. Today, when that factory is collecting dust, we are setting up huge cement plants in Myanmar, Sri Lanka, Mozambique and Cambodia, besides Nepal. What I am trying to show is that I have unflinching commitment to my objectives, regardless of the challenges I face. If one project does not work out, I am always prepared to switch to the next one to achieve my goals.

Market astuteness

Business does not run on the lines of elaborate theories outlined in thick books. Books may be helpful in generating business experts, but not businesspersons. One becomes a businessperson through market awareness.

I would like to tell a story I heard a long time ago. There was a village where people did not wear shoes. The promoter of a slipper factory sent a renowned marketing guru to study the market feasibility for his product in that village. After surveying the region and interviewing the local residents for a month, the expert prepared his report: in the village where nobody had ever worn shoes, it was impossible to sell even one pair of slippers. After brooding over the report for a while, the owner of the company declared, 'I am going to take my products to that village.'

Everyone was surprised. He said, 'The people there have walked barefoot their entire lives. That is our biggest potential market. All we have to do is to teach them to wear slippers.' Shortly, as he had predicted, slippers became so popular in the village that he opened his new factory in the village itself. This is what I call market astuteness.

I had not done any market survey before collaborating with Thai Food. Nor did I do any feasibility study before setting up my plants in India. My awareness guided me. This is the main reason I do not undertake market research and stockpile reports submitted by consultants before venturing into a new business. I am fully confident of my market awareness. I have been guided by my astuteness in every business I have ventured into and every negotiation I have undertaken.

Conservatism brings benefits

I do not agree with the generally accepted norm that one should always be positive. This might be surprising coming from me, so let me clarify. I take notions such as 'it's okay' or 'everything happens for our own good' as complacency. My philosophy in life is that a person should never be complacent or satisfied to accept whatever comes his way in life. That attitude obstructs one's progress.

Whenever a new venture is started, people tend to think about its positive aspects. I, however, always focus on the negative. Consider the positive aspects before getting into a project but, once you embark on it, you should focus on the negative aspects such as the challenges to be faced and the likely response of competitors. I make my colleagues focus on the negative aspects of my projects. It helps us to identify the possible or imminent problems so that we can duly address them. You start to mull over contingency plans. If you do not have contingency plans, then you might end up losing what you already have.

Restlessness ruins negotiation

The more you appear restless at the negotiating table, the more you lose. The person in front of you tries his best to corner you. A deal hinges a lot on how you talk and how you present yourself. I give the highest priority to my terms, my competence and my stake when I negotiate. For instance, when I am seeking fifty points, I will start asking for 100. In most cases, I succeed in striking a deal at seventy-five. Also, since everybody wants the best deal in negotiations, you can get a better deal if you can create a win-win situation for both sides.

Making unnecessary demands can also lead to failed negotiations. I have already mentioned how I lost the Lands End hotel deal in Mumbai on account of my intractable stance on equal sharing of the management fee. I also failed to take the right position in my negotiations with Airtel. The telecom giant was ready to forge a partnership with us even before UTL and Mero Mobile had entered the Nepali market. It wanted at least 51 per cent stake in the venture, and would not settle for anything less than equal partnership. The talks broke down due to my intransigence. As a result, I had to put off my plans to invest in the telecom sector for a long while.

Nothing succeeds like success

As the saying goes, nothing succeeds like success. If you become successful in any venture, more successes will follow. You have to create a strong success story for the world to see if you want to establish yourself in business. You should create a persona that persuades others to trust you. However, if you try your hand at a new venture before your earlier business is established, you will not make your mark in the market. Try to look for a complementary sector when you are ready for a new venture. You have to put in a lot of extra effort if you venture into a field in which you do not have sufficient experience. I started Maha Laxmi Maida Mills to complement Pashupati Biscuits. I went on to start Wai Wai only after both these ventures were established. All three ventures are interrelated.

Costs must be pruned

The total cost of cement plants that we are launching simultaneously in Nepal, Myanmar, Sri Lanka and a few other countries is more than Rs 12 billion. These projects are at advanced stages of completion. However, you will not even get a hint of this if you visit our corporate office. There are only three people behind this huge project and they, too, are taking on the project simultaneously with their other, regular work. The cost to the company on each of these three people do not exceed Rs 250,000 a month. Other business houses would have probably set up project offices in all the countries concerned and hired a large number of staff. They would have already spent several millions by now. But we are working quietly and cost-effectively

Discipline

Discipline is about two things: personal conduct and time management.

How do you conduct yourself with your colleagues? How do you present yourself before your partners, sales agents and buyers? These things determine your personal discipline. Talking idly with everyone you come across will diminish your stature. I do agree with the notion that you ought to treat your colleagues like friends. However, there is a limit to everything. If you become too intimate with your junior colleagues, then you struggle to give orders to them or to counsel them if they do something wrong. Nothing is more detrimental to an organization than a situation like that. To sum up, you need to strike a balance between respect, affection and fear when it comes to your relationship with your employees.

Time is the most precious thing in this world. You cannot get it back when it is gone, regardless of how much you are willing to pay. How do we make the most of the limited time we have? This is a billion-dollar question. Do not forget that life is not just about business. We also have family and friends, and personal and social lives. You have to optimize the time you have allotted to your professional life to your maximum benefit so that you still have time left over for other things in life. If you cannot handle the most precious thing in the world with care, you may not be able to handle other matters either.

Keep yourself updated

I am a self-taught person. Whatever I have learnt is from observing others. I mingle with a lot of people. I make new friends wherever I go. I listen to them attentively. I study them carefully. I learn their tricks. They are my business school. Those who are happy limiting themselves to a narrow sphere cannot be big-timers.

It is really important to keep yourself updated and stay abreast of what is going on around you. The more you are in step with the world outside, the more your personality shines. I had many weaknesses, and still do. But I did not have the inferiority complex that often circumscribes one's world into a narrow zone of comfort. I have always striven to overcome my weaknesses so that I could grow as a person. That is why I never shy away from learning things I did not know anything about.

Since my childhood, I have always wanted to make my presence known in every new situation or role. This is possible only if you keep a tab on the developments around you. I am an avid reader. I try to collect information on many subjects that I feel may come in handy at some point. I have initiated a system in my office to keep myself constantly updated with the latest information, no matter which part of the world I am in. Success is related to your personality.

23

Self-evaluation

My temper

I always strive for optimum use of time and resources. To manage this efficiently, tasks must be completed as scheduled. I have a level of expectation from my colleagues in this respect, and if they fail to deliver or perform poorly, that becomes a headache for me. In that situation, I easily lose my temper.

Another factor that sparks my anger is my way of evaluating people. I always wonder why, if I can do something, others cannot do it too! I would have accomplished this task in this way if I were in his or her position. I would have met the target in this manner. And why couldn't this person have done the same? I know this is an illogical approach, but who thinks logically when they are angry? As a result, many of my employees have felt offended and even quit, which only adds to my burden.

To bypass this weakness, I have started to interact only with a small circle of employees. I used to meet with all the departmental heads during our monthly evaluation meetings in the past. These days, I invite only a handful of senior executives to the meetings.

My aggressive nature

When I lose my cool, I start to become aggressive. Due to this aspect of my nature, I have quarrelled bitterly with many people, including members of the FNCCI and the CNI. When in a fit of anger, I use harsh words, intentionally or unintentionally. Though I do not harbour any ill intent towards the people to whom my words are directed, they take it personally. I soon forget about the incident, but those who have been offended remember the insult and look for an opportunity for revenge. They harm me when the opportunity arrives. My aggression has overshadowed my good qualities. Perception has a stronger impact than truth itself. Nobody analyses the person behind my conduct. They form their opinion of me from my projected image.

My management of human resources

I expect more than I should from my employees. I want them to accomplish everything as soon as possible. What I tend to forget is that not all people are equally capable. Some of them plunge into nervousness when pressed to deliver, further spoiling the task at hand. That eventually harms the company.

The society and the environment in which we work have their own limitations too. We cannot meet all our targets even if we strive relentlessly. Governmental red tape or the different priorities and working pace of one's partners can be impediments. As managerial leaders, we should expect outcomes only after considering our social milieu. Sometimes I become extremely impractical, focusing on my targets even if the world around me turned upside down. This must have been disheartening to many of my colleagues.

Even though I am aware of the shortcomings in my conduct, I cannot always help it. In the battlefield, a commander is guided by his strategy and not by his compassion. He expects even injured soldiers to put up a tough fight. There is no room for sympathy because a battle cannot be won with compassion. You need unremitting drive to win a battle. I have always sought that level of drive from my colleagues. But I have lost many trusted colleagues because I have driven them up the wall. As I think about how I may have hurt their self-esteem, I sink into deep self-criticism. I say, from the bottom of my heart, that I hold them in high regard for their contribution to the Chaudhary Group.

To Be Continued . . .

'You have to sacrifice something to gain something else,' my father had told me.

This was a piece of fatherly advice I never took very seriously. I want everything in life, not one thing at the cost of another. In my opinion, compromising on something to get something in return is not good management.

Have you seen how a tent is erected? It is supported by four poles at the four corners and by one in the middle. A perfect tent is erected only if all the pillars are placed in a coordinated manner; otherwise, the tent would be loose here and taut there. The journey of life is like putting up a tent. It is supported the most by the central pillar—our professional life.

If you are not happy and fulfilled in your professional life, then you are unlikely to feel fulfilled in life itself. I am not just talking about entrepreneurs like me but about people from any walk of life. Only those who have done their best in their profession can be happy and make their family happy too.

Professional success is not everything, however. If you focus only on professional success, one day you will realize that though you have reached your destination, your personal life has been left behind. If your room is filled with trophies and medals but there are no photographs of your parents, spouse and children, then such a success is futile. Family life is the second pillar of our life.

The third pillar is your personal life, and by that I mean your truly personal, inner life, the things that even your spouse and children cannot see. You may be a spiritual aspirant, a music lover, or love to chill out with friends or enjoy solitude. That is your inner personal life. Only those whom you choose can go there with you. Those who limit themselves to their professional and family lives alone lead a mechanical life. Find time to fulfil your inner life, and happiness will radiate from your face.

We belong to many social spheres—those of neighbours, friends and colleagues in society. Social life is about interacting with them. If we fail to dance with them in merriment and cry with them in sorrow, we become an outcast. If we do not recognize our social responsibilities and shoulder them, our life is not in balance. Therefore, social life is the fourth pillar.

The fifth pillar is public life.

What is the difference between social life and public life? We have a two-way involvement in social life. Society expects something from us and we want to do something for society. For instance, today I interact with the mass media, politicians, social activists and international figures. This is part of my social life. I share happiness and sorrow with the members of my society. This is another aspect of my social life.

Public life is a one-way involvement. You do not recognize the people, but they know you. They analyse your actions as good or bad. Some revere you as an ideal while others loathe you. All those activities that have an impact at the public level are part of our public life.

Those who can set up the tent of their life supported by these five pillars will lead a successful life. This is my ideal. I have always tried to strike a balance between these five pillars of my life; my lifestyle and my achievements are the outcome of this.

My life and achievements have also been shaped by my dreams. Businessmen are dreamers.

Dreams are boundless. But human capacity is limited. Those who recognize this but still keep raising the bar for themselves are bound to realize their dreams. They are sure to be successful. The heights achieved by the Chaudhary Group is the outcome of my tireless and steadfast determination, backed by my father, brothers, wife, sons and dedicated colleagues.

Epilogue

25 April 2015

That day I was in Meghauli of Chitwan in central Nepal, inspecting our upcoming resort along with my colleagues from Taj. Suddenly, everything around us started shaking. It felt as if we were standing on a boat on rough sail. 'Oh an earthquake!' somebody yelled. Near us was a trench that would be the resort's swimming pool. The six-inch-deep accumulated rainwater started spilling out of the one and a half meters deep trench! What a tremor! A great earthquake had struck Nepal.

I immediately thought of Lily. 'Oh God, Lily is alone in Kathmandu! At least we were together in Chile.' We think of our most loved ones at the time of crisis. Solace came when she called me and exclaimed, 'Babu! Are you alright?' She was also thinking about me! We were able to talk over phone after much difficulty. Telephone networks were extremely congested after the quake.

Surprisingly, I was still able to think clearly despite the mega disaster. Thank God, you put me through the Chile test first! I had passed, and passed well—I realized then.

To me, the Chile earthquake had come as a great revelation. I was face-to-face with the transient nature of life. You cannot postpone your cherished dreams and callings. Your duties and responsibilities can't wait. You do it now or never. You could be making plans for ten years, but how do you know what comes your way in the next ten days or in the next ten minutes!

When I returned to Kathmandu, my heart wept to see the ruins and rubbles. Many of our heritage sites were destroyed, including the Bhimsen Stambha, popularly known as Dharahara, the icon of Kathmandu. The streets, the people, the houses, the monuments—these were inseparable parts of me! I was born here. I grew up in these streets—among these houses, among these people. I had such an innate connection to this place. Oh God, what had happened to the city where my heart belonged!

As soon as we ensured the safety of our employees, I called a meeting of my senior executives and we immediately sprang into action for earthquake relief. Thousands of people had lost their lives (the death toll came to almost 9000), 700,000 houses were destroyed, and about 36,000 schoolrooms damaged. That was a great loss for a country staggering with slow economic growth and suffering from high political instability. We couldn't wait even a single minute before we came to the fore to help. While I was still in Chitwan, I had instructed my senior staff over phone to open up the gates of our schools so that the people had a place to spend the night in safety. I asked them to start distributing packets of Wai Wai and bottles of Rio juice and water so that nobody had to sleep hungry or thirsty.

Houses were damaged everywhere. My office building in Sanepa was not spared either. It housed my office and the international headquarters of CG Corp Global. It was the place where I started the Chaudhary Group and where I spent my crucial years building the business. I was troubled to see the damages as the place meant a lot to me. Our whole operation was bound to be disturbed for some time. We did not even get a chance to take out our important documents. Many of our employees' houses were destroyed. But that was nothing when compared to the sorrow and trauma my fellow countrymen were facing.

Fourteen districts around Kathmandu were seriously affected. Villages were flattened and people were sleeping hungry under the sky. We immediately decided that we would run relief programmes in these districts. 'There shouldn't be a moment's delay in reaching out to the needy people in these places,' I decided.

Putting our usual business aside, we started taking relief materials to these districts. Our whole team volunteered. In the first phase, we ran emergency relief programmes comprising food, water and medicines. Two weeks later, we announced through a press conference that the Chaudhary Foundation would build in total 10,000 transitional shelter homes and over 100 school buildings in the most affected districts. Out of the 10,000 shelter homes, 1000 would be solely funded by us and the rest through partnership. Now we have reputed names from around the world like Tata Trust, Alibaba, LG, Sapoorji Pallonji, MoneyGram as our partners in building these homes. Our total financial commitment was NPR 25 crore (approximately two and a half million US dollars). That was the first relief initiative of such big scale ever taken up by a corporate house in the history of Nepal. We ran the relief programme as a humble effort to help the people whose lives were devastated by the most damaging crisis of our times.

The nation was in a state of shock. Leaders, donors, corporate bodies and people from around the world had joined hands to run rescue operations and provide material relief to Nepal. Aircrafts from around the world came with rescue teams, relief materials, volunteers and experts to help. Our only international airport was so congested that the aircraft had to make rounds in the air for hours before landing. Despite total commitment and effort by the friends of Nepal, we as a country were struggling to manage the overwhelming relief support. On the one hand, the relief material was stockpiled, and on the other, people were suffering for want of basic supplies.

This was an example of our inefficient management system and lack of preparedness in times of crisis. There are examples around the world where such crises were so effectively handled that the whole scenario changed in a few years. Sichuan in China and Gujarat in India suffered great earthquakes in the recent past. But they not only recovered, but entered a new phase of development after the crisis. All it takes is a visionary leadership and an effective government. While I am awestruck by the examples of successful state management elsewhere, I am troubled to see that at home we are still entangled in the ideological debate of whether to go for rehabilitation or reconstruction after the earthquake.

Nevertheless, we the private sector never gave up. We took up the task of helping the earthquake-affected people around us. Today, while writing the final chapter of my autobiography, I feel happy to have already handed over shelters and school buildings. My sons, Nirvana, Rahul, and Varun, are actively supporting me in this social service initiative. It gives my heart great joy when I see the smiles on the faces of the people when they receive the shelter homes through us. I was fortunate to be at a school handover ceremony organized by the Chaudhary Foundation recently in the Kavre district of Nepal. I cannot express how happy I was when I saw the smiling faces of the children who would study in the classrooms we built.

During the Chile earthquake, I was shocked and terrorized. It changed my outlook towards life. But the Nepal earthquake changed my life itself! My priorities have changed. I have come to see life from a new angle. The joy you get by bringing joy to others' lives transcends all other joys. Your happiness cannot be absolute. It cannot be independent of others. Life is transitory, its worth can be measured only through the happiness you bring to others' lives. When you start thinking that way, your whole life changes. A new world dawns for you.